ON BICYCLES

ON BICYCLES

A 200-YEAR HISTORY *of* CYCLING *in* NEW YORK CITY

EVAN FRISS

COLUMBIA UNIVERSITY PRESS
New York

Columbia University Press
Publishers Since 1893
New York   Chichester, West Sussex
cup.columbia.edu
Copyright © 2019 Evan Friss

Library of Congress Cataloging-in-Publication Data
Names: Friss, Evan, author.
Title: On bicycles : a 200-year history of cycling in New York City / Evan Friss.
Description: New York : Columbia University Press, [2019] |
Includes bibliographical references and index.
Identifiers: LCCN 2018045873 (print) | LCCN 2018049808 (ebook) |
ISBN 9780231544245 (electronic) | ISBN 9780231182560 (cloth : alk. paper)
Subjects: LCSH: Cycling—Social aspects—New York (State)—New York. |
Cycling—United States—History. | Cycling—New York (State)—New York—
History. | Urban transportation—New York (State)—New York. | Bicycle
commuting—New York (State)—New York—History. | Bicycle sharing
programs—New York (State)—New York—History. | Cycling—Government
policy—New York (State)—New York.
Classification: LCC GV1045.5.N72 (ebook) |
LCC GV1045.5.N72 F565 2019 (print) | DDC 796.609747/1—dc23
LC record available at https://lccn.loc.gov/2018045873

Columbia University Press books are printed on permanent
and durable acid-free paper.
Printed in the United States of America

COVER DESIGN: Julia Kushnirsky
COVER IMAGES: Nastasic / DigitalVision Vectors / Getty Images (top);
New York City Skyline from Jersey City, Postcard, c. 1915 /
J. T. Vintage / Bridgeman Images (bottom)

For Amanda, Miles, and Quincy

CONTENTS

ON BICYCLES

INTRODUCTION

New York is a city in motion. New Yorkers walk—and walk fast. Cars lurch. Buses crawl. Intersections are battlefields. Ferries ferry. Planes take off and land. Helicopters shuttle one-percenters from Greenwich, Connecticut, to Wall Street and from Wall Street to the Hamptons. Commuter trains carry workers home at night and return them to overcrowded stations in the morning. A cacophonous symphony of subway cars, hurtling under and over the city, never ends.

On Manhattan's grid, locals know that one uptown-downtown block equals one twentieth of a mile. Unfailingly (and without a compass) they can find the southwest corner of an intersection. They also know not just which subway line to take, but which subway car to stand in, on which side the doors will open, and through which set of stairs to exit the station.

How New Yorkers get from A to B is not just a means. It is a force, a shaper of the city and the life inside it.

About one quarter of the earth on which New York City sits is a street, roughly equal to fifty-eight Central Parks. Those streets reveal as much of the soul of the city as any place. What they look like and whom they serve are questions so fundamental that the answers dictate what the city looks like and whom it serves. The daily dance on the streets—what the abstract artist Piet Mondrian called the Broadway Boogie Woogie in a

1942 painting—is a definitional aspect of life in New York. Over the last two hundred years, countless vehicles (horse-drawn carriages, streetcars, elevated trains, cars, trucks, and buses, to name a few) have boogie woogied up, down, over, and across the city. But it is the bicycle that has the longest-running claim to New York's streets: two hundred years and counting.[1]

This is the story of how that happened. Of how bicycles came and went and came back again. Of how the relationship among New York City, its people, and their bicycles evolved. Of how bicycles went from being a novelty to commonplace. Of how the city came to reflect the bicycles and bicyclists who occupy it, and how the city shapes our understanding of those same objects and people.

Where, exactly, the bicycle fits within the city has always been contested because New Yorkers have never been able to agree about what, exactly, a bicycle is. A 1973 New York City Department of Transportation report described it as the "step-child of the transportation world." City staff knew how to accommodate cars. They knew where the walkers should go. Bicycles were a different and more complicated story.[2]

In the nineteenth century, bicycles were compared to horses (sometimes called "steel horses"), to carriages (sometimes called "horseless carriages"), and even to flying creatures ("My new wheel is a bird!" one enthusiast declared, no doubt with a smile on his face, in 1896). Cyclists sometimes raced against railroad cars; other times they brought their bicycles on board. Toddlers rode them in playgrounds, but so did racers in velodromes. Over the years, bicycles have also been exercise machines for the health-conscious, surveillance units for cops, a way to explore for the curious, instruments of commuters, and cargo ships for messengers.[3]

Since the bike's first appearance, cheerleaders have lauded its many uses. But the bicycle's versatility has also raised critical questions that dominate the two-century, on-again, off-again history of cycling in the city. Who is a real cyclist? What is a bicycle really for? How New Yorkers viewed cyclists (whether as childish, hypermasculine, countercultural, white, ethnic, elite, or working-class) and what they believed the bicycle's principal purpose was (recreation, racing, commerce, or transportation) has forever shaped where and how bicycles belonged in the city—if they belonged at all.[4]

In short, as New Yorkers' understanding of the bicycle changed, so did the city.

From the moment the very first velocipedes (early bicycles) arrived in 1819, residents fought about what to do with them. Should they be allowed on the streets? In the parks? On the sidewalks? The answer was, apparently, "none of the above," as lawmakers soon banned them from the places they had been most used. Those first velocipedes lasted only a summer, but the wheeled contraptions, and the questions, would return.[5]

And so began a recurring pattern—a peak of interest followed by a period of decline. Yet, each time, the booms lasted longer. Just as a novice rider is first able to balance only a few seconds without falling, then a minute, then two, then three . . . New Yorkers rode for longer and longer with each revival. Ever since the 1870s, whether velocipedes, high-wheelers with their almost comically oversized front wheels, safety bicycles, tricycles, cruisers, ten-speeds, fixed-gears, BMX bikes, Citi Bikes, or e-bikes, there have always been bicycles in New York.

The question about where they belonged never disappeared either. New Yorkers remained divided on the issue because they remained divided on the nature of cyclists and cycling. In the nineteenth century, carriage drivers may well have frequented the six-day-long bicycle races at Madison Square Garden, but they objected to cyclists "scorching" through Central Park. CEOs in the 1980s may have enjoyed mountain biking at their summer cabins, but they did not want tank-topped messengers tramping through their lobbies. And twenty-first-century Hasidic Jews in Williamsburg may have been happy to put their children on a bicycle, but they did not want hipsters wheeling through their neighborhood. Calls to restrict bicycles came with each boom—in 1819, 1869, the 1890s, the late 1930s, the early 1970s, and the twenty-first century—and each new notion of cycling.

Bike critics were not simply lumped together either. In recent years, articles railing against cyclists could be found just as easily in the tabloid *New York Post* ("bubble-brained traffic-busting" bike lanes serve only "amphetamine-propelled deliverymen") as in the highbrow *New*

Yorker ("it is time to call a halt to [Transportation Commissioner] Sadik-Khan and her faceless road swipers"). Both truck drivers and passengers leering from limousines grumbled about the cyclists. Even cyclists complained about other cyclists.[6]

At the same time, New Yorkers continued to conjure up various, often distinct images of the cyclist archetype. Was it an immigrant delivering Chinese food? A young white commuter? A middle-aged man in Lycra (known as a "MAMIL")? New York has never had one singular cycling culture. But it did have cultures, whether it was cyclists hanging out along Lower Manhattan's "Bicycle Row" in the mid-1890s or racers congregating in a Harlem bike shop in the late 1960s. Never have all types of cyclists been perceived equally. The same holds true even by the end of this story, when the city embraces the bicycle as fully as it ever has.

Indeed, this book ends a long and remarkable way from where it begins. When they first came ashore two hundred years ago, bicycles were quickly banned. In the decades that followed, leaders and lawmakers reacted in piecemeal and often knee-jerk fashion to requests and complaints from bike advocates and critics. But in the end, infrastructure was built not just to satiate but to spur demand, and to change the way New Yorkers thought about bicycles, their streets, and their city.

On Bicycles is *A 200-Year History of Cycling in New York City*. It is not the complete and total history; neither does it document every bike path laid or every bicycle policy written. Instead, it tells stories that highlight key moments of New York's long cycling history.

There is, for instance, the story of Arthur Hyde, who, like hundreds of thousands of other New Yorkers in the 1890s, caught bicycle fever. Over the course of three years, he logged 6,811 miles, commuting to work, running errands, catching baseball games at the Polo Grounds, taking "the girls" out for a spin, touring the city and its surroundings, and riding through neighborhoods filled with bicycle shops, along asphalted bicycle lanes lining otherwise cobblestoned streets, and on the greatest bicycle path in all the world.[7]

There is the story of Violet Ward, who, while Hyde was pedaling across Manhattan, Brooklyn, and beyond, opened her own bike shop on Staten Island, organized a cycling club for women, and wrote a book, *Bicycling for Ladies*, that offered "common sense" advice: how to power up hills and coast down them; what to wear and more importantly, what not to wear; what the many bicycle parts were for and how to fix them; and how the bicycle, with its "limitless possibilities," could provide exercise, pleasure, and even freedom.[8]

There is the story of Robert Moses, the "master builder" famous for expressways, who also proposed one of the most ambitious bike-infrastructure plans ever announced. And the stories of Alice, Betty, Irene, Barbara, Gwendolyn, Muriel, Neil, Audrey, Sybil, Joan, Marlene, and Alan, elementary or junior-high kids who wrote letters that landed on Mr. Moses's desk and made clear that the city he helped build was hardly a cycler's paradise, even for the children expected to benefit from Moses's narrow view of the bike: as a toy for the parks, not a vehicle for the streets.[9]

There is the story of Steve "The Greek" Athineos and Mayor Ed Koch, adversaries in the 1987 battle of the Bike Ban. Sometimes a bike advocate, Koch was not a fan of the mostly nonwhite messengers who darted through Manhattan's streets and raced up and down in its signature office buildings. The mayor announced that bicycles (the thing messengers needed most) would be banned from three major avenues in midtown Manhattan (essentially the messengers' main office). Athineos led an army of messengers in protest and challenged the perception of what bicycles were for and where they belonged.

And then there is the story of Janette Sadik-Khan, the Department of Transportation Commissioner who (at a pace that would have impressed Robert Moses) installed protected bike lanes, closed streets to motor traffic, and launched the nation's largest bikeshare program. And of the bloggers and borough presidents, journalists and congressmen, deans and former Transportation Commissioners, who thought she was mad.

To tell these stories and to write this history, I have drawn from a diverse collection of primary sources: wheeling diaries; scrapbooks;

maps; rare books; records of bicycle advocacy groups, bike clubs, city councils, the Housing Authority, mayors, and parks commissioners; photographs; newsreels; and more. From elegant libraries to a Manhattan Mini-Storage, my research has taken me across the boroughs and has led to some unexpected finds, including material that, as far as I can tell, no historian has ever seen before. Since the book incorporates recent history, I have also conducted a series of interviews with regular cyclists, bike messengers, outspoken advocates, anti-bike lane protestors, and Department of Transportation employees.[10]

These stories, whether from the 1980s or the 1890s, offer a way to consider fundamental questions about the very nature of the streets, and of life, in New York City. How did Koch, Moses, Bloomberg, Sadik-Khan, business owners, cyclists, and skeptics influence the shape of the city and the ways people move through it? What can we see from the perspective of a bicycle (history) that might have otherwise been obscured? How can history help us understand the place of the bicycle in today's city and tomorrow's?

This book is not a story of fate. The path was neither neat nor linear. Change came about because of real people who made real decisions that had a real impact on the lives of New Yorkers, sometimes for generations to come.

While I make no claim that New York was *the* capital of American cycling, the city is the setting for a singular story. It is true that Boston was an important player in the early years, and, despite its hills, San Francisco has long been home to vibrant cycling cultures. Someone could certainly write a terrific book about the history of cycling in Portland (I would like to read it). But there is good reason to focus on New York. Its density has long attracted more utilitarian cyclists than anywhere else in the United States; its crowds and grime have spurred recreational riders to flee the urban core for the natural splendors that live beyond; its cathedrals of sport have hosted the biggest bike races and its streets the most massive bicycle parades; its policies and regulations have produced the fiercest debate.[11]

The stakes have often been higher here as well. New York's streets, bridges, tunnels, waters, sidewalks, and parks have been, and remain, contested grounds, teeming with people and vehicles fighting for space, priority, and in the largest sense, the city's identity. (Where else could there have been a *Pushcart War*, real or imagined?) Bike messengers could be found in plenty of other cities, but nowhere else were their services needed more, and nowhere else were they more maligned, than in New York. Home to some of the first bicycles imported to the United States, the oldest bicycle manufacturers, the original laws regulating bicycles, and the earliest signs of a cycling culture, New York has a cycling history as long and as deep as that of any other American city.

Undeniably, one of the distinctive features of New York's cycling history—the sheer number of people riding—is largely a consequence of another of the city's distinctive features—the sheer number of people who live there. Following that logic, New York might reasonably be called the toilet capital of the world. Indeed, part of what differentiates New York's experience relates to its scale. Much of New York's history and landscape (think skyscrapers) owes its shape to the fact that the city has long been home to so many people. The New York cyclescape is no different. Certain kinds of bike infrastructure—racks, lanes, paths, bikeshare—generally appear only when there is a large enough set of potential users. Bold solutions were proposed to solve a big population's big problems. Thus, although it will occasionally journey beyond the five boroughs, the book is set in New York and New York alone.[12]

Necessarily, bicycles—and their advocates and foes—stand at the center of this narrative. Even in the cycling heydays, many a New Yorker never rode a bicycle or thought twice about it. Over the course of history, the impact of bicycles on the physical landscape of the city compared to, say, automobiles has been minor. Many more New Yorkers have commuted to work on the subways. Even more have experienced Gotham by boogie woogieing on foot.

But after two hundred years, and in a city known for change, New Yorkers are still pedaling. How and why they have been doing so, how they have changed the city, and how the city has changed them is a remarkable story. One worth telling.

CHAPTER ONE

ROUGH START

The history of cycling in New York begins in 1819—and not with the bicycle but with its ancestor, the velocipede.

Also known as the draisine, hobby horse, dandy carriage, accelerator, Tracena, and pedestrian curricle, the wooden velocipede looks like a bicycle even to twenty-first-century eyes, with one notable exception: no pedals. Instead, like on today's balance bikes for toddlers, riders propelled the "swift walkers" by pushing off the ground with their feet or coasting down hills.

Word had traveled from Europe, where velocipedes were invented, that they could be put to practical use, achieving speeds upward of ten miles per hour. The first shipments of velocipedes had already floated to Boston, Baltimore, and Philadelphia, drawing curious crowds in each harbor, and in May 1819 the first of the wheeled contraptions reached New York. It was the beginning of what one magazine would dub "the summer of velocipedes."[1]

Ever dubious, New Yorkers demanded "ocular demonstration to be convinced" of its merit. The owner of the first imported velocipede was happy to oblige, offering a public unveiling outside Washington Hall, the headquarters of the pro-Federalist Washington Benevolent Society on the corner of Broadway and Reade Street. In an act that the local papers termed "outrageous," "the self styled proprietor" demanded a half-dollar admission fee from the inquiring spectators.[2]

Velocipedes could soon be found in action. Riders wheeled through Vauxhall Gardens, bobbed down the hill to City Hall Park, and circled Bowling Green. Although there was talk that a special ladies' version with four wheels for two women was on its way, it seems that only men rode this first generation of velocipedes in New York. But all New Yorkers could play the part of spectator. On a rainy summer evening (according to a perhaps hyperbolic press report) crowds lined the street and women and children gathered at "every window" to watch a velocipedist who promised to go from Chatham Square to St. Paul's Church in under two minutes. Much to the chagrin of the women whose "lovely tresses of every curl" had been ruined by the humidity, the braggart and his velocipede were no shows. In truth, there were never that many velocipedes to be found.[3]

Yet within three months of seeing their first one, New York lawmakers enacted the city's first "bike" ban. With roughly 120,000 residents, New York (composed only of Manhattan at the time) was the most populous city in the country, and the bumpy cobblestone or muddy dirt-paved streets were already crowded by carts, carriages, pedestrians, horses, and hogs. Riders were more likely to take to the parks—City Hall Park, the Battery, and Bowling Green—or the sidewalks, and it was from those spaces that velocipedes were officially banned in August 1819. Failure to comply resulted in a hefty five-dollar fine. If slaves somehow managed to violate the ordinance, then their masters were on the hook.[4]

Whether as a result of the prohibition or of a natural decline in demand, New Yorkers and Americans at large stopped riding velocipedes within months of when they started. Neither the city nor the bicycle was quite yet ready, and velocipedes were rarely seen for the next fifty years.[5]

Nevertheless, the summer of velocipedes foreshadowed some of the challenges to come and, in certain ways, shaped those later experiences. It established the velocipede not as a serious form of transport but as a "whimsical invention"—an identity the bicycle would long have difficulty shaking. In essence, those first velocipedes also raised doubts—doubts that persisted—that they had a right to the parks and the streets, that they offered a viable form of transportation, and that their devotees were sane.[6]

"By all means let the age of velocipedes be hastened," the *Brooklyn Daily Eagle* cheered in 1868, welcoming what it thought would be a new era of "every-man-his-own-team, and every-woman-her-own-horse." The velocipede was back.[7]

Most New Yorkers had not seen or thought about a velocipede for decades. In the papers, they were more likely to read about the English steamer, *The Velocipede*, than the kind with wheels. Yet during the interregnum, inventors kept tinkering. A Brooklyn man earned a rare American patent in 1858 for a three-wheeled velocipede propelled by a complicated mix of treadles, springs, levers, and a bearing board. For the most part, though, bicycle innovation occurred in Europe.[8]

In the 1860s, when Frenchmen began attaching pedal cranks to the front axle, the modern bicycle was born. Exactly how this happened and who deserves credit was controversial then (with lucrative patents at stake) and remains so today among bicycle historians. However they came to be, the new velocipedes seen spinning on Parisian boulevards by

1867 and warmly welcomed by the *Eagle* in 1868 were in fact bicycles—and while still commonly called velocipedes, started to also be referred to as bicycles.[9]

Nowhere in the United States was bicycle enthusiasm greater in the late 1860s than in New York and adjacent Brooklyn, which, thanks to decades of explosive growth, were particularly poised for bicycle mania. When the first velocipedes arrived in 1819, most New York residents lived on the crooked streets of Manhattan's southern tip. That began to change as the grid transformed rolling hills and farms into a network of rectilinear streets and avenues, inviting residents to imagine an entire island brimming with life.[10]

Imagination turned into reality quicker than anyone thought, in no small part thanks to the Erie Canal, which, when it opened for business in 1825, expedited shipping times, lowered costs for merchants, and brought foodstuffs, timber, and other heartland resources to the nation's financial capital. Soon, factories, markets, and storefronts dotted the increasingly large urban canvas. But New York was not just investing in industry; in 1858, Frederick Law Olmsted and Calvert Vaux won first prize in a design competition for the giant playground to be known as Central Park. Although the city was not immune from riots and damage during the Civil War, it was hardly destroyed. In fact, by the time the newest version of the velocipede arrived in 1868, New York was the vibrant home to more than 900,000 people.[11]

Brooklyn, which would remain independent from the City of New York until 1898, was growing too. In 1820, "Brooklyn town" (one of several towns that composed King's County) had only 7,175 residents and, as a period painting from Francis Guy makes clear, looked like a rural village. Guy's painting shows dogs, cows, pigs, and chickens roaming snowy streets. Off to the side, though, stand two men—a carpenter and a fat-bellied speculator fluffed by a fur coat—portending the expansion and industrialization soon on the way. By 1870, Brooklyn had nearly 400,000 residents of its own, making it the third largest city in the country.[12]

Into this expanding metropolis arrived the bicycle, seen by its boosters as an antidote to the ills of urban life. As the bicycle ascended, horses and their stench would disappear, the evil railroad companies would go bankrupt, the countryside would be brought nearer, suburbanization would boom, space would be annihilated. Instead of riding on the ever-delayed streetcars, which "never take you exactly where you want," the second-generation velocipede offered a "convenient means of locomotion" that would "revolutionize travel for all time."[13]

Not only an instrument of change in terms of transit, the bicycle was also lauded as a cure-all in a city prone to outbreaks of smallpox, yellow fever, measles, and cholera. Doctors predicted a new age of "Velocipathy," declaring the velocipede "the most excellent tonic and appetizer of our modern Pharmacopoea." New Yorkers on wheels could "fly from infection" and infectious sufferers. The velocipede would be the hero to finally defeat the city's dark side.[14]

With velocipedes reappearing (now with pedals) on city streets, the *New York Times* and the *Brooklyn Daily Eagle* soon began publishing regular columns on all things velocipede. Enthusiasts formed the Brooklyn Velocipede Club, which may have been the first bicycle club in the country. Entrepreneurs began setting up production facilities, making New York the American capital of velocipede manufacturing with firms like Pickering & Davis (144 Green Street), A. T. Demarest (620 Broadway), Mercer & Monod (3 William Street), and Calvin Witty (638 Broadway). Over the course of two years, New York designers registered fifty patents—a subject of frequent discord between producers—and sold bicycles not just to local Brooklyn and Manhattanites but also to people in cities across the United States. At first, they could not keep up with the demand.[15]

The early bike builders were more than just designers—they were also marketers, publishers, riders, and racers. Pickering & Davis, for example, put out *The Velocipedist*, an industrywide magazine with the broad and not so humble goal of "record[ing] everything of interest in the Velocipede world." It was the first bike-centric periodical in the United States. The manufacturers also opened their own riding academies.[16]

At the time, no one knew how to ride a bike. Compared to later bicycles that sported lighter frames, pneumatic tires, multiple gears, and soft saddles, the new velocipedes in 1869 were particularly difficult to master. There was a reason people called them "boneshakers." Staying atop them required learning a new set of skills: pedaling, balancing, and

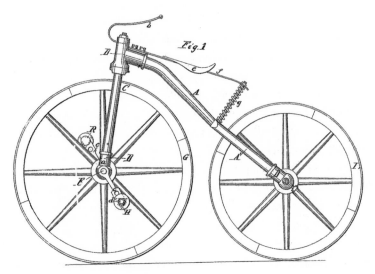

FIGURE 1.1 Like other New York builders, Thomas Pickering of Pickering & Davis contributed to a particularly American form of the velocipede. In this 1869 patent drawing, Pickering introduced a number of mechanisms intended to make the device lighter, less top-heavy, and easier to ride, including a tubular "back-bone" (A) (instead of a solid bar), a hollow fork (C), and a specially designed "polygonal-shaped stirrup" (H). Pickering's velocipede also featured a sprung steering handle and saddle, smaller wheels, and a lower frame, all intended to make riding on America's bumpy roads more comfortable.

Thomas R. Pickering, Velocipede, US Patent 88,507, issued March 30, 1869

steering, all at the same time. They also required courage. "To get on is not difficult. To stay on is a labor of genius," one rider quipped.[17]

In 1869—the year of peak use—dozens of bicycling schools opened. On Broadway alone there was an academy at Tenth Street, another at Twenty-Second Street, another at Twenty-Eighth Street, and yet another at Forty-Seventh Street. Elsewhere across Manhattan and Brooklyn, the uninitiated could take a lesson at the Empire City Velocipedrome, the Capitoline Velocipede School, the Phoenix Velocipede School, Fearing's Velocipede Rink, Burnham's, Byldenberg's, Pangburn's, Steinway Hall, Merchants Hall, or Central Hall. Art galleries and armories turned into riding academies. Really, any space big enough could be transformed. The popular schools hosted 200 "scholars" a day and catered to thousands of patrons, each of whom typically paid a monthly membership fee. With membership came access to the facilities, sometimes rather expansive. The Pearsall School, for example, hosted beginners on its upper floors, reserving space on the ground floor for spectators to watch the more accomplished riders. There was even a twenty-foot "artificial hill."[18]

Adult students often required several one-hour lessons from "professors" before they could roll around the rinks themselves. From there they graduated to the streets, sidewalks, and parks. (The original velocipede ban from 1819 seems to have been forgotten.) Inside the academies there were smooth wooden surfaces, railings to grasp, experts on hand, and only selective, and presumably sympathetic, onlookers, making the prospect of falling just "a little embarrassing." The bumpy, muddy streets were a different story. "Sliding down hill on a hand-saw, tooth side up, would be two degrees more comfortable" than riding a velocipede, one novice reported, lamenting that the experience left his muscles sore and clothes ruined. Another newbie in Brooklyn had such trouble navigating and avoiding the "ash barrels" that lined the street that no one in the neighborhood got a " 'square' night's rest."[19]

The academies were more than just schools. In the evenings, they held races where riders would circle the track nine or so times (roughly one mile) as spectators eyed the clock. At a race held at the Empire Rink, one manufacturer cum racer won in a time of 3:35. Another match pitted a pedestrian against a man on a velocipede. Could a velocipedist travel five miles before the "walkist" covered three? (No. The pedestrian bested him by five seconds, finishing in nineteen minutes.) More than pride was at stake. Winners often took home substantial prizes, sometimes measuring in the thousands of dollars.[20]

Racing was not the only spectacle on offer at the schools. On a Saturday evening in March a baker's dozen riders entered Burnham's rink as part of a grand opening performance. As a band played, stuntmen rode in with their arms folded, one with a "small boy seated upon his shoulders." At Calvin Witty's school on the corner of Fulton and Flatbush avenues (one of three he operated in the neighborhood), Fred Hanlon, who with his brothers helped popularize the velocipede through acrobatic performances, took off his coat and put it back on while riding sidesaddle. Another crowd favorite was when riders going at full speed picked up two chairs, one in each hand, and paraded them around the room.[21] Part school, practice rink, racing track, open gymnasium, and circus tent, the academies embodied the confused nature of the velocipede itself—a means of transportation, a machine made to race, and a novelty.

No matter their usefulness, velocipedes were beyond the means of most New Yorkers. While certain models could be had for less, velocipedes typically cost $100 or more, with fancy models fetching roughly $200, and the fanciest models, fashioned with ivory and silver components, upward of $500. Aside from bankers, merchants, lawyers, and their ilk, few could afford one. Certainly not an Irish dockworker or the many other recent immigrants that made up the 44 percent of New Yorkers who were foreign born. Middle-class salaried employees earned about $2,000 per year, skilled mechanics about $1,000, and unskilled workers considerably less. Even for the salaried types, a velocipede cost roughly three weeks' pay. It is not surprising that Mr. J. G. Pangburn chose to open his riding academy in Lower Manhattan where "business men" congregated and could easily "drop in" for a quick lesson. Yet there was much talk about how cheap velocipedes would soon replace expensive horses: "It costs but little to purchase and still less to keep . . . It does not . . . eat cart-loads of hay . . . it won't bite."[22]

For those who could afford it, there were certainly plenty of chances to buy. At the evening performances there was almost always a sales pitch. For example, the "Velocipede March and Galop" overture that began the nightly festivities at the Pearsall School featured a commercial masquerading as a parade: the Pearsall Brothers atop the "patented" Pearsall Velocipede (on sale at the on-site store for $125), the Pickering Brothers on the Pickering Velocipede ($125), and the Messrs. Monod on their branded velocipede ($115). After the showcase, visitors were invited down to the floor to examine and purchase the models.[23]

Despite the elaborate salesmanship, most riders probably never bought a velocipede. Instead, whether attending a class or cycling on ever-popular Clinton Street in Brooklyn or through Central Park, they rented them. Renting out velocipedes became another of the many ways New Yorkers

FIGURE I.2

An advertisement from 1869.

Patent Medicine Labels and Advertisements,
Lot 10632–3, 1869, Library of Congress Prints
and Photographs Division, Washington, DC

sought to profit from the budding interest. Stuart's Hotel in Canarsie advertised that it would lend its guests velocipedes to use on the special course it was building just for them. A "velocipede photographer" opened a studio on Manhattan's Broadway. Others sold velocipede accessories—parts, wrenches, lanterns, locks, and gloves. Even those not in the business sought to profit from it, including one entrepreneur who marketed a special velocipede hair oil to women.[24]

Whether it was appropriate for women to ride was "the question of the day." According to at least one enthusiast from Chicago (where riders bought New York-made velocipedes and patronized riding academies owned by New Yorkers), "There are a thousand reasons why it is a misfortune to be a woman, but just now the chief of all of them is, she can't straddle a velocipede. Like shaving, the machine is an exclusively masculine appurtenance." Because of the constraints of traditional dress and because mastering the bicycle required daring and athleticism, virtues traditionally bestowed upon men, he was not alone in thinking that women and bicycles did not mix. The same writer claimed that men with skinny (weak) legs were also ill suited for riding. In this case there was an easy solution: hire "a colored man" to push.[25]

In New York, despite suggestions that "the tyranny of fashion forbids" women from velocipeding, a select group of women did bike, albeit in distinct ways. First, convention required that their bicycles be different than those of men. Some rode tricycles, which were not exclusively for women but designed in a way to make them appear less masculine. With three wheels instead of two, they were more firmly grounded and required less effort to balance. Some models also had lower frames and seats, making riding in a dress easier and in appearance more like sitting in the back of a carriage instead of straddling a machine. Sometimes manufacturers even referred to the saddle as a "chair," emphasizing the ease and relaxation that came with riding a tricycle. "What is lost in speed is made up in comfort," is how one expert described the distinction between three- and two-wheeled velocipedes. But not every woman was willing to forgo the true velocipeding experience. There were two-wheeled velocipedes modified to have an extra-plush "willow seat" or an especially low frame that diminished the awkwardness of stepping over and straddling the high bar.[26]

Even with these changes, modified attire was required—flowing dresses were not exactly ideal cycling wear. A distinct riding outfit emerged: a tight-fitting bodice, a knee-length skirt worn over bloomers, slender sleeves, and a circular hat topped with a feather or ribbon. While the typical dress maintained femininity, there were reports of women in "bilegular garments." When women riders did violate proper decorum, New Yorkers made their feelings known. At the Empire Rink in mid-April, for example, two French "roughed-faced women in flesh-colored tights nearly to their hips" prompted female spectators to leave "in disgust."[27]

As usual, people were more interested in and critical of what women were wearing than men, but men on wheels sometimes pushed the limits of fashion too. An 1869 lithograph from the New York-based team of Currier and Ives depicts a velocipedist with unmowed sideburns; tight, sky-blue pants; brown jacket; and mustard-colored vest and cap, the latter encircled by a ruby-red ribbon.[28]

Not surprisingly it was the men most invested (literally) in velocipedes who encouraged women to ride. After all, women represented half of the potential market. Back in 1819 New York, there was only talk of a women's version of the velocipede. Now there were many ladies' models from which to choose. By differentiating the bicycles and therefore the experience, perhaps the businessmen could have it both ways. Maybe they could sell velocipedes to women and not offend their neighbors.

The academy owners welcomed women to attend ladies-only classes. Some even asked their wives or sisters to serve as models, demonstrating that it was possible for women to ride and to do so without "objectionable *exposés*." On a spring afternoon in Brooklyn, for example, velocipedes

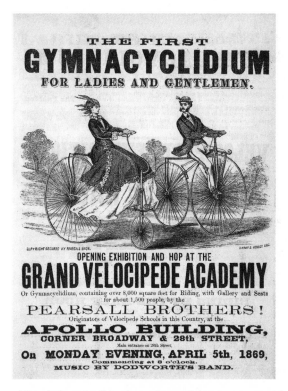

FIGURE 1.3 Although the Pearsall Brothers advertised their new room as the first "gymnacyclidium" for both men and women, women could only take lessons during a special ladies' hour and only so long as a family member served as a chaperone.

"The First Gymnacyclidium," Printed Ephemera Collection, Lot 10632–3, Library of Congress, Washington, DC

rolled along Clinton Street, including one pedaled by Miss Pearsall, who managed to "attract great attention." Just a couple of weeks earlier she had debuted the "Peerless" velocipede designed for skirt-wearing women at the family's "Pearsall's Gymnacyclidium" (on sale, on site, for $135).[29]

While women riders were welcome in the academies, the streets were not always so friendly, and not just because of their bumpy nature. Nineteenth-century New Yorkers often perceived the streets as dangerous spaces, places for women without a proper family and home, and the offices of prostitutes. But the streets also afforded the chance for independence and a flourishing culture, even if mediated by social conventions. The relationship between class, gender, and public space in New York was evolving. And even though women were much more likely to ride indoors at chaperoned classes, when bourgeois women, who had tended to emphasize the importance of home and domesticity, did ride through the city atop a sporting machine, they complicated the ways New Yorkers understood women's place in the public sphere. "A pretty young woman astonished the gray-coated policemen and pleased the public generally," by velocipeding through Central Park, a February 1869 news report documented. She rode "a splendid two-wheeled turn-out, which she managed with perfect skill." The praise came despite an important detail: she was dressed in "manly costume."[30]

For the first time, riders began to ask the city to change. There were enough of them to warrant some public infrastructure and the numbers would only increase, enthusiasts thought. In particular, as more riders succeeded in the rinks, they clamored for smooth surfaces on which to ride outdoors. Pavement—consisting of concrete, wood, or some combination thereof—was much preferred to the bone-shaking cobblestone. Riders also asked for ramps to climb curbs without having to dismount. Even critics began to wonder if, for the benefit and safety of everyone else, the city should designate a "special place" for velocipedes in the parks. A bolder plan came from former assistant secretary of war and editor and part owner of the *New York Sun*, Charles Dana. The weighty-bearded velocipede enthusiast proposed a pine-planked, elevated bicycle path that would run all the way from the Battery to Upper Manhattan. While the thirty-foot-wide roadway would be primarily for velocipedists, the pedestrians below would benefit too: they would no longer be "endangered by the carelessness or awkwardness of velocipedists." The elevated veloway never came to be, but velocipedists scored small victories, like when city officials agreed to pave Bedford Avenue in Brooklyn at their behest.[31]

With more velocipedes on the streets came more questions. Were they toys fit for the parks or too terrifying to be admitted? Should they be allowed on the streets and the walks or just on exclusive paths? Who were the velocipedists and why were they riding? The answers were complicated. In some instances, one use seemed to threaten another. "Racing on the street must be frowned down," the *Brooklyn Daily Eagle* cautioned, if velocipedes are to "come into general use."[32]

Although velocipedes never did "come into general use," those living in 1869 had good reason to think that they soon would. Early that year, the *New York Times* estimated that there were roughly 5,000 velocipedists in the city and its immediate suburbs. Not long before, there had been zero. Later in the season, another paper estimated that 16,000 New Yorkers rode.[33]

With increased popularity came more calls for restriction. And no ground was more sacred than Central Park, which saw 2,786 velocipedes roll through over the course of one spring month in 1869. It was an impressive number, to be sure, but a far cry from the 148,310 other vehicles and 280,143 pedestrians. Still, traditionalists worried. If the park was further invaded by thousands and thousands of these new machines, it would cease to become the park as they knew it.[34]

In January 1869, *Scientific American* reported that the parks commissioners had banned velocipedes in Central Park, citing a lack of space and cyclists' propensity to frighten horses. The magazine argued that the ban was nonsense: "The park was made for the public not the public for the park." If New Yorkers were voting with their velocipedes, the Central Park commissioners needed to accommodate their constituents. But fifteen days later, the *New York Times* declared that the issue had not in fact been settled and threw its weight behind the velocipede cause, saying it would be foolhardy to prohibit the "velocipedal public" from enjoying the city's greatest park, especially since the commissioners of Prospect Park in Brooklyn invited velocipedists to ride along its bridle paths, eventually opened up the carriage drives, and even promised to build a special velocipede course.[35]

To the relief of riders (and despite what subsequent historians have written), the Central Park velocipede ban did not materialize. While it is possible that the commissioners made statements to the press about their intention to enact such a ban (several articles referred to the commissioners as vacillating) or to prohibit bicycles from sections of the park (several reports mentioned that velocipedes were excluded from the carriage drives, but permitted on the bridle paths and walks), the official record includes no such prohibition. To the contrary, the commissioners included velocipedists in official tallies of park users.[36]

Although velocipedes were allowed within the park, there was growing talk that they should not be allowed outside it. In the spring of 1869, lawmakers considered banning bicycles from the streets. In this case, the *Times* supported the ban, arguing in a May 1869 editorial that while a velocipede was "a pretty toy" and a good source of exercise, it belonged only in the indoor academies, the contained parks, and perhaps on the more northern and more deserted streets. The roads of Lower Manhattan were just too crowded for the riders who "fly like shuttles." The roads way uptown could be treated like playgrounds, but the downtown thoroughfares needed to be free from the "nuisances which imperil life and limb, and impede free and easy locomotion." Instead of thinking of velocipedes as a means of locomotion, the *Times* labeled them obstacles, comparing the vehicles to "boys' sleds." Whether or not they could effectively be used as such, velocipedes, if actually banned from the streets, could never become a legitimate mode of transportation. But like the Central Park ban, the broader antibicycle proposal never came to be.[37]

Similar debates arose across the rivers. In Jersey City and in Newark, lawmakers agreed to let velocipedes wheel through the streets but banned them from the sidewalks. Brooklyn politicians were about to follow suit until they realized that an existing ordinance barring wheeled vehicles from the sidewalks already prohibited such activity. When it suited their purposes, lawmakers defined velocipedes as vehicles; other times, they classified them differently.[38]

In the summer of 1873, the Brooklyn Common Council went a step further, banning bicycles from city streets between 1:00 p.m. and 8:00 p.m., effectively relegating velocipedes to toys. The council members had considered banning them for the entire day, but in order to let "the boys exercise," left the mornings free. The velocipedists did not protest en masse. Nor did the manufacturers. There were no legal challenges or public refusals to pay the two-dollar fine for disobeying.[39]

Why? Because by the time the council passed the ordinance, most of the velocipedes were already gone. The mania for velocipedes ended as suddenly as it began. In April, May, and June 1869, more than 2,200 riders, on average, entered Central Park each month. By July, something had happened. There were fewer than 900. By not terribly cold October, the number dwindled to 141. With crowds flocking to circuslike velocipede performances in the evening and riding rinks during the day, it seemed as if the most natural habitat for the bicycle was indoors. And, in fact, the mania died just as the weather was at its cycling best. Over the summer of 1869 when other outdoor activities beckoned, the *Times* noted that attendance at the riding academies had thinned and the schools had become "the resort of roughs." The *Velocipedist*, the monthly magazine that had promised to keep up with all things velocipede, lasted just three issues. Shop owners auctioned off velocipedes for a fraction of the price they had fetched months earlier. (In 1873, a stolen velocipede was said to be worth "about $5.") In the coming years, the major manufacturers shut down or turned their attention to the children's market, as velocipedes were typically understood as toys for youngsters. Children and their toys had no place on the streets.[40]

What happened? Historians have argued that the velocipede was too flawed a device, that while it may have been fun to ride on indoor rinks, it was ill suited for the uncomfortable nature of riding on the roads. One writer in 1869 did describe taking a spin on the street as the equivalent of "riding a hog." Similar reports suggested that New Yorkers were beginning to realize just how impractical the velocipede was. The unsteady machines required skill to ride, not easily attained by adults who never learned as children. And they were believed to make horses skittish and to disrupt the established ways of using parks and moving along the streets. Others blamed one segment of cyclists—racers who made velocipeding seem less respectable—and one segment of spectators—young boys who teased adult riders and their silly getups (recall the "bilegular garments" for women and tight, sky-blue pants for men). Considering the expense of becoming a velocipedist, the size, scope, and potential of the market had been overstated to begin with.[41]

Although (slightly) longer in duration and more widespread, New York's experience with velocipedes in 1869 was similar to that with its nonpedaled ancestor in 1819. In both cases, people enjoyed imagining how their lives and their city would change. In both cases, people disagreed about where velocipedes belonged and how they should be regulated. In both cases, the velocipedes disappeared quickly.

Yet, in this second era, the bans on bikes did not come to fruition until after most had already disappeared. Not exactly a potent political force, velocipedists were nevertheless strong enough in number and held enough clout to ward off the restrictions. And some velocipede businesses survived, even if sellers had to reorient their efforts toward the children's market. When those children entered adulthood, they might again become cyclists interested in trying a new kind of bike. For it would not take another fifty years for the bicycle to return.

Within a decade of velocipedes coming and going, a new and unusual kind of bicycle revitalized Americans' interest in wheeling. By the mid-1870s, batches of high-wheelers with oversized front wheels that promised greater speeds found their way from Europe into the hands of an enterprising Bostonian, Albert Pope. Pope soon set up shop in Hartford, Connecticut, and emerged as the most important player in the domestic bicycle market, selling his bicycles under the Columbia brand.[42]

Although New York was no longer the center of the bicycle industry, it was still a center of cycling. In the late 1870s, indoor riding rinks began to pepper the landscape once again. Clubs devoted to racing, riding, and defending the rather unordinary machines mushroomed. (The high-wheel-style bicycles were later dubbed "ordinaries" in order to distinguish them from subsequent models.) Throughout the 1880s, even outside of Manhattan, bicycle clubs, like the Staten Island Wheelmen, the

Brooklyn Bicycle Club, the Kings County Wheelmen, the Long Island Wheelmen, and the Nassau Wheelmen, proliferated.[43]

As was true in the past, bicycles were a hobby for the elite. High-wheelers generally cost $120 or more and to join a club, members also had to purchase a club uniform and pay regular membership dues. They were also required to have good taste, at least enough to appreciate a seven-course banquet like the kind the Citizens Bicycle Club served up in 1886. Members feasted on Blue Point oysters, Gumbo de Volaille, grouse, and petits fours inside the club's spacious Manhattan headquarters, the city's first building constructed solely for use by a bicycle club. Only adults were allowed inside. In this moment, bicycles were meant for adults. Adult men, that is.[44]

However improper it may have seemed for women to ride velocipedes, the idea of a woman in a dress mounting a soaring bike with a saddle five feet off the ground was a nonstarter. For the most part, anyway; a select group of women rode and even raced on them. But in general, the high-wheelers became synonymous with men, and young, white, and sporting ones in particular. Even with the help of a small step, getting on the bicycle required skill; so did successfully riding it. Headers (a crash in which the rider falls forward) were common. Deemed more appropriate by Victorian standards, tricycles continued to offer women a safer alternative, but were even more expensive than the already pricey high-wheelers.[45]

Riders were also nearly all white. In part this reflected the demographics of the city population, which was overwhelmingly white too; the influx of African Americans, Latinos, and Asians would come later. Whether they were immigrants or not, the enormous number of poor people who crowded into the narrow, dumbbell-shaped tenement buildings were not among New York's riders.[46]

Nevertheless, the number of New Yorkers riding, whether on a bicycle or a tricycle, increased once more. By the summer of 1880 there were hundreds of cyclists and by the mid-1880s there were several thousand. In a city with well over a million people (close to two million if you include Brooklyn), they still comprised a tiny minority. But atop their giraffelike bikes they were hard to miss. And they once again prompted questions about the nature of cycling and the nature of city space.[47]

Initially, the tide turned in favor of the riders. The first major piece of bike policy passed in the high-wheel period was not regulation but deregulation. In May 1880, the Common Council of the City of Brooklyn lifted the seven-year-old prohibition on cycling in the street. Wheelmen and women regained the right to ride; the only requirement was that they carry a lantern at night. The *Brooklyn Daily Eagle* probably summed up the general mood when it threw its support behind the resolution even as it belittled the latest bicycle craze as a "nuisance," proclaimed that only men infected with an "extraordinary lunacy" would dare to ride the tottering bicycles, and predicted that the fanatics and their ridiculously large wheels would disappear in short order. After all, the previous bicycle incarnations lasted less than a year.[48]

But just a few months after the council lifted the bicycle ban, controversy struck. On October 19, 1880, at 5:30 p.m., a coachman lost control of his horses just as Mary Porter, face "flushed with the glow of health," was returning home on horseback from Prospect Park. One of the horses rammed into the seventeen-year-old, and she died on the scene. The coachman blamed her death on a bicycle, which had allegedly spooked his horses.[49]

Within weeks, Brooklynites were pleading with the Common Council to take the dangerous bicycles off the street, citing the recent accident and the general disregard of the cyclists who "only laughed" as they frightened horses. "The gilded bicycle should be abolished altogether," one petitioner demanded. Another suggested the need for traffic signals, speed limits, and restrictions on which streets bicycles could travel.[50] As pleas for regulation came in, the growing concern that bicycles would scare horses and that "bicyclers would take a sort of pleasure" in doing so prompted the Manhattan Department of Public Parks Commissioners to enact a resolution written in unusually plain language: "That no bicycles or tricycles be allowed in the Central or city parks."[51]

The only dissenter was Commissioner Andrew Haswell Green—who commonly found few allies among commissioners but had a major hand in shaping the city as we know it today. It was Green who led the campaign to combine five boroughs into one city; who helped build the Metropolitan Museum of Art, the Museum of Natural History, the Bronx Zoo, and the marble-encrusted New York Public Library; and who oversaw the implementation of the Greensward Plan for Central Park. As a bushy-faced octogenarian, he was mistakenly shot and killed and then so deeply mourned that New Yorkers lowered flags and closed city courts. (Subsequently, he was largely forgotten.)

Green thought bicycles should be allowed in the park, at least during certain hours. But his lone vote was not enough. The other commissioners were steadfast. When a handful of cyclists returned a few months later asking for permission to ride on a sidewalk abutting Central Park, the answer was the same: No.[52]

But by this time, bicycles had been around long enough that more formal advocacy had developed. There were now several bicycle clubs that formed part of an emerging bike lobby. Leading the fight for Central Park were Kirk Munroe and Downing Vaux.

Munroe was a writer, adventurer, Staten Island resident, and, in 1880, cofounder of the League of American Wheelman (LAW), a national organization that promoted the bicycle and the rights of riders, hosted races, and offered a social network. He was an avid, early, and prominent cyclist, having also organized the New York Bicycle Club in 1879 and allegedly imported the third high-wheeler in all of New York. Downing Vaux was a landscape architect better known as the son of Calvert Vaux, codesigner of Central Park. Now Downing, sporting a full beard that seemed to swallow his mouth whole, was asking if he and his friends could ride in the park his father had built. Perhaps their reputations were solid enough or the number of riders was now large enough that the commissioners felt the need to make a small concession. In March 1881, they granted the LAW permission to hold a bicycle parade through Central Park later that spring.[53]

But anticyclists were increasingly organized as well. A group of wealthy and well-connected residents, including a Russian ambassador and a patent attorney, fired off petition after petition encouraging the commissioners not to give in. Adding his voice was another lawyer who later made headlines by trying to remove an insane asylum from his Morningside Park neighborhood. Lunatics and cyclists both threatened the sanctity of his neighborhood and his park.[54]

Tensions escalated in the summer of 1881 when three cyclists, with the support of the nation's leading bicycle manufacturer and the backing of the LAW, openly defied the bike ban. The instigators included William M. Wright, captain of the Mercury Club and rider of "the largest wheel in America"; S. C. Foster (a.k.a. Knick O'Bocker), a writer for *Bicycling World* and the "Poet Wheelman" of one of the three local bicycle clubs to which he belonged; and Henry H. Walker, a member of the Manhattan Club known for doing "fancy business" on his wheel. They knew that violating the prohibition would lead to arrest, which would then allow them to argue their case in court. As planned, officers apprehended the men and, because they refused to pay the fine, sent them to prison.[55]

The trial began shortly thereafter. On the cyclists' side were thirty-four witnesses representing a cross section of the kinds of New Yorkers who became cyclists—a lawyer, a civil engineer, a glass importer, a lumber businessman, etc. Their testimony revolved around the contested issue of whether bicycles irritated horses. They all said essentially the same thing: they had been cycling for the last two years, they had seen many a horse, and while a few horses shied away, rarely did they seem terribly bothered.[56]

Thirty-nine witnesses for the other side told a different story that echoed what had happened to the young woman killed in Brooklyn the year before. Thanks to careless cyclists, one driver testified, he had suffered a black eye, a concussion, and lost "part of his eyebrow." A mother and daughter reported that they had been violently tossed from their buggy. Another driver recounted being thrown into a ditch in a hit and run.[57]

Despite claims of bad behavior, the cyclists and their defenders emphasized that the riders were "gentlemen," not "inexperienced boys." Whether or not bicycles belonged in the park depended on what bicycles were for, how cyclists behaved, and the degree to which bicycles moved like carriages, which were, in fact, allowed. Although the early cyclists had money, their adventurous streak often put them at odds with the more traditional elite. Tricycles—slower, safer, and more carriagelike—appeared tamer, which is why two of the three law testers rode them instead of the precarious two-wheelers. To underscore the point about the suitability of cycling in the park, when lawyers for the city asked the cyclists how fast, on average, bicycles travel, they answered, "Seven miles an hour," citing a speed closer to a trotting pace than that of someone zipping down a hill. Could they stop as fast as a carriage? The witnesses reported that they needed between five and fifteen feet to stop, explaining that cyclists braked by applying backward pressure on the pedals (proudly, most did not use actual brakes). One witness claimed to be able to "vault right off" in an instant.[58]

Their tactics failed. The cyclists lost their case, though the decision did not weigh in on the bigger question of whether bicycles endangered public safety. Instead, the court merely affirmed that the parks commissioners had the authority to ban bicycles, which they continued to do for the next two years, allowing cyclists only a yearly parade.[59]

Those parades turned out to be no small matter. They helped to demonstrate that cyclists could behave themselves (and were not all that different than the other parkgoing elite), and that the horses would not mind. Meanwhile, the number of cyclists kept increasing. Unlike in the earlier velocipede eras, bicycles proved to be more than just a fling. Finally, in June 1883, the commissioners granted cyclists access to the park. But there was a catch—two, in fact. First, they had to be "proficient" riders, not reckless novices. Members of the "established bicycle clubs," which often had strict admission requirements in terms of money and class, could apply for a permit to ride. Even those allowed in could only ride on the park's west drive and do so only before 9:00 a.m. The commissioners probably expected to find just a handful of riders between sunrise and 9:00 a.m. In fact, cyclists—many without the required permission slip—took to riding in the middle of the night since it was technically legal beginning at midnight each day. Within weeks, the commissioners opened up Riverside Drive too, with less severe time restrictions and soon, none at all.[60]

The parks commissioners swiftly banned bicycles from other places in their jurisdiction, including two Harlem River bridges, the Macomb's Dam Bridge, and the Third Avenue Bridge. In the days before municipal consolidation and long before Robert Moses would create complex authorities governing bridges and tunnels, the political authorities that controlled the bridges varied. In this case, the Department of Public Parks

FIGURE 1.4 Tricycles also catered to couples riding tandems, like the two varieties (one in the foreground and another in the background) seen in this 1886 drawing of Riverside Drive. Riding on Riverside Drive at night became so popular that a bicycle livery opened nearby with 100 bicycles/tricycles for riders to rent and offered storage to those who wanted to keep their wheels near the park. It was open twenty-four hours a day.

T. De Thulstrup, "Wheeling on Riverside Drive," and "Wheelmen in New York," *Harper's Weekly*, July 17, 1886, 455–57

maintained control of the two heavily trafficked crossings. According to the superintendent of the Macomb's Dam Bridge, horses jumped in panic and women "screamed and hollered" when bicycles rolled by.[61]

In 1885, the Brooklyn park commissioners introduced their own regulations, even as they acknowledged that there had been few problems in Prospect Park (6 crashes involving bicycles and one with a tricycle, compared to 110 carriage crashes, 10 skating accidents, and 2 people who "fell in the lake"). Noting that most riders were "expert in the management of their machines," the commissioners allowed bicycles and tricycles on all of the parkways and footpaths but prohibited speeding, coasting (riding with one's feet off the pedals), and bugles (which club

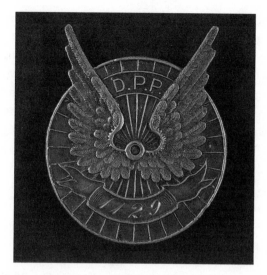

FIGURE 1.5 Only members of an established bicycle club who applied for permission could access Central Park and Riverside Drive during select hours. Approved riders were expected to don one of these numbered metal badges issued by the Department of Public Parks.

Museum of the City of New York. 50.335, ca. 1886

captains used to bark orders to members). They also required that riders keep to the right, give warning when passing, and carry a lantern at night.[62]

These rules applied only to those wheelmen permitted in the park. Riders had to register with the park superintendent and, like their friends in Central Park, wear a metal badge on their left breast to gain admission. Enforcing compliance were members of five Brooklyn bicycle clubs, the same groups that suggested the regulations in the first place. Apparently, cyclists had just as much to lose from cyclists behaving badly as anyone else.[63]

Throughout the early years of the high-wheel era, politicians passed regulations in piecemeal fashion, often responding to particular petitions from particular constituents. In Central Park and Prospect Park, commissioners agreed that only certain cyclists belonged: those expert enough not to scare horses and, more importantly, those sophisticated enough (well-behaved members of the bicycle clubs) not to demean the character of the space.

But as the number of cyclists (most of whom were voting-age men) grew and cycling persisted, so too did their political power. By 1887, nine years after the first high-wheelers rolled through Gotham, the bicycle lobby secured a landmark victory. With cyclists hovering nearby, almost all of the lawmakers in Albany, Governor David Hill included, endorsed the "Liberty Bill," which afforded bicycles the same status as carriages. No longer could New York aldermen, parks commissioners, bridge superintendents, mayors, or anyone else ban bicycles unless they were willing to ban carriages too. Even though most cyclists rode for recreation, the law now upheld bicycles as also vehicles for transportation. The parks commissioners were not happy.[64]

Neither were the many New Yorkers for generations to come who would try to push bicycles off the road. Although modified and always open to interpretation, the "Liberty Bill" is still on the books.[65]

Over the course of the first seven decades of New York's cycling history, there were three distinct eras, each richer than the last. The pedal-less velocipedes that came in 1819 numbered only a few and lasted only a few months. Still, they were banned. The velocipedes fifty years later were more popular, and the buzz lasted slightly, but just slightly, longer. There were some signs of the very beginning of a culture of cycling—a magazine, a club, and people devoted to velocipedes. There was not much infrastructure, but there were dreams and proposals. In the end, lawmakers banned bikes once again.

By the time the high-wheelers had become more established (over years, not months) without ruining the parks or the city, cyclists earned rights instead of prohibitions. They eventually won access to the parks and the streets. They did not yet have their own spaces, but the lobbying forces had been marshaled and they would be in a position to demand those in due time.

Although the landscape of the city did not change much, New York's early experiences with bicycles had lasting repercussions. The debates that started in the very beginning—about where bicycles belonged, how they should be ridden, who should be riding them, and whether they should be welcomed or discouraged—persisted, as did some of the laws, as did the bicycles. While the popularity of cycling would continue to ebb and flow, never again would bicycles disappear completely from the city.

In fact, bicycles were about to become more popular than ever.

CHAPTER TWO

UP AND DOWN

The 1890s was a decade for the cyclists. Despite an economic tail-spin, thousands of American workers produced millions of bicycles. Miles and miles of bicycle paths flowed in and out of metropolises. Bicycle clubs formed in big, medium-, and tiny-sized cities. New York was at the heart of the American cycling renaissance. As Stephen Crane wrote about his adopted hometown, "everything is bicycle."[1]

In 1896, just in Manhattan, there were at least fifty-six bicycle dealers and scores of how-to-ride-a-bicycle academies. Newspapers featured daily stories of the wheelmen's "gossip" and entire pages devoted to cycling. New Yorkers rode on the greatest bicycle path in the world, argued the most about where and how bicycles belonged, and invented a future in which bicycles crisscrossed the city, reshaping the physical, social, and cultural landscape along the way. Teetering on the edge of modernity, New Yorkers dreamed of a new kind of city: a cycling city.[2]

In 1898, New York became Greater New York, as the five boroughs joined in a massive metropolis home to more than twice as many people as the nation's second largest city. Already the well-worn seat of American capitalism, New York City was still growing in size and significance. Age-old questions about how to manage—how to govern, how to deliver public services to the masses, how to cater to industrial titans and protect the vulnerable—took on new meaning.

Bicycles tapped into these larger conversations about the failures of urban life and utopian visions of a city remade. New Yorkers in the 1890s were already desperate for ways to escape crowds, navigate freely and independently, and exercise mind and body in a city perceived as toxic. It was in New York—big, dense, chaotic—where bicycles appeared in the greatest numbers and where they seemed to offer the greatest promise: of faster commutes, healthier bodies, a cleaner city, richer social opportunities, independence from streetcars, and the freedom to roam. Before the age of the automobile, it was the bicycle that promised private transit for all and a new way to envision an old city. In short, the bicycle offered hope.

Among a sea of more than 3.4 million New Yorkers, hundreds of thousands of whom could reasonably be called cyclists, were Arthur Hyde and Violet Ward. Their accounts, documented in "wheeling diaries," scrapbooks, letters, and photographs, tell a larger story about cyclists and the city, revealing that bicycles and bicyclists did not always live on the periphery. Hyde, Ward, and New Yorkers at large honestly believed that the bicycle was reshaping their city—for better or worse.

Arthur Hyde

Arthur Penrhyn Stanley Hyde was born in 1875 and lived first in Newark and then Manhattan, with regular time spent in and around the New York area. While he toyed around on a child-sized velocipede as a boy, adults rode high-wheelers. But as he aged, so did the bicycle.[3]

By the time he was eighteen, the disproportioned two-wheelers had largely disappeared. In their stead, and in much higher numbers, "safety" bicycles, with two equal-sized wheels, a diamond frame, and pneumatic tires, exploded in popularity. Although it typically had only one gear and no brakes, the safety bicycle was heralded as a technological marvel—deservedly so, considering that the bicycles New Yorkers ride today look quite similar. Easier and safer to ride, deemed more appropriate for women (because they were easier and safer to ride), and much cheaper than the high-wheelers, safety bicycles enchanted New Yorkers and Americans at large.[4]

Hyde's first ride on a safety did not go well: "I thought it was an easy thing . . . the next thing I knew I had pitched over into the gutter." But before long he was off exploring the city and beyond. At first he rented from a dealer on Lenox Avenue and 125th Street, and within days he bought his very first bike, a "Referee Cushion Tired Wheel" from a shop downtown on Chambers Street.[5]

We know these details, and many more, from Hyde's meticulous recordkeeping. In and of itself, the practice of documenting one's mileage, the routes taken, and bicycles bought and repairs rendered was not altogether unusual. But Hyde's "wheeling diary" is unusually rich. From 1893 to 1896, covering some 6,811 miles, and over four volumes and 364 pages, Hyde's diary illuminates many dimensions of New York's cyclescape.

Hyde's first bicycle, according to the list price, was just over $100 and, like most bicycles at the time, was a luxury item. But many buyers, Hyde included, never paid full price. He fed his appetite for bikes through active participation in the secondhand market. His first bicycle was a used version that set him back only $40. He later traded it in to help pay for his second one, a Liberty Scorcher, and when he purchased a Bohemian in 1895—already discounted from the retail price of $85 down to $60—he

FIGURE 2.1
In his wheeling diary, Arthur
Hyde documented each of
his rides and also included
photographs, ephemera, letters,
and drawings, including this
portrait of himself drawn by his
good friend and frequent cycle
companion, Harry White.

Arthur P.S. Hyde Diaries, 1892–1896,
Volume 1, sketch p. 39–41. BV Hyde,
Arthur P., New-York Historical
Society Library

offset the cost by raffling off his old bike. Hyde raised $45 and the win-
ner paid just 28 cents. The effort was well worth it: "It is a bird!, 23
pounds, 72 gear, 24 inch frame, T saddle post, Sager A Saddle, Morgan
and Wright tires, Elm-Plymouth interlocked rims, in fact a genuine up-
to-date 1895 wheel." But soon it was time to trade in the Bohemian for
a Model D road racer ("she is a cooker! 80 inch gear!! Gee whiz!!!").
Though it was listed in the catalog for $100, he owed only $30 "to boot"
after a trade-in.[6]

Over the course of three years, Hyde bought five bicycles, never paying anywhere close to catalog price even when he did splurge for new
models. Dealers also encouraged purchases on installment plans. After
a trade-in and for a mere $5 deposit, Hyde rode his Liberty Scorcher
home. Moreover, retail prices fell steeply over the course of the 1890s as
production swelled.[7]

Even though he was always looking for a deal, Hyde had money. He
lived comfortably with his family on the Upper East Side. His mother

did not work, his family was listed in the *Social Register*, and he was able to attend private schools. His family also had deep American roots. With ancestors dating back to the mid-seventeenth century, the Hydes faced few of the challenges that met the million recently arrived immigrants who also called New York home.[8]

Recent immigrants or not, most New Yorkers still would have considered the bicycle an extravagance. Even those with secure wage work would have had to save carefully to afford one. Button backers earned, on average, $1.66 a day. Silk dyers made $1.83 and bookbinders $2.83. Even for those with more skilled jobs, like plumbers ($3.50 day) and bricklayers ($4 day), a new high-quality bicycle meant several weeks' worth of wages. Nevertheless, when a Lower East Side factory worker recorded in her 1897 account book that she was putting aside $1 out of her regular $12-per-week paycheck to pay off a bicycle, she was not alone. The poorest New Yorkers might never become cyclists, but many others did. And as was the case with the earlier bicycle booms, boosters imagined that everyone would soon be able to afford a set of wheels and enjoy the mobility it offered.[9]

For the New Yorkers who did ride, bicycles often proved the speediest way to get around a city with streetcars limited by fixed tracks and schedules. The bicycle was now a viable form of transportation. Hyde, an assistant instructor in military tactics, biked his way up to the Barnard School for Boys on 125th Street, where he had once been a student. He also found cycling the easiest way to make day-to-day stops, riding to church, the post office, and the homes of friends and relatives. He regularly pedaled to recreational spots, including the Polo Grounds, the Upper Manhattan horseshoe-shaped home of the New York Giants baseball team. From his residence on Eighty-Fourth Street just east of Fifth Avenue, it took about twenty-five minutes each way. And on one occasion, it was by bicycle that he could most quickly deliver the sad news to his siblings: Grandpa Hyde was dead.[10]

As the number of cycling trips increased, so did the demand for bicycle parking. Bicycle racks sprouted outside ice cream parlors, churches, and office buildings. (With such public outdoor parking came bike theft, and thus, bike locks.) Some destinations even had bicycle valets. Private residences, like three French-inspired limestone townhouses built in 1898 near Riverside Drive, had dedicated space for bicycles. Each unit came with a bicycle room tucked away off the first-floor hallway. Stately apartment buildings catered to cycling tenants too. The Woodbury and Elmscourt on the corner of Madison Avenue and Ninety-Fifth Street and the Cherbourg on Ninety-Second Street and Central Park West advertised shared bicycle rooms in the basement.[11]

The same bike could serve multiple purposes. Hyde often rode to get somewhere and, like most other cyclists, took even more trips just for the fun of it. When on one of his regular "runs" to bicycling hotspots—along Riverside Drive, around Grant's Tomb, and down the Boulevard (as New Yorkers called the stretch of Broadway north of Columbus Circle)—Hyde found crowds of men and women on wheels doing the same thing, delighting in seeing and being seen. The Boulevard was an especially crowded

FIGURE 2.2 A woman hands off her bicycle to a valet at the Bronx Zoo.

Woman checking her bicycle, New York Zoological Gardens, Bronx, N.Y. undated, [c. 1899], glass negative. George Ehler Stonebridge Photograph Collection, New-York Historical Society PR066_1461

FIGURE 2.3 One of Hyde's favorite places to ride was around Grant's Tomb on River-side Drive. Frequently, he would make several loops around the memorial. He was not alone. As Hyde wrote in 1895: "at almost any hour of the day, may be seen scores of wheel-men and wheelwomen, their wheels standing in the gutter, while they are reclining on the benches, enjoying the cool breezes which one almost invariably finds here."

Cyclists on Riverside Drive near Grant's Tomb, 127th Street, 1898. Photograph, PR 068, New-York Historical Society Library, 82477d; "A Tour of New York's Parks," *The LAW Bulletin and Good Roads*, August 16, 1895, 15–17

spot. Traffic counters standing at one corner on a spring day in 1896 observed more than 14,000 cyclists cruising by over a 16-hour period (roughly one cyclist every 4 seconds).[12]

The crowds of cyclists included men and women together, a much more common sight than in previous eras. While the practice of cycling did not alone revolutionize how women and men socialized in the city, it did play a role in challenging social conventions, including how they inter-acted in public and how they dated. For Hyde, the bicycle proved a useful tool to meet women. In April 1894, he rode to Madison Avenue in mid-town to make a "call on Elsa"; a few months later they were playing tennis

FIGURE 2.4 Many cyclists, Hyde included, enjoyed social rides in the evening. Indeed, traffic counts on the Boulevard indicated that the most popular hour was between 8:00 p.m. and 9:00 p.m. and the second most popular was between 9:00 p.m. and 10:00 p.m. Here is a busy Fifth Avenue (at Forty-Fourth Street) after dark.

Charles W. Jefferys, Fifth Avenue at Night, Looking North from Delmonico's at Forty-Fourth Street, 1899. Wallach Division Picture Collection, The New York Public Library, Astor, Lenox and Tilden Foundations

together. In the summer of 1895 he bicycled over to Lena's house. Soon they could be found sitting together "under the trees." A couple of days later, he went back to see her, but "Mr. V." would not let him in. Unfazed, Hyde biked over to Alice Robinson's house to make another call.[13]

On more than one occasion, he hired wheels for "the girls" to try out. At least once, he gave a young woman riding lessons, practicing in front of the Museum of Natural History. On a multiday bicycle trip, he enjoyed dinner with "a charming girl from Germantown," and when on a steep hill near Douglaston, he met "a very pretty girl" who could not quite pedal up the climb. He regularly went for bicycle rides with Mable and others—never with a chaperone. For a period in the spring of 1896, Hyde rode nearly every day to visit Helen, one of his occasional riding partners, near her 126th Street home. Circling the neighborhood on two wheels, he sometimes found her. Sometimes he spied her only at a distance, and sometimes, to his terrible disappointment, he could not find her at all. It was by bicycle that he rode to Helen's graduation, seeing her for "probably the last time for two years." But he was not one to wait around. Within a week, he was out riding with Ethel. And in 1900, he married Lena, presumably the very same Lena with whom he had "sat under the trees," biked to an ice cream parlor, and often visited via two wheels.[14]

Dating is conventionally understood as a twentieth-century phenomenon with young couples venturing out, replacing the intricate system of making calls and getting to know one another inside parlor rooms with family members watching, or at least hovering nearby. Thanks to the mobility it afforded and the changing customs it portended, the bicycle offered a way to recast social relationships.[15]

Aside from dating, the bicycle unlocked new social opportunities. Bicycle clubs began to appear in nearly every neighborhood. Between 1894 and 1898 there were about 220 bicycle clubs in Manhattan and Brooklyn. (That is almost as many bicycle clubs as there are Starbucks locations today! And with less than half as many New Yorkers back then.) As costs dropped throughout the decade and as consumers, like Hyde, found ways to lessen purchase prices, the pool of riders became much more diverse. The individual organizations, a handful of which were holdovers from the high-wheel era, included clubs for immigrants; Chinese Americans, Japanese Americans, Danish Americans, and Italian Americans started their own groups. There was the Alpha Wheelmen for "colored" members; up to this point, almost all New York cyclists had been white. The Pioneer Cycle Club was for women and run by women (though it later admitted men), a far cry from when male entrepreneurs encouraged women to attend ladies-only classes at their indoor velocipede rinks. The Fanwood Quad Club consisted entirely of "deaf mutes." There was the Apothecaries' Bicycle Club for pharmacists, the

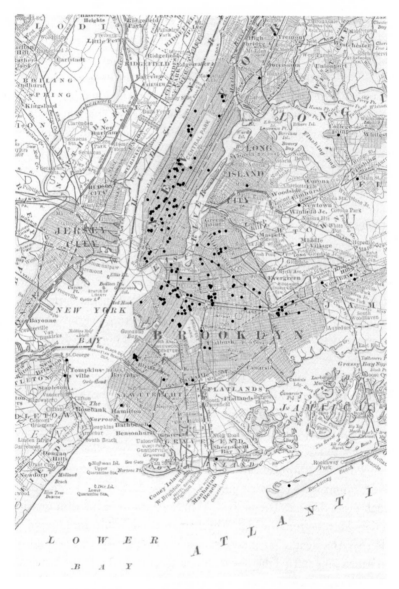

FIGURE 2.5 Between 1894 and 1898 the headquarters of two hundred bicycle clubs spanned much of the city, but were clustered in the lower half of Manhattan and the western section of Brooklyn. There were many more clubs, some of which did not have an official headquarters and others for which an address could not be located.

Map by the author

Federal Wheelmen for letter carriers, and the Metropolitan Stenographers in Manhattan (Brooklyn had its own stenographer bike club). Neighborhoods boasted their own clubs, including the Bushwick Wheelmen, Chelsea Wheelmen, Greenpoint Wheelmen, Park Slope Wheelmen, Windsor Terrace Wheelmen, and Yorkville Wheelmen. Some clubs, like the Ocean Parkway Wheelmen, even organized around particular streets.[16]

Clubs both promoted the idea of the bicycle as a democratizing and Americanizing force—a tool for New Yorkers to socialize and express their identity—and exposed its limits—most clubs catered to the well-to-do and were segregated by race, class, ethnicity, or gender. The official clubhouses were often guarded spaces and quite elaborate. The Long Island Wheelmen, for example, built their headquarters on Bedford Avenue in Brooklyn, a hotspot for biking since the velocipede days. The three-story facility decorated with frescoes on the inside and a large, window-studded copper oriel on the outside was hard to miss. The Long Island Wheelmen (members, who averaged thirty-seven years of age, jokingly

THE LONG ISLAND WHEELMEN'S CLUB-HOUSE, BEDFORD AVENUE, BROOKLYN.

FIGURE 2.6
The Long Island Wheelmen's Club Headquarters, 1890.

Harper's Weekly, August 30, 1890, 672

referred to themselves as "Old Fossils") enjoyed full use of the space, out-fitted with a bowling alley, billiard room, gym, parlor, lockers, fireplace, and separate rooms for officers, ladies, and servants.[17]

Hyde belonged to the Tiffany Wheelmen, a group of cycling enthusiasts who worked at Tiffany & Co. His father was a longtime employee, and Arthur worked intermittently for the firm between 1893 and 1895. Like the New Yorkers who shopped there, Tiffany & Co. caught bicycle fever. In 1896, bicycles began to show up in its annual catalog and store-fronts. Most famously, the company began to "Tiffany-ize" existing wheels for wealthy clientele, including a Columbia model embellished with a silver frame and ivory handlebars that eventually sold for $5,000. Members of the club included its captain, John T. Curran, famous for designing the "Magnolia Vase," an ornate heap of silver put on display at the 1893 Chicago World's Fair, and Frank Spengler, a silversmith from the Lower East Side who learned the trade from his German-born father. As was typical, the Tiffany Wheelmen took group rides to Long Island, raced to Coney Island, and fraternized with fellow members.[18]

Hyde was also a member of the largest and most powerful organization of cyclists: the League of American Wheelmen (LAW) that Kirk Munroe cofounded in 1880. By the late 1890s, it boasted over 100,000 members; as a sign of New York's prominence in the cycling world and national bicycle politics, roughly a quarter of LAW members hailed from the Empire State. It had also greatly expanded its political influence. Presidential nominating conventions included "good roads" platforms pushed by the league; President William McKinley (and many other politicians) wooed members and sought the wheelmen's vote; and when Theodore Roosevelt was a vice-presidential candidate in 1900, he was also, the league magazine made sure to note, a card-carrying member from New York.[19]

So was Arthur Hyde, who convinced his friends to join, stayed at LAW-sponsored hotels while on long trips, and contributed to the weekly *LAW Bulletin and Good Roads* journal. One of his articles offered advice on how best to exit the man-made city and find natural splendor in the Hudson Valley and out on Long Island. But one need not go that far; as Hyde wrote (in the third person): "The writer believes that one may see more of nature in her primitive loveliness, visit more interesting, historical

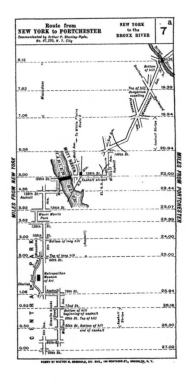

FIGURE 2.7

To create the cycling maps that would be included in *Fifty Miles Around New York*, Hyde conducted his own research, measuring distances and noting turns, hills, paving conditions, and landmarks. This particular map was the first, southern section of three maps intended to guide cyclists from midtown Manhattan to Portchester. His other maps illustrated preferred routes to Poughkeepsie and Tarrytown.

League of American Wheelmen, *Fifty Miles Around New York: A Book of Maps and Descriptions of the Best Roads, Streets and Routes for Cyclists and Horsemen* (New York: New York State Division of the League of American Wheelmen, 1896)

and romantic ground, and in general, spend a more enjoyable day within the city limits of New York than by going a hundred miles into the country in any direction." Hyde also compiled maps and bicycling routes for the popular *Fifty Miles Around New York*.[20]

One favorite club activity was the bicycle parade. In their earliest iterations, the marches on wheels often had a political bent, like the annual high-wheeler parades the LAW had organized that aimed to convince the Central Park commissioners to lift the ban on bikes. But throughout the mid-1890s, most bicycle parades were social and celebratory in nature. There was a lot more to celebrate now: new bicycle paths, throngs of new riders, and city politicians listening attentively to the cyclists' demands. As a show of the force and volume of city bicyclers, the parades were mutedly political too. Hyde participated in two of the largest. The first was in Brooklyn and on the most remarkable pieces of bike-specific infrastructure yet built in the United States.

Bicycle traffic to the island (Coney) had become so heavy that local wheelmen successfully lobbied for a 5.5-mile bicycle path starting at another favorite cycling destination, the park (Prospect). Then they began asking for, and got, a "return path," thereby providing two one-way expressways just for them. The majestic, extra-spacious Frederick Law Olmsted and Calvert Vaux-designed Ocean Parkway was particularly well suited for the two generous bike paths, one sixteen and the other eighteen feet wide, that ran alongside the main drive with a healthy buffer, lined with trees, separating the bicycles and the carriages. The path was not without controversy; some wheelmen expressed concern about segregating, and therefore delegitimizing, bicycles, especially when they learned that cyclists would be forced to use the path and would be prohibited from the main drive.[21]

Regardless, the Coney Island Cycle Path set off a wave of bike path building around the country. In New York, lawmakers made room on Riverside Drive, already overly populated with cyclists, by laying a bicycle path and creating separate spaces for bikes, walkers, carriages, and saddled horses. Although they were not primarily built in the service of a larger transportation network and intended largely for recreation, the paths gave riders a sense of what it meant to have their own roads. And they did begin to request some paths that would serve as transportation corridors, including unsuccessfully campaigning for a separate bicycle path on the Brooklyn Bridge.[22]

Though he lived in Manhattan, Hyde regularly pedaled to Coney Island, joining thousands of other wheelmen who left one island for the sandy shores of another. And to mark the opening of the new Coney Island Cycle Path, he joined thousands of other riders for a grand parade in June 1895. Spectators sitting in any of the viewing stands that lined the new bicycle way would have had no trouble spotting Hyde leading a division of 2,000 "unattached" (meaning unaffiliated with any cycling organization) riders. Not all notice was positive. The *Brooklyn Daily Eagle* reported that "the great army of the unattached was without organization or discipline." Nevertheless, Hyde enjoyed the fanfare that followed—photographs with the participating officers and a pit stop on the way home for cigars and sarsaparilla.[23]

FIGURE 2.8 The newly opened Coney Island Cycle Path in 1895.

Scientific American, August 24, 1895, 120

The following June, the *Evening Telegram* organized its own colossal parade. The *New York Times* estimated that 20,000 people watched "the largest parade of cyclists ever seen on this side of the Atlantic if not in the whole world." Parading divisions included "uniformed schoolboys," women, military men, riders on tandems and exotic bicycles, and one group organized by the bicycle manufacturers. (Capitalism was hardly invisible in the 1890s.)[24]

On the morning of the parade, Hyde set up shop on Sixty-Eighth Street and the Boulevard, standing alongside his "brand new 'Remington'" bicycle bought especially for the occasion and picked up earlier in the morning. Designated a parade marshal, Hyde barked out orders to his aides, including his older brother, Ralph Jr., whom Arthur had converted to a cyclist. Clad in "very becoming uniforms consisting of braided blouses, white duck trousers, brown canvas leggings, campaign hats and white gloves," they did their best to keep the eleventh division in neat lines of four riders (with six feet of space in between each group) and in separate companies (with twenty feet of space in between). It was not easy. Because of the clogged streets, Hyde's group fractured in several places. Still, at least according to its leader, the division managed a "fine appearance." The highlight of the whole affair for Captain Hyde, headed to West Point, was when they came upon General Grant's Tomb. He and his fellow officers paused for a moment and removed their caps in salute.[25]

There was plenty of silliness too. Dogs and parrots paraded alongside the humans. Wheelmen dressed up as "Indians and Zulus." Some wore women's clothing. Harry Dewey, a Weehawken resident who dressed as a "Jersey Mosquito," won an award for being the most "grotesque rider." A woman from the Upper East Side won a prize for going as "Queen Zenobia," the third-century Queen of Palmyra.[26]

FIGURE 2.9 Here, cyclists riding in the (fan favorite) fancy costume division are vying to win prizes and enjoying the chance to play dress-up without derision. The photograph also highlights a number of black cyclists. There were occasions, like the parade pictured here, when black cyclists could participate alongside others. But even then, racism was hardly invisible. Fourth from the left is a rider who appears to be in blackface.

E. Benjamin Andrews, *History of the United States from the Earliest Discovery of America to the Present Time, Volume V* (New York: Charles Scribner's Sons, 1926), 116

Clubs were involved in the parades and bicycle races, increasingly popular in a society obsessed with speed and record setting. New Yorkers got caught up in a game to see how fast and far bicycles could travel. Could a cyclist keep up with a train? (A member of the Kings County Wheelmen, Charles "Mile-a-Minute" Murphy, managed to do just that, at least for longer than most thought possible.) How fast could someone ride to Philadelphia from New York? (6 hours and 17 minutes.) How many times could someone circle a track over the course of not one, not even two, but *six* straight days?[27]

This last question tantalized fans at Madison Square Garden who paid to watch exhausted riders try to outpedal one another on the banked wooden one-tenth-mile track. In a memorable 1898 race it was Charles Miller who earned first place. Like everyone else, he took short breaks to sleep. Unlike his competition, he also spent thirty minutes getting married. Nonetheless, he completed a dizzying 21,050 laps over the six days of racing. Some riders wore goggles to see through the smoke-filled air (some even smoked cigars while riding) and competitors regularly fell asleep at the wheel. New York lawmakers ultimately decided that riding for that long was dangerous. They declared it illegal for anyone to race for more than twelve hours a day.[28]

Although Hyde also dabbled in racing, he found the real beauty of the bicycle not its ability to go fast around a track but rather its ability to transport a person far away from the city. Hyde regularly took multiday tours, enjoying the geography (e.g., "a charmed valley filled with farms," "the blue hills of Long Island," etc.) that lay well beyond home. He would often stop for food (at Dingman's Ferry in August 1895, he put his 77¾ mile trip on pause to dine on chicken and huckleberries and, for 75 cents, drink an "exorbitantly priced" cup of coffee) and stay overnight at wheelmen-friendly hotels, which offered discounts for riders, storage for their wheels, and special menus to sate their appetite.[29]

Through it all, he delighted in the mode of travel. "I went on a regular exploring expedition," Hyde remarked, relishing the "quite wild" scenery and the various towns he visited that were otherwise unreachable by rail. The bicycle offered a way to curate his experience of his community, to define its boundaries, and to reconsider the relationship between the individual and the collective.[30]

Hyde also enjoyed cycling to historic sites. He rode to a Civil War marker in White Plains, a monument to President Washington in Dobbs Ferry, an Iroquois Indian memorial in the Rockaways, and the bronze statue of Simón Bolívar on a horse in Central Park. (Hyde never recorded his impressions of the statue, but the *Times* dubbed it among the most "unsightly" in the city.) Some of his favorite sites had meaning only to him. Long after his family had moved from the Bronx to Manhattan, Hyde cycled back to the old house. The city had since acquired the property to build Van Cortlandt Park. Gone were the chicken coop, the house, and the "massive iron gates" that had once seemed so permanent. But the memories—of Rollo, the family dog buried beneath his feet—and the smells—of grapes, tomatoes, and corn that once sprinkled the landscape—came back to him. Hyde's new bike brought him back in time.[31]

Despite its value in offering door-to-door transportation, the bicycle had significant limitations. It could only take riders as far as their legs could muster, which is why cyclists often relied on several forms of transportation. Hyde regularly biked to train stations and ferry docks and would carry his wheels aboard. He took plenty of long "runs," but spending a day casually touring the Hudson River towns required getting there more quickly than by bicycle. Understandably, cyclists fought for the right to be able to bring their bicycles on trains—and to do so for free.

Aside from distance, cyclists were limited by the quality and placement of roads. Cycling maps detailed preferred bicycle routes, and Hyde kept copies indicating which roads had been asphalted and made his own notes about dangerous terrain: for example, a stretch near Peekskill, he wanted to be sure to remember, was littered with stones the "size of a pigeon's egg to the size of your head."[32]

As the most vocal group within the "good roads" coalition of the 1890s, cyclists lobbied local governments to asphalt (a relatively new technology) popular bicycle thoroughfares. Cyclists in Brooklyn and Manhattan, often through a LAW subcommittee or one of the local bicycle clubs, proposed specific paving projects, complained about lackluster roads, and celebrated new asphalt. The Commissioner of Street Improvements "made nearly every improvement suggested" by the Associated

Cycle Clubs of New York and the LAW, the *Times* reported in the summer of 1897, before presenting a long list of recently completed work along First, Fifth, and Seventh avenues and across Forty-Sixth Street, Seventy-Ninth Street, and 126th Street, among many others.[33]

The report also noted the spots in which "asphalt strips have been laid" for the benefit of cyclists. If paving the whole road was too expensive, then at least a portion could be smoothed. These ribbons of asphalt were essentially bicycle lanes, and cyclists hoped to build a network of them for both commuting and recreational cycling. Quickly, though, cyclists called their value into question, noting that wagons, carts, and trash regularly obstructed the paths.[34]

Whether on the ribbons of asphalt or not, a select group of New Yorkers regularly commuted by bike. On Arthur Hyde's commute from his Eighty-Fourth Street home to Tiffany & Co., then headquartered on

FIGURE 2.10 Asphalt "ribbons" alongside Hudson Street (and Perry Street). The bicycle lanes stretched from Thirteenth Street to Chambers Street and were expected to attract "streams of people" commuting back and forth between the residential district on the West Side and the "downtown business district."

Wheel and Cycling Trade Review, September 18, 1896

Union Square, he spent about 22 minutes riding the 3.75 miles (according to both his nineteenth-century cyclometer and today's Google Maps). He almost always took the same route, riding most of the way along Madison Avenue before snaking over on Twenty-Sixth Street, south on Lexington Avenue, around Gramercy Park, and down Irving Place, choosing paved streets all the way. When he cut back west toward Union Square from Irving Place, for example, he always pedaled along the smooth-surfaced Eighteenth Street. Neither the neighboring stretch on Seventeenth nor Nineteenth Street was paved. Cyclists like Hyde developed their own mental maps of the city.[35]

For many riders, cycling was a seasonal activity. Although no form of transportation was weatherproof, cyclists were especially vulnerable to the elements, and even enthusiasts like Hyde recorded more miles during the spring, summer, and fall than they did in the winter. (No longer was cycling an activity best enjoyed indoors in the winter.) But the cold did not discourage Hyde entirely. In 1895, he rode to a cousin's house in Yonkers for Thanksgiving dinner, biked to church on Christmas, and went touring on New Year's Day. More than the cold, rain was Hyde's chief irritant, forcing him to stop and find shelter, sometimes even to leave his bicycle behind at a clubhouse or restaurant and find another way home. Rain was "anything but pleasant" and could quickly make unpaved roads impassable. On one winding bicycle tour to the Delaware Water Gap, Hyde stopped for dinner as soon as the rain began. When it showed no signs of abating, he booked a room. "When I woke up this morning, I found, to my disgust, that it had been raining all night and the road in front of the hotel was mud about two inches deep." It was "something horrible," he recorded in his diary on August 12, 1895. "I lounged around after breakfast and cleaned my wheel," waiting for the conditions to improve.[36]

Stopping for a bite and a drink to escape the weather presented its own complications, as Hyde learned while out on a trip to Mineola with Ralph Hyde Jr. in January 1896. Realizing that it was too cold and windy to make it back home, the brothers stopped for a gulp of brandy and hatched a plan. They would take a train to an elevated railway to a ferry that would get them in the vicinity of their Upper East Side neighborhood. But "the condition Ralph was in, together with the fact that he took the brandy on an empty stomach and then got into a heater car, made him quite tipsy." When they finally landed in Manhattan, Ralph Jr. could not even get on his bicycle, let alone ride. So Arthur stood his brother's bike up in the gutter, cycled past it, and grabbed the handlebars, driving both sets of wheels back home. He wondered how it would look. What if a police officer spotted him?[37]

He had good reason to be worried. New York had just commissioned its first corps of bicycle police officers. Their mission was simple: rein in reckless cyclists. New York police commissioner and future president Theodore Roosevelt soon expanded the squad and their charge. On Roosevelt's command, the bicycle police force multiplied from a pair of riders possessing "extraordinary daring" to a force of 100, large enough to warrant their own station. Within a year, police officers on wheels had made 1,366 arrests.[38]

Roosevelt fondly reminisced (and employed classic ethnic stereotypes) about his three favorite bike cops: a "native" American, a German, and an Irishman. "The German was a man of enormous power." The "Yankee" was "tall" and "powerful" and doggedly pursued his "natural prey—scorchers, runaways, and reckless drivers." The ability to hunt down "scorchers"—the pejorative term applied to riders who disobeyed traffic laws, zoomed around city streets, and frightened pedestrians—was essential. The Irishman had a "sinewy" figure and "flaming red hair, which rather added to the terror he inspired in evil-doers." He worked the toughest neighborhoods where there was "an occasional desire to harass wheelmen." Roosevelt, the "progressive," especially loved that this Irish officer treated all criminals the same, from the wealthy carriage driver who did not have his lantern lit after dark to the "street-corner tough who had thrown a brick at a wheelman."[39]

Aside from having bricks, stones, or insults hurled at them, wheelmen and -women were imperiled by other vehicles competing for city space. Crash rates are impossible to determine, but it is clear that adding bicycles to the already busy mix of pedestrians, streetcars, and carriages caused serious complications. Hyde was involved in several crashes himself. In one case, he sounded his bell to warn the buggy in front of him that he was about to pass. Instead of trotting straight ahead, the driver swerved, cutting Hyde off and causing him to fall head first over his handlebars. In another instance, he was "run down by . . . a potato dealer" in Greenwich Village. His front wheel was broken, but not his enthusiasm for riding.[40]

Cyclists could also be the perpetrators. "It seems as if I am fated to knock someone down once a year," Hyde sighed. On his way to catch the Forty-Second Street ferry, he "ran down an old woman." Another time he "ran a man down" on Second Avenue. Neither pedestrian was seriously hurt, according to Hyde at least. In the spring of 1895, Hyde bicycled up to Yonkers and along the Croton Aqueduct (oh, how he longed for the proposed and much talked-about Croton bicycle path). On his way back home, he struck "a little girl" who "cried considerably." She was clearly in more pain than he was, even though he had fallen from his bike and was still recovering from a three-hour dentist appointment that morning. Hyde helped the girl up, but "lost no time" speeding away. He consoled himself by wishfully assuming that she was not seriously hurt.[41]

Plenty of crashes did result in serious injury and sometimes even death. "There are many thoroughfares in the city," explained the Chief of Police in 1896, "where the traffic on vehicles of all kinds, and especially bicycles, is so great that it is necessary for the protection of life and limb that such traffic should be properly regulated."[42]

How bicycles should move through the transportation network was a hotly debated question with widely divergent answers. That different types of people rode for different reasons on vehicles that were unlike any others would forever make it difficult to reach consensus about where bicycles belonged. One solution was to separate different kinds of traffic. After a lengthy debate with politicians, bicycle advocates, streetcar operators and others, New York aldermen formally divided traffic on the ever-crowded Boulevard, creating de facto bicycle lanes.

And in 1897, New York became the first city to pass a comprehensive set of traffic laws, restricting (and thereby legitimizing) how bicycles could move vis-à-vis other vehicles. Born in the debates about how to regulate traffic on the Boulevard and essentially drafted by local cyclists, the new rules required that cyclists keep to the right side of the road and off the sidewalks, carry a lantern at night, signal turns with their hands, sound a "bell or gong" when turning corners or passing, travel at less than eight miles an hour, and keep their feet on the pedals. Most of the rules (many of which were ignored) applied to all legally defined vehicles, which now included bicycles and tricycles, carriages and carts, and even the new and very few "motor wagons."[43]

Regardless of the other vehicles on the road, laws designed to improve safety, and considerable efforts to improve road conditions, it was impossible to stop cyclists from tripping themselves up. On a long ride to Amenia up in Dutchess County and over a stretch of "vile" road, Hyde was "thrown" from his bike. A couple passing by in a wagon later found him unconscious. After a dram of whiskey (it helped "considerably") he was back on his way, bloodied head and all. Another incident occurred on a frigid January day in 1896: "I was riding . . . with my sweater pulled up around my head, and a pair of smoked glasses on to keep the wind out of my eyes." Before long he was on the ground, having run into a stalled wagon. This "closest call and most Providential escape" left him largely unscathed, but he promised to always keep his head up and eyes on the road. Thank goodness, since neither Hyde nor other cyclists wore helmets.[44]

Given all the crashes, it is not terribly surprising that Hyde's bike was regularly in the shop. Reliable data are hard to come by, and Hyde's experiences might have been atypical since he logged so many miles, but he and his riding companions seemed to always be breaking their machines. On a moonlight outing of the Tiffany Wheelmen, Hyde and friends rode through scenic Brooklyn. On the way back, a member broke a pedal and was forced to ride home one-legged. Another cyclist's light went out long before they made it home at 1:25 a.m. Hyde suffered his own share of mechanical problems. At least four times he lost or ruined a nut, leaving him without a pedal. In other instances, he needed to have his "front tire cemented on," his front fork bent back into shape, his split rim repaired, and his cranks replaced. He regularly punctured his tires too. Among all the New York sites he visited, one of the most frequent was the repair shop. Over the course of three years, he made twenty-four separate trips to Spalding's down on Nassau Street near City Hall.[45]

Considering the number of repairs Hyde needed, the number of bicycles he bought and rented, and the pace at which New Yorkers became cyclists, it should be no surprise that bicycle shops opened year after year, in neighborhood after neighborhood—including over on Staten Island, where an enterprising enthusiast opened her own shop in 1895. Her name was Violet Ward.

Violet Ward

Born in February 1863, Maria Ward was better known as Violet, a nickname she said was given to her by Abraham Lincoln on account of "her delicate beauty." Although that story might be apocryphal, her father, a general turned banker, did know President Lincoln, General Grant, and other lions of American history personally.

A descendant of several generations of notable military men and financiers, Violet grew up in an equally prominent home. Sitting on the wrap-around, vine-covered porch with her dog, she looked out onto the family's exquisite gardens, stand-alone icehouse, and lawn tennis court. Built in 1865, the sprawling, eighteen-room mansion sat on twenty acres of prime grounds in Grymes Hill, a sleepy neighborhood in the northeastern section of the steak-shaped island known for sublime vistas and affluent residents. Like many of their neighbors, the Wards enjoyed Staten Island as a rural retreat but also kept a foothold in Manhattan. Violet would regularly shuttle back and forth between "Oneota," as they called the Staten Island estate, and her Lexington Avenue residence (which Arthur Hyde regularly biked past).[46]

When she was a teenager in the late 1870s, Ward's schooling consisted of copying passages from Byron, reading Greek history, and at least informally learning how to be a society woman. She excelled in each, acing history and composition and soon earning a perennial spot on the *Social Register*. She took dancing classes in the evening, participated in the horse show at Madison Square Garden, attended dramatic club performances, and served as a director for Staten Island's "Ladies' Club." In the 1880 census, Violet's occupation was listed as "housekeeping," a not unusual designation for women (often wives) finished with school and not working outside the home. Considering that she lived with four servants, Violet probably did not have a lot of housekeeping to do.[47]

Among her various interests, none surpassed her enthusiasm for sports. She loved to golf, which was also experiencing a surge in popularity in the 1890s. Ward joined the Harbour Hill Golf Club in New Brighton and was later named among the "best golfers" to compete in the Women's Metropolitan Championship. (That she lost in the first round of match play and had scorecards littered with 9s, 11s, and 14s suggest she may not have actually been among the very best.) She also joined a local tennis club for women and an ice-skating club in Manhattan.[48]

But no athletic activity enchanted Ward more than cycling. Already an avid cyclist, she organized group rides for women starting in 1894. There was just one condition: participants needed to learn how to "take down, clean, assemble and adjust their bicycle." What good was it to ride a bicycle you could not repair? She also joined several bike clubs, including the most elite one in New York—the Michaux Cycle Club.[49]

Organized in December 1894, the Michaux distinguished itself, at least according to the hyperbolic journalists of the time, as "the smartest" and "wealthiest and most exclusive organization of its kind in the world." Initially headquartered on Broadway and Fifty-Second Street, the club moved to a more fitting space along the Boulevard and Sixtieth Street. While many clubs catered to the wealthy, the Michaux was the pinnacle of elitism. Its 250 members included financiers, judges, newspaper editors, colonels, and captains, largely culled from the "Four Hundred," the unofficial list of the four hundred New Yorkers who mattered the most (meaning those invited to the lavish balls hosted by socialite nonpareil Mrs. Astor, a child of the illustrious Schermerhorns who joined a family with an even greater fortune when she married the grandson of John Jacob Astor, the fur trader and real estate tycoon). Despite the $50 annual dues, there was a healthy waiting list.[50]

In the winter, members wheeled around an indoor rink and bike-danced the Virginia reel. In the summer, there were bicycle picnics, "fancy-dress carnivals," and group "runs" to favorite destinations: Westchester, Inwood, Coney Island, and the High Bridge. No matter the season, members could take riding lessons at the club headquarters, which included ample space to unwind—a reading room, lockers, showers, baths, and dressing rooms. "Competent" valets, butlers, and maids stood ready to serve.[51]

While members included aristocrats and earls, most notable was that women joined too. The majority of Michaux women, including Edith Mary Kingdon Gould (wife of George Jay Gould, the son of financier Jay Gould), Alva Vanderbilt (wife of William K. Vanderbilt, the grandson of railroad tycoon Cornelius Vanderbilt), and Bessie Smith White (wife of the famed architect Stanford White) were married to men of note. Ward herself was unmarried. No matter their marital status, women members were subject to extra scrutiny. Journalists, for example, paid particular attention to the Michaux women's trendsetting "costumes."[52]

Female members were invited to participate in special club races. Ward was not one of the six members who competed, but she surely applauded at the closing ceremonies of a two-week race in which Michaux women looped (for several hours a day) around Bowman's Cycling Academy. That a respectable club endorsed such an endurance event is surprising; bicycle racing was a sport dominated by men. Racers and organizers generally thought women had no business participating, even when they managed to do so successfully. In January 1896, for example, Madison Square Garden hosted a special "ladies" six-day race. Although thousands of spectators showed up for the finale, the *New York Times* judged the event a failure. "The better element in bicycling circles had frowned" on the race, so the writer gloated. He further sniped that "a majority of the contestants were young girls, but several were old enough to know better."[53]

Women sometimes competed in long-distance road races too. At a 100-mile race organized by the Long Island City Wheelmen, "Miss Nellie Benson" finished fifth. The female member of the Riverside Wheel-*men* clocked in at an impressive 6 hours and 21 minutes. She earned a "survivor" medal just like the men. But shortly after the race, Miss Benson and the 99 men she bested were put on notice that sanctions would be coming. Participants had violated two rules: racing on a Sunday and racing with women.[54]

Although official sanctions never came, many cycling clubs took matters into their own hands. One of the largest groups, the Century Wheelmen, barred women from their hundred-mile rides. The measure faced some criticism, but the Century men pleaded their case to the public. First, there was the physical toll. Doctors worried about women's supposedly frail constitutions. Second, tired men would have to endure the onerous responsibility of looking after the women. Finally, women at the end of a century ride hardly looked like themselves. As one man reported: "few men will be found who respect the dusty, perspiring, disheveled woman seen at the finish of the 100 miles."[55]

Women were not the only ones deemed unfit for sport. In this age of Jim Crow, black cyclists were often barred from both the clubs and the races. There were some who pedaled to work, leisurely rode through the city, and raced. The most famous, Marshall "Major" Taylor, a onetime member of the South Brooklyn Wheelmen who took eighth place (1,732 miles) at one of the marathon sixes at Madison Square Garden, set records, won championships, and earned a national following. And there were a few "colored" cycling clubs. But by and large, black cyclists were disproportionately underrepresented—on the streets, in the clubs, and on the track.[56]

Black riders faced the same obstacles to becoming a cyclist as anyone else, in addition to challenges all their own. That bicycling was an activity suitable only for white, privileged, athletic men had been a truism for a segment of New Yorkers ever since the first bicycles arrived. Those beliefs did not suddenly disappear in the 1890s. Popular cartoons and caricatures, like Currier & Ives's Darktown Bicycle Club series, linked the bicycle with degrading stereotypes, depicting black men and women riding like buffoons—adopting poor form, frequently crashing, and losing races. "I knowd we'd have busted de record if it hadn't bin for dis misforchin," says a fallen cyclist with a wheel stuck around his head in an 1895 lithograph. New Yorkers consumed media perpetuating racism, and race organizers shivered at the thought of integrated competitions.[57]

But groups of black cyclists resisted and, like black boxers and other athletes, saw racing as a way to assert their manhood. When a "colored" member of the Alpha Wheelmen was told that he could not participate in a race sponsored by the Metropolitan Association of Cycling Clubs, for example, he promised to take his case to court before the organization reversed its decision. The Calumet Cyclers, another "negro" bicycle club in Manhattan, applauded the decision in a way that linked race with gender. "Feeling our position keenly at the continued effort to keep the negro below the level of manly sports," the Cyclers thanked the association for "bringing forth the true American principle and manly straight-forwardness that we believe all true-hearted men should be endowed with." In this telling, cycling was American and manly; it was not about being black or white.[58]

The League of American Wheelmen thought differently. Bowing to the demands of its southern faction, the LAW in 1894 required that all of its members be white. That did not seem to bother Ward, who, like Arthur Hyde, was a proud league member. She joined in the spring of 1895 and by summertime had accepted the position of consul, serving as a liaison between the local and national office, hosting touring wheelmen, reporting on local road conditions, and identifying hotels, repair shops, and other sites for league endorsement. Ward stuck out in an organization dominated by men, and she was often reminded of her status. In some of its correspondence to Miss Ward, the League of American Wheelmen addressed her as "Dear Sir." In one letter, "sir" was crossed out and "Madam" handwritten in its place—but the same letter referred to her lapsing dues and need to renew "his membership."[59]

Perhaps she had just forgotten to pay. After all, she was busy starting her own bicycle club. This one was for women.

In June 1895, the Staten Island Bicycle Club officially welcomed its first members. In that initial season, seventy-five "well-known young women" joined the "most fashionable society on the island," the local papers reported. Later on the club invited men to join too, but even then, the leadership remained all female. Members had to be at least fifteen years old and able to afford $10 for six months' worth of dues.[60]

With regular bicycle teas and group rides, the club appears to have been successful. But Ward sensed something was missing and decided to open a bike shop adjacent to the club headquarters near the ferry station in the St. George neighborhood. Having encouraged her friends to ride and having learned firsthand that Staten Island was home to too few bike shops, Ward "felt the responsibility" to build "a flourishing business" before allowing someone else—with the need for income—to take over. She was not interested in the daily affairs of running a bike shop.[61]

But in the interim, that is exactly what she did. The shop repaired wheels (one dollar to fix a flat), tuned-up customers' bicycles (twenty-five cents for oiling and adjusting), and offered bicycles for hire, long-term

FIGURE 2.11 Violet Ward, standing in the center with the black hat, joins fellow members of the Staten Island Bicycle Club at the start of a group ride.

Alice Austen, Staten Island Bicycle Club Tea, photograph, June 25, 1895. Collection of Historic Richmond Town

bicycle parking, and riding lessons from a "speedy" cyclist. Ward shopped around for inventory, talking to dealers at a sporting show at Madison Square Garden, getting samples, and purchasing stock—bolts, nuts, plugs, pedals, rubbers, cement, child seats, lanterns, luggage carriers, bicycle stands, varnish, enamels, oils, cyclometers—from bicycle dealers in Lower Manhattan. There were so many bike shops downtown on "Bicycle Row" that someone standing on Broadway next to City Hall could, in just a few minutes, walk to more than thirty, including Arthur Hyde's favorite, Spalding's. There were dozens more throughout Manhattan plus scores more across the rivers.[62]

In addition to managing the shop, Ward was still president of the Staten Island Bicycle Club. The secretary was the club's cofounder and fellow League of American Wheelmen member, Alice Austen. Also a

Staten Island resident and three years Ward's junior, Austen was one of Violet's closest companions. Decades later, Austen would earn her due as a brilliant American photographer. For the time being, her artistic talents were known only to Ward and a handful of others. Aside from photography, Austen shared Ward's passion for sports, playing tennis and golf and joining Ward for exercise classes taught by a gymnast friend of theirs named Daisy Elliott. An 1893 Austen photograph captures one such class. Inside a gym crowded with pulleys, bars, targets, and dumbbells, a stone-faced Elliott hangs from rings; another woman wields Indian clubs; and Ward, dressed in the same dark, heavy, baggy bloomerlike uniform as her classmates, clutches a football.[63]

This was an image that would have looked foreign in previous decades, but Ward, Austen, and their friends composed a group of progressive, athletic "New Women." They pushed back on the notion that females were weak and challenged conventions about the kinds of activities, clothes, and spaces deemed appropriate for women. Ward never married and instead developed close relationships with other women, creating, as the historian Carroll Smith Rosenberg has described, "single-sex familial institutions which would foster women's autonomy and creative productivity." Austen, who was later in a five-decade-long relationship with another woman, took many photographs of her close circle of female friends that, had they been public, would have caused a stir. Collectively, Austen's photographs created "photographic tableaux of herself and friends feigning drunkenness, in bed together, and dressed as men."[64]

Ward and Austen started working together (Ward as author, Austen as photographer) on a book to spread the gospel of cycling. When it comes to the bicycle, "women and girls bring upon themselves censure . . . almost invariably deserved." So begins Ward's 1896, two-hundred-page treatise, *The Common Sense of Bicycling: Bicycling for Ladies with Hints as to the Art of Wheeling—Advice to Beginners—Dress—Care of the Bicycle—Mechanics—Training—Exercise, Etc. Etc.* While the title is a mouthful, it only begins to cover the range of topics she explored over twenty-two chapters.[65]

At the outset of the book, Ward extolled the seemingly endless possibilities of the bicycle: a tool for exercise and recreation, a way to travel the countryside, an excuse to get outside, a symbol of modernity, a democ-

FIGURE 2.12 Violet Ward (seated) and an unidentified woman in front of Alice Austen's home in Staten Island. In her letters, cards, journals, and scrapbooks, Ward does not discuss her sexuality or mention any romantic relationships. Nevertheless, and although people living in the 1890s described same-sex relationships differently than we do today, some modern New Yorkers have labeled Ward and Austen as "lesbians."

Alice Austen, photograph, 1892. Courtesy of the Alice Austen House

ratizing machine, a means of "absolute freedom." Although it was in a sense magical, the bicycle, in Ward's mind, was more a product of science. Fascinated by machines since childhood and already an inventor, with a patent for an improved bodkin needle to make threading easier and a patent application for a golf club with a "whale bone neck," Ward stressed that riders need to understand the bicycle as a piece of technology. "Most women can sew on a button," she reasoned; wrenches and screwdrivers were hardly more difficult to master than needles and scissors. They would need those tools to develop the skills of a true cyclist: being able to repair a flat; remove, clean, and reattach the chain; polish the metal; and lubricate the many moving parts. Every rider should be able to identify each valve, screw, washer, nut, and bolt and understand the concepts of friction, inertia, gravity, suspension, elasticity, velocity, resistance, and centripetal force. No one should ride without knowing how bicycles move the way they do and why riders do not fall over (and why they do). If not, they would be subjected to "ridicule" and should expect "little sympathy from experienced cyclists."[66]

There were other rules that applied to both women and men. No cyclist should ride too soon after eating, nor should anyone travel too far without toting along some "chocolate or beef tablets." And it was always in poor form to gloat about the number of miles recorded on their cyclometers. (Arthur Hyde never got the message.)[67]

Bicycling for Ladies made few explicit distinctions between men and women, but her female audience likely understood much of what she had to say in gendered terms. For example, as a prelude to a discussion of bicycle-related traffic laws, Ward also took the opportunity to talk about something much grander:

> Mounted on a wheel, you feel at once the keenest sense of responsibility. You are there to do as you will within reasonable limits; you are continually being called upon to judge and to determine points that before have not needed your consideration, and consequently you become alert, active, quick-sighted, and keenly alive as well to the rights of others as to what is due yourself. You are responsible to yourself for yourself; you are responsible to the public for yourself; and you are responsible to the public for the rights of others.[68]

In this telling, the bicycle was a tool for women to reshape their world, to reconsider the public sphere and their relationship to it. Women cyclists had to learn the rules of the game before they could change them. "Riding the wheel, our own powers are revealed to us, a new sense is seemingly created . . . You have conquered a new world."[69]

The independence that Ward so celebrated was at the heart of critics' concerns about the moral behavior of female riders. Anxieties about how women behaved in public were nothing new, and the stakes in urban spaces, with countless watchful eyes, had always been particularly high. For much of the nineteenth century, gendered geography meant that while men could wander alone, "the women who walked the streets" as one historian put it, did so "as either endangered or dangerous women." On bicycles, women were even more visible, even more subject to the male gaze; but they also could disappear out of sight. One woman was so worried that she launched a full-fledged antibicycle crusade in hopes of removing the "hellish thing" from the streets of New York and the entire country.[70]

Ward understood that women were held to different standards. "There is much prejudice against athletic exercise for women and girls." The way to fight back was to prove that they could ride over tough terrain, up steep hills, and across great distances. To do so, they needed to train. Just like bicycles, Ward analogized, "the human body is constructed for use, and will suffer from want of use, rust out, as it were; and it will from over-use." She did warn her readers not to ride too long or too strenuously, but she did not see the constraints in gendered terms. All cyclists have limits.[71]

The health benefits of cycling were similar for everyone, including "thin women," "stout women," and, although she does not say so explicitly, men. The industrial age produced sedentary people and polluted air, and it was widely believed that urbanites were diseased—New Yorkers more so than anyone else. Doctors recommended regular doses of exercise and the countryside. Bicycles delivered both, even if certain doctors, and many others without any medical training, continued to insist that women were ill suited to riding.[72]

Part of the problem was that women's conventional clothing—tight-fitting corsets and flowing dresses—was impractical for bicycling. "If you possess a pair of knickerbockers, so much the better," Ward advised, emphasizing the need to wear something "comfortable" that would permit "absolute freedom of movement." For critics, pantlike knickerbockers and bloomers crossed a line. Indeed, ridiculing wheelwomen and their outfits became common practice in the streets, in newspaper columns, and in humor magazine cartoons.[73]

To be sure, much of what Ward endorsed went even beyond what some advocates were willing to support. "Now, if there is one thing I hate it is a masculine woman," opined one writer in 1894. "It has made my heart sore to see the women who have been putting on knickerbockers, riding the diamond-frame wheel [as opposed to the lower, drop frame intended for women] . . . and racing and scorching with the men." That author

COASTING.

FIGURE 2.13 (TOP) Violet stands next to her friend Daisy Elliott, the gymnast who posed as a model in *The Common Sense of Bicycling*, demonstrating the proper way to ride, mount, dismount, and repair a bicycle.

FIGURE 2.14 (BOTTOM) Here, she models how to coast, a practice that was, because it involves taking one's feet off the pedals, widely looked down upon, especially for women. The photographs (rendered as engravings in Ward's book) are among the few Austen photographs to be published during her lifetime.

Alice Austen, Violet Ward and Daisy Elliott with Bicycle, ca. 1895. Collection of Historic Richmond Town; Ward, *The Common Sense of Bicycling*, 72

FIGURE 2.15 New-York based humor magazine *Puck* had a field day satirizing the popularity of cycling in the 1890s with cartoons featuring wheelwomen in colorful, fashion-forward bicycling costumes. This 1897 cartoon and the associated caption also poke fun at the ways the bicycle (parked behind the chair) changed domestic roles. Five years prior (depicted in the inset), Clara agreed to marry George and become a "a young man's slave." Today, it is a different story: "Now, George, don't let Willy get into mischief; don't forget to give the twins their bottle; when the groceryman calls give him that order I told you to remember; if you get a chance, I wish you would dust out the library; don't let that roast burn in the oven, and if Mrs. Smithers calls, tell her I will be home this evening. I am going to take a spin on my wheel, and will be back in two or three hours."

"Her choice. The young man's slave [five years later]," *Puck*, July 7, 1897

was not only a female rider but also an enthusiast who had even started her own magazine, *The Wheelwoman*. Among devotees there was hardly consensus.[74]

While many supporters maintained that women cyclists ought to ride like women—moving at a measured pace, sitting erect, and dressing like a lady—Ward gave advice on how to power up climbs ("Never let a hill get the better of you, if it is one that you have a chance to attack a second time set to work and study it"), scorch (a term generally reserved for reckless male cyclists), coast, and sprint. Even if she admitted that there was only a certain time and place for these less dignified forms of riding, the very acknowledgment that women could engage in those cycling practices was unusual.[75]

Although the bicycle did give women a tool to successfully challenge existing social norms and offered hope for change—of status, position, wardrobe, opportunity, and movement—progress did not come easily. In the process of breaking convention, convention was often replicated. The media, race organizers, club leaders, and others insisted on rooting women's experience with bicycles in traditional storylines. Unlike men, women vied for the prize of prettiest rider. And newspaper columnists showed women how to use bicycle parts to decorate the home (like making "bicyclely" ornaments and dressing up an old wheel with ribbon and hanging it over the mantle).[76]

Ward's book was reviewed in several newspapers across the country, and the "excellent little manual" received full-page coverage in a May 1896 issue of the *New York Herald*. Not atypically, that same Sunday edition featured all things bicycle: stories about the latest innovations in bicycle technology (e.g., adjustable bicycle umbrella holders); songs about bicycles; news from dozens of local bicycle clubs; cartoons about bicycles (e.g., ten men cycle into space and land on Mars, where they end up stuck after Martians trash their "double quint" bike); ads from local dealers selling new and secondhand bicycles, bicycle suits, bicycle lanterns, trouser guards, oils, cyclometers, bells, pumps, saddles, and tires; bicycle riding academies selling memberships; announcements for a forthcoming bicycle parade; an invitation to visit Hubert's Museum on Fourteenth Street, which offered "Pretty Girls, attired in the latest bicycle costumes, in hourly contests for superiority"; a lengthy story about a Bicycle Tea and "some of the Pretty Women and Pretty Costumes That Were Observed"; a piece about a scorcher who was caught on Eighty-Seventh Street by a "bike cop"; another story about a drunk cyclist and suspected bicycle thief; and news of a rider who had been run over by a horse. The *New York Herald*, like the *New York Recorder*, the *Brooklyn Daily Eagle*, the *New York Times*, and nearly every other New York-based paper, fought to win the attention of bicycle-hungry readers with daily columns about cyclists, competing with the many bicycle-centered magazines and journals that flourished in the 1890s.[77]

Even before finishing her book, Ward began drafting two others. The first was a narrower reference book on bicycle tires and other parts. The guidebook would, so she promised the bicycle admen whom she doggedly solicited, result in more knowledgeable and satisfied customers. In return, the entrepreneurial Ward asked each manufacturer to sponsor the book—to the tune of $100.[78]

Ward shopped for advertisers at Madison Square Garden's 1896 Bicycle Show. The annual exposition featured dazzling displays of the latest bicycle models, complete with electric signage. Local dealers met with national firms, trying to gauge what and how much to order. At the trade show, Ward found plenty of freebies and sales pitches, and at least a few manufacturers interested in doing business with her. In the summer of 1896, the Spencer Brake Co. of Chambers Street in New York sent her a bicycle equipped with one of its "invisible coil brakes," hoping Ward, an emerging name in the women's bicycling world, would endorse it.[79]

Evidence suggests that Ward was also planning an even more ambitious book. Just after *The Common Sense of Bicycling* was published in summer 1896, she began amassing newspaper articles related to cycling from across the country, pasting them into a scrapbook, and eventually creating a vast collection of several thousand pages. More than just gathering clippings, Ward, to borrow a phrase from scholar Ellen Gruber Garvey, was "writing with scissors." Scrapbooking had become a common practice by the late nineteenth century, particularly among activist women; in this case, Ward used the scrapbooks as both a reference project, to form a kind of bibliography of cycling that she could draw from for future writing projects, and a personal journal, with private correspondence related to her cycling interests, cycling ephemera, etc.[80]

A typical page in her scrapbook contains several glued-on articles, covering a range of topics from papers scattered across the country. Some of the clippings, like reviews of her own book, chronicle her successes. Other clippings cover cycling in general: bicycle technology, new bicycle ordinances, debates about taxes on bicycles, discussions of the bicycle trade, accident reports, and even a picture of an orangutan riding a bike. Most of the stories relate specifically to women, with headlines including: "The Bicycle Girl's Fads," "How Women Should Ride," "Handsomest Wheelwomen," "Racing by Women to be Stopped by the L.A.W.," "Death to Bloomers," "What Should be the Length of a Girl's Bicycle Skirt," and "Ugly Hands Threaten the Women Who Indulge in Wheel Exercise." One article featured drawings of the "clay model" saddles that belonged to New York's most fashionable women. Ward's seat was not included, but several fellow Michaux Club members were, each of whom had to sit on a mound of clay for half an hour to develop a mold for their custom aluminum saddle. The maker took pains to mention that the concept was "neither ridiculous nor vulgar," therefore suggesting that it was perhaps both.[81]

As it turns out, her scrapbooks were the last things she ever "wrote" about cycling.

In the late 1890s, Violet Ward put away her bicycle. Although she continued to participate in club life and civic-minded groups—she would become a member, for example, of the New-York Historical Society—and kept playing golf, her public presence began to fade. As time wore on, Violet and her sister, both unmarried, became known as eccentrics who rarely left their decaying mansion on Grymes Hill. She died in 1941.[82]

Arthur Hyde's wheeling diary ends in the summer of 1896, right before he shipped off to West Point. As a cadet, he spent a year as future general Douglas MacArthur's roommate. Hyde graduated in 1900 and began a distinguished career in the service, ultimately earning the rank of colonel and authoring several books on military strategy. On the side he studied theology, and when he retired in 1922, Reverend Hyde began a second career in the church, leading several congregations throughout the country before settling back in New York, where he died in 1943. He was buried in Peekskill—one of his favorite wheeling destinations back in the 1890s. Whether or not Hyde kept riding at West Point or while in the army is uncertain. His career path probably gave him much less time to cycle, but even if he had remained in New York, he probably would have stopped riding anyway. After all, most everyone else did.[83]

As the century turned, bicycles disappeared from the streets, paths, and parks. Why did hundreds of thousands of New Yorkers and millions of Americans stop cycling, and so abruptly?

It was not because everyone started driving cars—that would not be the case for decades to come. Nor was cycling rendered obsolete by vast subway systems—those would come later too—or terrific improvements in the streetcar network or other forms of transportation. Bicycles had been used mainly for recreation, and there were no regulations or new restrictions that suddenly endangered the pastime. Nor was it because of some inherent flaw in American cities—too sprawling, too hilly, or too foul weathered. None of these factors stopped millions of Americans from gleefully pedaling about in the 1890s. Indeed, as a practical matter, the decision whether or not to bike from Hyde's house on the Upper East Side to Spalding's bike shop downtown should have been no different in 1902 than it was in 1896. But it was.

The change, rather perversely, was something enthusiasts had long advocated: less expensive bicycles and more types of cyclists. The fashionable bicycles were no longer considered such when prices dropped and as more New Yorkers became cyclists. Used by an increasing (even if still decidedly minority) number of women, nonwhites, working-class, and utilitarian riders, bicycles seemed, to some, less sporting, masculine, and privileged than they had been. In short, the bicycle lost its power as a status symbol. As its social value began to fade, so did hopes that the bicycle was the magic solution to cure the ills of modern society and the modern city.

For Ward, Hyde, and the army of city cyclists, the bicycle provided a new perspective from which to see the city and offered real advantages and opportunities. They used it to commute, run errands, exercise, meet people, join clubs, escape the city, and challenge social conventions. And just at the moment that the bicycle was beginning to usher in real change—new traffic laws, paved streets, bike lanes, bike paths, bike shops, bike clubs, different clothes and dating rituals, and increased feelings of freedom and independence—cycling fell out of favor.

When bicycles came back in fashion decades later, government and its leaders would play a much more central role. In particular, one person, a child of the 1890s, would go on to shape the cycling experience like no other had. His name: Robert Moses.

CHAPTER THREE

MOSES

To say that Robert Moses had more of an influence on the land-scape of modern New York than anyone else is not hyperbole. It is consensus.

Although the man is long dead, Moses's bridges, tunnels, and park-ways; playgrounds and beaches; sporting venues and housing projects are very much alive. Millions of New Yorkers encounter them every day, and many stand as monuments to a distant past when the city built things quickly, beautifully, and sometimes even on budget. In today's New York, it is hard to imagine that a new public restroom would look anything like the curved, two-story, blue terra-cotta-tiled bathhouse that Moses commissioned at Orchard Beach. Or that a new swimming pool could compete with the one large enough for 6,800 people that Moses, a former collegiate swimmer, built in Brooklyn's McCarren Park. Or that another Lincoln Center will pop up in midtown or downtown or anywhere, for that matter. Which is why some New Yorkers and historians of recent vintage have praised the master builder, perhaps the last one we will ever see.[1]

Yet in equally plain sight is a landscape of poor choices and missed opportunities: homes destroyed, lives transplanted, pedestrians ignored, and a public transit system that might have been. The Yale/Oxford/Columbia-educated New York City Department of Parks Commissioner, Chairman of the Triborough Bridge and Tunnel Authority, New York City Construction Coordinator, member of the City Planning Commission, chairman of the Committee on Slum Clearance, and chairman or member of many other organizations has been accused of viewing the city from above, failing to understand life at the neighborhood level, and building a city for rich, white New Yorkers at the expense of all others.

The bushy-browed man who never drove a car is most remembered, and rightly so, for his highways—both paved and proposed. But bicycles also moved, and still move, through a city fashioned by Moses. Indeed, from the 1930s through the 1960s, the question of where bicycles belonged in New York was in large part answered by one man. It was Moses who prioritized the kinds of infrastructure that would be built, where such projects would go, and how people and vehicles would use them. In the grandest sense, it was Moses who shaped how people moved. And his decisions had lasting importance. In fact, they were often cast in concrete.[2]

Robert Moses moved to New York in 1897. He was eight years old. He was grumpy. The greatest bicycle boom that the world had ever known was roughly the same age. When Moses's family left the dirt streets of New Haven, Connecticut, for Manhattan, bicycles cruised about the city that was a center of the cycling world. Mere blocks from his home on East Forty-Sixth Street (paved with asphalt), Lurie & Ross opened a bike shop; the New York Tourist Wheelmen, a local cycling club, maintained its headquarters; and three different cycling schools—the Spalding-Bidwell Cycling Academy, Johnson's Cycling Academy, and Golden's Cycling Academy—promised to turn novices into experts. The schools were not for children, for in the 1890s Americans conceived of bicycles as a toy and sometimes tool (and sometimes both) for adults. Children were far less likely to ride, and it is quite possible that Moses never rode a bicycle. But he would have seen them. They were everywhere.[3]

But as the century turned from nineteen to twenty, bicycles were disappearing from Gotham's streets. With sales to adults slumping, manufacturers increasingly pitched their wares to children. "Boyhood without a bicycle is like a summer without flowers," a *Boys' Life* advertisement proclaimed in 1922. With marketing campaigns promoting the bicycle as the ideal way to instill character and the perfect gift for an eighth birthday ("the beginning of the bicycle age!" nudged the Cycle Trades of America), the bicycle industry strengthened the link between bikes and kids.[4]

By 1928, the *New York Times* guessed that the average age of a cyclist was "easily a decade younger" than it had been in the 1890s. Girls "may ride up until their graduation from elementary school, but the high school miss usually regards the 'bike' as considerably beneath her dignity." Bicycles started appearing in the windows of FAO Schwartz. Toddlers on tricycles zoomed down the sidewalks. Younger than the cyclists in the 1890s and older than the children who rode in the early twentieth century, Moses belonged to a kind of lost generation of cyclists.[5]

Even within what was ultimately a three-decade lull of adult cycling, a select group of New York men and women kept pedaling. As other municipal police departments switched to motorcycles, New York's 1915 force included 135 bike cops. In the 1920s some bicycle advertisements still targeted "business men and industrial workers" looking for a convenient and economical way to commute. Admen were less likely to woo the socially minded, middle- and upper-class New Yorkers who had once dominated the market. There was still a smattering of cycling-related social events, and the city sometimes hosted a "Bicycle Week" in May. There were up years (which often came with, for cyclists and bike sellers anyway, great and unrealized expectations that a long-term trend was just beginning) and down years (which often came with great and unrealized expectations that increased bicycle usage was just around the corner).[6]

Despite the few bicycles on the streets, New York remained home to a vibrant racing scene. The popular six-day races, now featuring teams of two switching on and off (because of the law limiting individuals to twelve hours of racing a day), continued to call Madison Square Garden (which moved locations in 1925) home. The biannual, near week-long competitions often drew more than 100,000 fans. Bike racing, especially in the 1920s, was among the most popular sports in America—and the most lucrative. The purse of a Garden Six Day could total $50,000. Top riders earned $1,000 per day in appearance fees, and invitations from Calvin Coolidge to visit the White House. Celebrities, including Babe Ruth, Jack Dempsey, Will Rogers, Douglas Fairbanks, Mary Pickford, and Al Jolson, watched races from the stands or assumed the honorary role of firing the starter's pistol.[7]

Elsewhere in the city, racers circled one-sixth-mile tracks at open-air venues. The New York Velodrome opened in 1922 on Broadway and 225th Street in the Bronx and accommodated 16,000 fans at what was one of the largest and most popular tracks in the country. In 1930 the wooden velodrome burned to the ground, but a new 10,000-seat space opened a couple of blocks away from the famous boardwalk in Coney Island. Both stadiums hosted sprint races, endurance contests, and motor-paced races in which cyclists rode in the slipstream of motorcycles. Even without the assist, the fastest riders achieved speeds nearing 40 miles per hour on the steeply banked tracks.[8]

Although the Great Depression sapped some of the enthusiasm for racing, the Garden Sixes remained popular throughout the 1930s. A 1937 British newsreel depicts 14,000 rowdy fans waiting for Mayor Fiorello La Guardia to signal the start of a race featuring an international field of fifteen two-man teams taking turns riding on the track and sleeping on tiny cots parked in an infield overcrowded with trainers, mechanics, spare parts, and "pounds of beefsteak." A team from Germany, competing under the Nazi flag, won the race, logging 2,565 miles.[9]

Despite the depression, bicycle sales rose steadily, nearing and eventually surpassing the records (though not on a per capita basis) set in the 1890s. In 1936 and 1937, Americans bought about 1.25 million bicycles per year, roughly double the rate from 1934 and 1935, and roughly five times the 1930–1933 average rate. In 1938, The Cycle Trades of America estimated that there were 6 or 7 million bicycles on the road. The industry expected the growth to continue (as industries are wont to do). The media started paying attention too.[10]

The first issue of the *Cycling Herald*, a monthly newspaper published in Brooklyn "whose sole and only purposes are to publish news relating to bicycling," appeared in the summer of 1938. Bicycle clubs were forming again. The League of American Wheelmen, which had lapsed in 1902 as Americans' interest in bicycling waned, was by 1939 informally revived and within a few years officially back in business. New York was again home to a number of clubs: The Acme Wheelmen, Century Road Club Association, Empire City Wheelmen, German Bicycle Sport Club, Gotham Cyclists, Unione Sportiva Italiana, and Long Island Wheelmen's Association, plus a handful of smaller organizations.[11]

Although the much larger boom of the 1890s was in part prompted by a new kind of bicycle, the uptick in the 1930s had little to do with bike technology. What seemed to be spurring sales now was what had hastened the end of the last boom: bicycles were cheap. Prices were down to about twenty-five dollars—still not affordable to all New Yorkers, but much less expensive than automobiles. The comparison was made more obvious by the speedometers, faux gas tanks, and other automobile-style features that adorned bicycles from the period. Although more affordable than in years past, bicycles were also increasingly fashionable. As other historians have shown, a group of Hollywood-cool movie stars began to ride and endorse bicycles, helping stir the revival.[12]

With the economic woes came a wave of nostalgia, and bicycles served as reminders of an imagined past: a simpler, cleaner, less crowded, and less depressed New York. The previous bicycle boom of the "gay Nineties" was referenced again and again. A depression-era parade in Central

Park, for example, included participants dressed in cycling garb of times past and riding (or more exactly, trying to ride) vintage bicycles.[13]

In popular forms of entertainment, bicycles symbolized the 1890s and all of its supposed merriment. The New York World's Fair, which opened in 1939 and for which planning began (with the help of Robert Moses) in the mid-1930s, is often remembered for Futurama, the General Motors-sponsored exhibit that celebrated highways, cars, and gasoline. But the fairground in Flushing Meadows, Queens, also played home to a historical pageant, *American Jubilee*, in which the bicycle had a starring role. Alongside flags, stars and stripes, and bald eagles, seventy-five cycling performers (on bikes donated by the Cycle Trades of America) outfitted in 1890s costume wheeled around the giant outdoor stage as part of a nine-minute number, "My Bicycle Girl." The act was "pure nostalgia in its representation of the good old days and romance," one historian of dance concluded. Indeed, by the late 1930s, what was remembered of the

FIGURE 3.1
A New York World's Fair poster.

New York Public Library,
Manuscripts and Archives Division,
New York World's Fair 1939–1940
Records, Image ID: 201477

1890 bicycle boom was that cycling was purely fun and social, a reminder of a happier city.[14]

Although the 1890s were often invoked in the 1930s, few of the new riders were old enough to remember the previous boom. Still used by small children, bicycles by the mid to late 1930s started to attract "older younger people" in their late teens and early twenties, looking for exercise, entertainment, and nothing too "strenuous." Unlike the previous booms, there was no sudden rush to open riding schools. Having learned to ride bikes as children in the 1910s, a generation of adults already knew how to ride by the 1930s.[15]

Women composed a significant portion of the new riders. "Keep fit on a bicycle and you won't keep fat," a female advice columnist swore in 1938. She also promoted the magic bicycle as a savior for the "too thin." Get a bicycle, eat right, and "watch the weight add on." Women initially outnumbered men on the special weekend trains that began transporting cyclists from city to country in the mid-1930s. Like "snow cars" and "fishing cars" that took New Yorkers to surrounding mountains and lakes, the "cycle train" to Canaan, Connecticut, provided day trips—complete with a boxed lunch and a route map—to a twenty-six-mile stretch of road "guarded by railway representatives" and with few cars, little noise, and crowds of bicyclists. There was also a "cycling steamer" that took New Yorkers and their bicycles up the Hudson River by boat. Compared to more rural areas and compared to the 1890s, the city had less cycling appeal. Back in the 1890s, a writer for the *Brooklyn Daily Eagle* explained in 1936, "cycling was much simpler." There had once been smooth bicycle paths, asphalt ribbons on the street, and ample spots to park one's wheels.[16]

Because of the boom/bust nature of cycling interest, infrastructure created during one boom was likely to be repurposed before the next one took hold. Indeed, most of the 1890s bike infrastructure had been erased or reallocated. And because of the differing views of bicycles and the changing environment of the city, advocates in one boom were not always asking for the same type of infrastructure found in another. In the 1930s, the focus was even less on transportation than it had been in the 1890s. The new cyclists wanted recreational paths and wanted to feel safe. They began lobbying the city to (re)build infrastructure. And they had one man to direct their plea to: Robert Moses.

By the time Moses was sworn in as the New York City Parks Commissioner in January 1934, he had come a long way from the quiet, unassuming boy he once was. Smart, hardworking (and still grumpy), and with a plan to make government more efficient, Moses trampolined into power. Shortly after earning a PhD in political science in 1914, he tested his academic theories of civil service reform in practice at the Municipal Research Bureau in New York. There, Moses, who had no formal training in planning, spearheaded a campaign to centralize government power by consolidating smaller agencies into larger departments and empowering the governor with new authority. His push to consolidate power—later, for himself—would become one of the things he was best known for.

In 1924, Moses became president of the Long Island State Park Commission and began building beaches and parkways at a scale and in a style never before seen. When he developed Jones Beach State Park on Long Island, for example, he transformed a tranquil expanse of sand into a crowded beachfront distinguished by elegant bathhouses and an expensive brick and limestone water tower made to look like a Venetian bell tower. In part so that New Yorkers could drive to his new beaches, Moses began drafting plans for an extensive network of parkways. The parkways, Moses insisted, should be more than just roads; they should be pieces of art, mimicking nature's curves and affording space for attractive landscapes. Though local property owners fought against the Southern and Northern State Parkways, Moses won and did so in what was becoming his trademark style: trumpeting parks to the public, announcing bold plans, seizing control of project finances and design, pushing detractors out of the way (almost no one was off-limits), and starting projects so quickly that opposition surfaced too late.

With a track record as the planner who could "get things done," Moses was Mayor La Guardia's top pick for the parks commissioner post in 1934. There was just one problem: Moses already had several jobs, including President of the Jones Beach Parkway Authority, Chairman of the Emergency Public Works Commission, President of the Bethpage State Park Authority, Chairman of the New York State Council of Parks, and President of the Long Island State Parks Commission. Moses vowed that he could take on the new job while keeping the others. La Guardia agreed. Moses also demanded that the new position come with greater authority, specifically that the five separate parks departments (one for each borough) be consolidated. La Guardia agreed. Moses also asked to write the legislation creating the newly strengthened commissionership himself. La Guardia agreed to that too.

Within weeks of taking the new job, Moses gained yet another title. As Chairman of the Triborough Bridge (and later Tunnel) Authority, he would ultimately oversee the design and operation of seven bridges, two tunnels, and all of the associated toll revenue. For someone never elected to public office, Moses wielded an enormous amount of power.

Moses's first major bike initiative came in July 1938: the Alley Pond Cycle Path in Queens. In the immediate years prior, Moses had overseen the construction of bits of path here and there, but nothing like this. It stretched 2.5 miles along the old Long Island Motor Parkway, the private road originally built in 1908 for racing sports cars by William K. Vanderbilt (in the 1890s, his wife pedaled alongside Violet Ward as a Michaux Cycle Club member). The road had since become city property, and Moses saw it as the perfect opportunity to satisfy the growing public demand for bike infrastructure. Like a new playground, the Alley Pond Path was entirely for recreation, portending Moses's long-term approach to bikes.

To mark the path's opening, Moses joined the parks department's fifty-piece band in a grand celebration filled with visible reminders of the nineteenth-century cycling world: high-wheel bicycles; Charles "Mile-a-Minute" Murphy, the bicycle racer who back in 1899 famously set a speed record while drafting behind a Long Island Railroad car; and sixty-two-year-old Alexander Ewers, introduced as the first bicycle cop to have arrested a speeding motorist. The irony that a road built for cars was now being remade for bicycles was not lost on anyone, let alone Moses: "The way to make progress, sometimes, is to go backward."[17]

The Alley Pond path, Moses told the crowd, was just the beginning. He acknowledged that bicycle facilities were the "biggest unsatisfied need facing the Park Department today" and promised that more "comprehensive" solutions would come soon. After Moses and the other dignitaries spoke, the three-year-old son of a parks department engineer cut the ceremonial ribbon. The riders took off on what was not just the longest and most attractive bicycle path in the city but also one of the grandest paths built anywhere in the country since the turn of the century.[18]

With plenty of room, bicycle policemen keeping watch, and guardrails lining the curves, the path was designed for recreational cyclists to pedal in peace. No honking horns. No speeding cars. No jaywalking pedestrians. Open every day from 8:00 a.m. until dark, the path attracted riders whether or not they owned a set of wheels. The Alley Pond Fieldhouse rented bikes (35 cents an hour) and sold and repaired them too. Lessons were $1 an hour, plus 10 cents if riders needed to check their clothes. Regulars could keep their bikes in long-term storage for $2 a month. Automobile parking was available for those who planned to rent a bike, were not within cycling distance of the path, or did not dare to ride on the streets. There was even a Sunday morning bus that ferried people from

FIGURE 3.2

The Cycle Trades of America, the leading bicycle industry trade group, envisioned the Alley Pond Bicycle Path as a sign of a more hopeful future filled with cycling infrastructure and, of course, increased bicycle sales.

American Bicyclist and Motorcyclist, September 1938

West Forty-Second Street to Queens's newest playground. In its first year, 38,000 cyclists used the path.[19]

By the time the path opened in the summer of 1938, Moses was already working on an ambitious plan for many more bike paths across the boroughs. To fulfill his vision, he would need far more capital than the city or even the state could provide. He needed help from Washington.

Mayor La Guardia had long had success lobbying President Franklin Roosevelt for New Deal money. New Yorkers needed jobs. And there was plenty to build and beautify in Roosevelt's home state. Despite lingering animosity between President Roosevelt and the parks commissioner (Roosevelt, elected governor of New York in 1928, was much less enchanted by Moses than previous governor Al Smith had been and sought to diminish his influence, removing Moses from his post as Secretary of New York State), Moses managed to win more than his fair share of New Deal monies, particularly from the Works Progress Administration (WPA) that employed millions of Americans to build roads and bridges, construct new parks and swimming pools, paint murals, and even conduct oral history interviews of former slaves. Moses knew that there were millions of dollars at stake and in almost no time had detailed blueprints for shovel-ready projects—something that usually took teams of mayors, engineers, and parks commissioners in other cities years to do. There were benefits to consolidating power after all. By 1936, New York City alone claimed roughly one-seventh of all WPA money. The Department of Parks benefited the most, netting an average of more than $59 million a year between 1935 and 1937, or more than eight times the entire department budget.[20]

Money came in. Buildings rose. Parks opened. Hoses dumped water into swimming pools. And playgrounds sprouted like tulips in April. On average, Moses and La Guardia opened one new playground every six days—for three years straight.

Bicycle-related programs were well within the WPA's sphere of interest. In a WPA-produced short film from 1937, the New Deal agency showcased a selection of its work in California. Included in the silent promotional film are scenes from a crowded velodrome in San Jose, an intense game of "bicycle polo" in Monterey, and two women on bicycles riding along a lakeside path. Whatever monies the WPA was willing to invest in bicycling would only last so long. The great wave of government spending in the first and second New Deal had already passed, and the political prospects for a third were slim. Ticktock.[21]

In August 1938 Moses announced his "Program of Proposed Facilities for Bicycling." In it, he outlined a comprehensive plan to build bicycle paths across the city at a spectacular scale. In all, he proposed adding 58.75 miles of bicycle paths. And he was starting almost from scratch. When Moses took office in 1934, the total distance of all bicycle paths in all boroughs had measured, according to one official, just 5.5 miles. Some might have said closer to zero, considering that this figure likely referred to the still standing bicycle pathway linking Prospect Park and Coney Island that had been built *for* cyclists and that Arthur Hyde had so proudly paraded down in 1895; in the interim, the bicycle path, since populated by horses, baby carriages, and motorcycles and crisscrossed by automobiles, had become barely recognizable.[22]

Running within the parks and stretching alongside several parkways, the new paths were intended for cyclists and cyclists alone. No New Yorker (and few, if any Americans) had seriously pushed such a comprehensive plan to accommodate cyclists since the century turned.

Moses's plan touched each of the five boroughs. In Manhattan, Moses assigned almost all of the new pathways to Central Park. For the Bronx, Moses drew up a plan for a 9-mile bicycle parkway, connecting Van Cortlandt, Bronx, and Pelham Bay parks. In Brooklyn, Moses focused on improving riding conditions within Prospect Park, reconfiguring the old Coney Island Cycle Path, laying a new path along the Shore/Belt Parkway, and building a loop around Marine Park. Queens was slated to receive six new paths, including a 9.5-mile stretch in Flushing Meadows Park (first to be used by pedestrians for the World's Fair and later to be repurposed for cyclists) and a 1.5-mile path in Kissena Park. Staten Island, where Moses dubiously claimed "the indulgence in bicycling may be heavier in proportion to population than in the other boroughs," would receive just a single 1.5-mile route, owing to the fact that the "lightly traveled highways can take care of most" of the demand. On most other occasions, Moses made it clear that bicycles did not belong on the roads.[23]

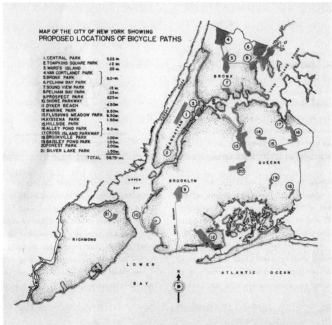

FIGURES 3.3 (TOP) AND 3.4 (BOTTOM) Moses's plan for bicycle paths, 1938.

Department of Parks, City of New York, *Program of Proposed Facilities for Bicycling*, 1938, New-York Historical Society

Indeed, Moses's program was as much about making the streets more car-friendly as it was about providing places to cycle. The twenty-four-page plan begins by acknowledging what the parks commissioner thought was obvious: "bicycles have no place on public highways." This was an assertion, but not a law. It is true that the New York City Department of Parks could regulate bicycle use in the parks and along the parkways and New Yorkers conceived of streets as primarily motor traffic thoroughfares; however, state law from the nineteenth century still granted cyclists the right to the road. Laws tended to survive longer than infrastructure. Nevertheless, Moses contended that cyclists did not belong on roads. Not only was it unsafe for them, but just as important, they "are themselves a hazard to motorists." Moses also went out of his way to ensure that the new paths did not impede automobile traffic. In Central Park, for example, he carefully planned grade crossings and designed the snaking layout of the 5.25-mile path so as to least vex motorists.[24]

In Moses's vision—and in the city he would go on to build—cyclists fit only on park paths. "Unless bicycling is confined to designated, controlled areas within the parks, it would be just as dangerous as on city streets," he wrote. Moses wanted cycling to be a contained form of recreation, like swimming pools and playgrounds. So long as the bicycles remained within the confines of the park and did not threaten to escape its bounds, then the exact locations of the paths seem to have been rather unimportant to the man famous for his love of details. "We have planned winding layouts," Moses went on, "which will lead in most cases from somewhere to some other place." Moses was building for only one of the bicycle's many uses: recreation. Therefore, no actual destination was needed.[25]

Although historical traffic data are scarce, it is clear that Moses had reason to be concerned about safety. As the number of cyclists increased, so did the number of crashes. Around the time of the bicycle program announcement, a survey found that overall highway safety was improving but that there had been an increase in the number of crashes resulting from "careless bicycle riding." (There was no category that included the number of cyclists injured or killed while engaged in careful bicycle riding.) Later statistics showed that the number of riders killed or injured on a bicycle doubled over the first eight months of 1939, compared to the previous year. As a result, Mayor La Guardia echoed Moses in warning that while cycling "may be healthful, and it may even be romantic . . . it is very hazardous when carried on in competition with the automobile."[26]

That Moses's 1938 plan was littered with cycling images from the pre-automobile era was a telling indication that he had no interest in integrating the two types of street traffic. Like many New Yorkers at the time, Moses had only a vague recollection of what the cycling mania at the end of the nineteenth century looked like; one drawing of a man straddling a velocipede from about 1819 was included as a pictorial reminder of the cycling craze of "The Early Nineties." The details were fuzzy enough for history to serve a political purpose. The hard-won legislative battles that manifested in laws granting cyclists the right to ride on the streets were buried. The cycling commuters, admittedly always a minority, were forgotten completely.[27]

When news of Moses's bicycle path plan hit the streets, one magazine said that it was "Heard 'Round the World" and predicted it would be "echoed throughout the U.S.A." That was hardly the case. There was a modest wave of path building, like the 3.5-mile, dirt-surfaced municipal bike path built in Cincinnati in 1939. And in this case and others, it was clear that Moses was not alone in seeing roads as places only for cars. Moses's view was far from unique. But the scope of his plans certainly was. So was the size of the checks that the federal government was doling out.[28]

But timing was not on Moses's side. The WPA approved his bicycling program in full in 1938, but it became clear by the following spring that WPA money was drying up. Certain promises from the previous summer would be broken. Not everything planned got built, and even most of the projects that did changed shape. The proposed 9.5-mile loop around Marine Park became just a 1-mile piece, and the Prospect Park path was more modest than originally planned. Within two years of Moses's announcement, the city had laid 20 miles of paths in total, including the "new" 5.5-mile path from Prospect Park to Coney Island that was reconfigured to give space back to cyclists.[29]

The most significant piece of Moses's program to actually materialize was the dozen miles of pathway running alongside the new Belt

FIGURE 3.5 While motorists are stuck in traffic, cyclists cruise along the Belt Parkway Bicycle Path.

Belt Parkway Bicycle & Pedestrian Path, Belt at Jamaica Bay, photograph, December 20, 1941. Courtesy NYC Municipal Archives

Parkway in 1941. Beginning on the western edge of King's County with a view of the Narrows that separates Brooklyn from Staten Island, extending past Fort Hamilton and Sheepshead Bay to Canarsie and hugging Brooklyn's waterfront along the way, the Belt Parkway offered cyclists an almost uninterrupted stretch of pavement, fresh water breezes, and the pleasure of not having to contend with cars or trucks. As planned from the outset, bicycles, pedestrians, and automobiles each had a separate space. Riders prized the new pathway even though the *Brooklyn Daily Eagle* warned them to watch out for the "cowboys," adolescents who "wobble along in a manner calculated to shake the nerves of the best riders" and liked to "sneer" at cyclists over the age of twenty-one.[30]

When the Belt Parkway opened in Brooklyn, Manhattan was home to just bits of path in two of its parks that had only been recently allocated

FIGURE 3.6 Cyclists in Central Park make use of the bicycle-only pathway. Pedestrians are warned to "keep off."

Marjory Collins, "Bicycling in Central Park on Sunday," 1942, Library of Congress Prints and Photographs Division, Washington, DC

for cyclists. The measly "few hundred feet of path" in Central Park was not enough for Clifton Fadiman, the wine-loving book editor for *The New Yorker* and witty, bantering host of the radio show "Information Please." In 1941, Fadiman wrote to Moses: "Everything, it seems to me, is being done today for motorists." On the other hand, he complained, bicyclists had almost no place to ride. Moses responded with characteristic ill humor: "Take the chip off your shoulder. As a distinguished moderator of experts of everything under the shining sun, you should be a little more cautious about generalizations." Moses did promise that the Central Park path would soon be lengthened to 1.3 miles, but this was still paltry considering that it was touted as the longest path in all of Manhattan and fell far short of the 5.25 miles that had been promised back in 1938.[31]

Fadiman further alleged that officers targeted cyclists, who were permitted to ride only in the designated areas and who, he claimed, had "better manners than motorists." A parks engineer saw it differently: "One summons for bicycle riding in Central Park for a three-week period is preposterous." Another New Yorker (who referred to himself as "A Taxpayer") agreed, writing to a sympathetic Moses about the speeding cyclists who wove between benches, frightened passersby, and on at least one occasion knocked down a small child. Another man reported seeing a boy on a bike riding at "full tilt, his posterior near the hind wheel, his hands, ape-like, wound about the handle-bars." Girls, supposedly, were no better; he fumed that the "embryonic Lady Godivas . . . do not believe in wearing street apparel" or even hosiery.[32]

Yet while some complained of unruly riders disturbing the peace in the park, many cyclists could not even get to the park. A group of twelve- and thirteen-year-old girls from the Upper West Side reported to the commissioner in the fall of 1939 that while "we wish to ride bicycles," it was nearly impossible to do so. Without a path to the paths, the relatively short distance was insurmountable. Ten-year-old Neil Langley also wrote to Commissioner Moses in 1939 on behalf of his frustrated "gang." "I am not permitted to ride my bike because it is too dangerous to ride it in the street. . . . My mother said she would let me ride it in the park, but not to the park." Instead of just complaining about the problem, Langley offered a solution that would help all of the "other boys who are in the same jam." He wanted bike lockers near Central Park for children to store their wheels. Another young girl asked about riding on the sidewalks as an alternative. Perhaps she did not know, but within the parks and across the city it was illegal to ride on the sidewalks, except for children under the age of ten. As her brief biography included in her letter to "The Hon. Robert Moses" indicated, she was exactly ten years old.[33]

In his response, Moses suggested that she "try the [Riverside Drive] path which has been built especially for you and the other children." The path he was referring to ran north from 100th Street for just six blocks alongside Riverside Drive and had been built with WPA money in 1937. The Riverside path had the "poorest possible" accessibility, the parks department conceded in an internal memo. Riders had to carry their bicycles down a flight of stairs before walking some 200 yards to the path's starting point, and had to dismount at the end of the path before turning back.[34]

Riverside resident Harold Dunk, who had been holed up in his apartment with an injury, watched cyclists schlepp their bicycles to the path and also watched day after day as city employees planted expensive flowers that would soon wither. Writing to the parks commissioner, he demanded to know why the money spent on Riverside Park flowers was not spent on improving the path. The park engineer asked the ailing man to keep count of the number of people enjoying the tulips.[35]

None of the paths was designed for serious cycling. As Moses himself wrote in 1939: "We have taken into consideration that riding up and down a short straight stretch of road is not the best kind of bicycling and, therefore, have planned as far as practical, winding layouts of such length and design that there will be no feeling of monotony." Riding back and forth on the six-block Riverside Park path would certainly count as monotonous, but the path did reflect Moses's vision that cycling was not a practical means to get from A to B.[36]

That bicycles were not conceived of as a tool for transportation was made more obvious in the summer of 1940 when the parks department proudly announced that it was going to cater to the ranks of cyclists who had recently taken up "the sport." Bicycles would now be allowed on all of the running tracks inside city parks. Officials hoped to satisfy a demand while improving safety for children, who continued to "create additional hazards to motorists." So, in 1940 New York, bicycles seemed more suited for the quarter-mile running tracks than the streets.[37]

As it turned out, the opening of the Alley Pond Path in Queens, the reopening of the Coney Island Cycle Path, and the beginning of construction on the bicycle path along the Belt Parkway—all of which occurred before the United States entered World War II—was not the beginning of a new era of path building but rather an isolated burst. By the end of 1941 most of the progress had ended. When Americans were forced to ration gas (and also bicycles) during the war, Moses predicted that automobile usage would drop and bicycle usage would rise. "As the preponderance of use changes from one to the other," he wrote in May 1942, "regulations governing the use of parkways and related facilities will of necessity have to be adjusted." Fewer automobiles took to the streets, especially for weekend trips to the beaches that Moses helped turn into an attraction. And there was anecdotal evidence that bicycles were more prevalent on Gotham's streets. But no new pro-bicycling regulations or infrastructure appeared. To the contrary, Moses's bike infrastructure campaign slowed to a halt, and when he was pitched forward-looking solutions, like when one woman suggested that "abandoned railroad rights of way" be transformed into bicycle paths, he did not share the vision.[38]

In the postwar period, total bicycle path mileage did creep upward, but much of it came in the form of facilities that were hardly cyclist friendly. By 1956, the city claimed 54.615 miles of paths (close to the 58.75 proposed back in 1938), but that included 6.4 miles of boardwalk at Rockaway Beach in Brooklyn and South Beach in Staten Island, which cyclists could not use at all in the summer, after 1:00 p.m. on weekdays, or after 11:00 a.m. on weekends. It also included 16 separate "paths" that were really just playgrounds and tiny designated park areas where bicycles were permitted. Since the opening of the Belt Parkway, no new path extended for more than 3 miles. The thought of adding bicycle paths and amenities only grew more foreign as the years went by and as New York (like most other American cities) redrew its map to invite more automobiles.[39]

One notable resident who did ride in the 1950s was Jane Jacobs. Best known for saving Washington Square Park from Moses and his planned expressway that would have cut through its heart (one of several proposed highways that threatened to swallow Manhattan), Jacobs was a Greenwich Village resident and avid cyclist. Her bicycle sat right off the kitchen in her Hudson Street home. On the weekends she and her family biked for fun, and during the week she was a regular bicycle commuter.[40]

To her writing post at *Architectural Forum*, she pedaled up from the Village, through the flower district and the garment district, and ulti-

FIGURE 3.7 Jane Jacobs on her bicycle in front of a gas station.

Architectural Forum, April 1956, 51

mately to Rockefeller Center, where she parked in a garage full of Cadillacs. It was legal to bike on the road, but few did. That Jacobs rode, and that she was a woman, made her a target of suspicion and comment. "Get a horse," someone teased. Others shouted, "Watch out, girlie, you'll get hurt," and "Whyn't you stay in the Park?" Rarely concerned about naysayers, Jacobs kept cycling, often beating traffic. As a colleague of hers at the *Forum* noted in 1956, Jacobs "knows a lot about NYC traffic. Lewis Mumford [an urban theorist] might learn a good deal on the handlebars of her bike." So too might have Robert Moses.[41]

While Jacobs's magnum opus, *The Death and Life of Great American Cities*, hardly mentions the bicycle, the critique she presents of Moses and autocentric planning generally must have been at least in part shaped by her own experience biking through the city. Rolling along streets designed for cars and feeling at the mercy of hulking steel vehicles, cyclists had a unique perspective on traffic, flow, and safety. And riding at a pace slower than motorists but faster than pedestrians, cyclists saw a different cityscape. As another famous New York cyclist, David Byrne, put it many years later: "I felt more connected to the life on the streets than I would have inside a car or in some form of public transport." Conceivably, part of Moses's vision of the city was cemented by having been chauffeured around. Had Moses been a cyclist, perhaps his view of neighborhoods, streets, and parks would have been different.[42]

Moses's view shaped not just bridges and highways, parks and playgrounds but also some of the city's largest and most important housing projects, through his role (among all the others) as city construction coordinator. One such project was the Pelham Parkway Houses in the Bronx, a sprawling public housing facility opened in 1948 that more than 1,200 families would soon call home. At $16 a month, apartments were affordable. But there were a number of drawbacks, including one that made a sixth-grader named Marlene rather unhappy: no bicycles allowed.[43]

Although a couple of housing projects permitted cycling, including Stuyvesant Town, which required riders to affix a license to their bikes, the New York City Housing Authority (NYCHA) banned bikes from most others, including Parkchester and Peter Cooper Village. Marlene could not ride around the Pelham Parkway Houses, and the parks were too far away. She was too old for the sidewalks. And the streets (according to her parents and Mr. Moses) were off-limits too.[44]

In the early 1960s, housing administrators did contemplate lifting the ban. A NYCHA commissioner admired a housing project in Bremen, Germany, with a lengthy bicycle path snaking across it and suggested that the same be built in the States. NYCHA lawyers wasted no time swatting down his idea, citing the need for expensive liability insurance. In reality, there had been relatively few accidents at the small number of housing projects that allowed cycling. Nevertheless, legal counsel concluded that bike paths would lead to "rowdyism, dangerous cycling, overcrowding, racing, and other disorderly activity." Part of the problem was that New York was no Bremen; in Europe bicycles were for adults, while in the United States "a bicycle is treated more like a toy."[45]

Americans largely saw it the same way. The bicycle industry had redoubled its efforts targeting children. A bicycle was "Young America's Top Choice" for Christmas, *American Bicyclist and Motorcyclist* declared in 1953, especially for boys. Marketers tempted tots with cartoon-inspired bikes and pitched bicycles to older children (and their parents) as tools to develop maturity and masculinity.[46] As a 1955 Phyllis McGinley poem, published in *The New Yorker*, began:

All of a sudden, bicycles are toys,
Not transportation, Bicycles are for boys[47]

And like Marlene (who demonstrated that girls, of course, rode too) ten-year-old Alan lamented that there was no space to ride in his neighborhood. In 1958 he wrote to Moses, asking "whether a bicycle path could be constructed" near his home. Alan lived on Bryant Avenue in the Bronx, one block away from Moses's Cross-Bronx Expressway that infamously sliced through the Tremont neighborhood. As construction was ongoing, Alan wondered why "children like me don't have places to go by bicycle."[48]

At this point Moses was finally, gradually losing some of his power. In 1959, he relinquished most of his titles, including that of parks commissioner, in exchange for the opportunity to oversee the planning of the 1964/1965 World's Fair in Flushing Meadows. The popularity of cycling had been higher when the World's Fair first came to New York in 1939, when Moses planned to leverage the opportunity to build a 9.5-mile bicycle path on site. The money never turned up, and neither did the path. In 1959 he again saw the World's Fair as a vehicle to build venues and parks that would long outlive the exposition. This time there were no plans for bicycle paths. But there were plans for a bicycle racetrack.[49]

To raise the profile of the fair, Moses secured a deal with the United States Olympic Committee to host fifteen different Olympic trials scattered across sites he had already built or soon would build, including the main pavilion at the fair, a pool in Astoria, a track on Randall's Island, and the waters off of Orchard Beach. Moses also won the privilege of hosting the U.S. Olympic Cycling Trials, including both road and track competitions. A 100-kilometer time trial and a 180-kilometer race took place in Central Park, while the track events were held on a new, Moses-commissioned velodrome in Kissena Park.[50]

In September 1963 the quarter-mile banked track marked its official opening with a series of sprints for men and women of different ages, from "cubs" to "old timers." The following summer, fans watched local kids and racers from across the country vie for a spot on the Olympic team in individual time trials, match sprints, and even tandem bicycle races. One New Yorker did make the team—Harlem-born Oliver "Butch"

Martin Jr., who regularly trained in Central Park and earned fame as a "Negro champion" in a sport dominated by whites.[51]

The trials drummed up at least some interest in a sport more popular in Europe that had never completely disappeared in the United States. As Joshua Freeman, a local teenager, later remembered, "Nothing ever happened in Queens"—so when the trials, the television coverage, and the "unbelievable" riders came to the borough, he was pulled into the bike racing scene. Soon Freeman was hanging out at the local bike shop, training on the Long Island Expressway service roads, and riding across the Queensboro Bridge in the wee hours of the morning to Central Park, where he raced on a used Atala. The park, as Moses had wanted it, was still the domain of cars, which was part of the reason riders ventured out so early.[52]

Freeman raced as a member of the Century Road Club Association, which traced its roots back to the 1890s bike boom and was among the most visible clubs (it boasted 130 members in 1969) of the handful of such groups, most of which were geared entirely toward racing. Freeman delighted in being part of an "esoteric" community that offered a "way to escape the world." Hardly anyone trekked to Times Square newsstands to keep up with the European grand tours. Only a select few knew what the "French Club Straight" meant (the spot along the Central Park loop where the French Sporting Club finished its races) or could share in the joy of buying Jacques Anquetil (a five-time winner of the Tour de France) cleats.[53]

With the new velodrome and with access to the more rural Long Island roads as training grounds, Queens was a center of 1960s bike racing in New York. It was also home to several bike shops. When the Kissena velodrome opened, a new shop popped up around the corner. Older shops included Ed "Pop" Perry's in the Jamaica neighborhood and Dick Power's Sunnyside Cycle Shop on Roosevelt Avenue. Together, they embodied the small-world nature of racing. Bike shop owners, custom frame builders, and occasional mentors/coaches, Perry and Power played host to gatherings of racers and wannabes. The shops functioned as manufacturing facilities, sales galleries, social spaces, and sometimes even club headquarters, attracting racers from across the five boroughs and bringing together New Yorkers who otherwise never would have met. Freeman, for example, fondly remembers hanging out at Tommy Avenia's shop in Harlem, a neighborhood that, he recalled, white kids from Queens rarely frequented.[54]

Nevertheless, the racing community was hardly diverse. Perry was black, but most of his customers were white. Many of the prominent clubs retained ethnic associations (French, German, and Italian) even if some members joined regardless of country of origin. And although the Century Road Club Association had previously amended its bylaws, removing the requirement that members be white, it was still thought of as an all-white (or at least mostly white) club—so much so that a black garment worker thought it wise to say he was Mexican when applying for membership. Despite the fact that the city was becoming home to an increasingly diverse population, segregation persisted in the cycling community, as it did in the schools and elsewhere. Racing remained dominated by whites and white men in particular. Women did compete and joined local clubs but were a small minority among an already small group. And because racing necessitated high-end bicycles, accessories, and membership fees, it was not for the poor. Yet participants were described as more bohemian and more blue-collar compared to the speedsters of subsequent generations.[55]

The racing world at that time was also fairly casual. Club meetings often took place in barrooms. After the November turkey race in Central Park (where a table full of giant turkeys awaited the winners), racers typically put their bicycles away until springtime. Some continued to compete, often in barroom match races atop rollers (stationary devices on which riders pedaled in place but still needed to maintain their balance as if riding outdoors). Some switched to ice skating until the weather turned warm.

Even though racers were among the visible riders in this era, few New Yorkers ever raced or paid much attention, no matter the season. Despite the Olympic trials and the opening of the Kissena track, racing in New York did not exactly take off. Years after the Queens velodrome was built, one rider remembered that the track was filled with kids on motorbikes—and the parking lot littered with "condoms and hypodermic needles."[56]

Like most New Yorkers, few racers, aside from training on the roads and riding to competitions or bike shops, seriously considered biking around the streets of New York.

Although his career was winding down, one of the most important stories starring Robert Moses and the bicycle had yet to be written. It took place on the Verrazano Bridge, one of the city's great connectors, linking Staten Island to Brooklyn. But for cyclists, the two boroughs would remain worlds away.

On November 21, 1964, thousands of people sifted through sixteen toll booths, forking over fifty cents for the privilege of being among the very first to drive across the bridge named for Florentine explorer Giovanni da Verrazzano (the city misspelled the name, forgetting the second "z"). A group of children, some on bicycles, began to dash up the bridge from the Brooklyn side. They did not make it across. Nor would cyclists thereafter.[57]

A lot had changed since Moses first started building bridges. On a hot summer day back in 1936, Commissioner Moses, Mayor La Guardia, and President Roosevelt marked the opening of the Triborough Bridge, a stunning combination of roads and ramps that connected three boroughs and provided the muscle for many of Moses's future projects. Down below on Randall's Island, celebrants delighted in a massive picnic of free beer, "salads and cold cuts, frizzled in the midday sun," while the very same day a brand-new 21,000-seat stadium played host to the U.S. Olympic Track and Field Trials. Also in the shadow of the bridge and sitting squarely underneath the Triborough toll plaza was Robert Moses's office. Money poured in, blueprints for future projects came out. In this signature project was a portrait of Moses: the colossal bridge and the recreational facilities beneath, the parades of cars pouring across, and the tolls that dripped into his hands.[58]

To mark the occasion, New Yorkers raced to be the first one to cross the bridge. A "boy on a bicycle" managed to win the race to the Queens side, edging out a motorist (and a serial bridge/subway opening aficionado) whose brand-new car stalled twenty yards shy of the finish. He was the first of many cyclists who were permitted to traverse the span for a ten-cent toll; pedestrians walked for free along the pathways on the edge.[59]

That bicycles were allowed on the bridge was not unusual. Bicycles were permitted and tolled on the George Washington Bridge (twenty-five cents for cyclists, fifty for motorists, and ten for pedestrians). Some cyclists took to the footpaths, but there was nothing illegal about riding on the main drive. On the Marine Parkway Bridge and the Bronx-Whitestone (both completed in the late 1930s), bicycles were also permitted and tolled (ten cents a crossing).[60]

In 1939, Moses lowered the bicycle toll to five cents on two of his bridges. While the tolls did not yield big bucks for the city, they did provide a means to "carefully control bicycles." Lowering tolls may have seemed like a boon to riders (they had requested it), but it also presaged a shift in policy. The change can be read as part of the process of delegitimizing bicycles: bicycles should not be tolled like cars, because they were not vehicles like cars. And if they were not vehicles like cars, then they certainly did not belong on the bridge roadways like cars.[61]

In 1940, the Kings Wheelers Cycling Club wrote to Moses proposing that he dedicate a lane for bicycles on the Manhattan Bridge. (At the time, they were permitted only to walk their wheels across the pedestrian path.) Club members even suggested that they would pay for it themselves through an annual fee. Moses was not interested.[62]

In fact, he was beginning to think bicycles did not belong on bridges altogether.

One reason for the shift may have been simple: the typically fastidious Moses did not even know what the policy was. In reference to the Marine Parkway Bridge, he wrote to one of his lieutenants: "I assume that the bicycles are always required to be on the walk and not on the drive and that they are walked over and not ridden over." Not quite. Bicycles were permitted on the roadways when traffic was "light"; otherwise they were supposed to (and according to a parks department memo, they often did not) walk their wheels across the pedestrian path. On the Triborough, cyclists could ride on the road in the lane nearest the curb.[63]

Also, Moses pointed out that fewer cyclists were now using the bridges. Traffic counts showed that monthly bicycle crossings across the Triborough Bridge peaked in July 1936 (1,193 trips) and across the Marine

Parkway Bridge in June 1938 (577). As motor vehicle traffic kept increasing, the reasons to permit bicycles and include bicycle/pedestrian facilities on bridges became less compelling. And with no dedicated bike lanes, it was increasingly treacherous and less attractive to bike across. From 1946 to 1954 the number of vehicles using interborough bridges and tunnels more than doubled. On the George Washington Bridge alone, the number of vehicle crossings more than quadrupled, to 33 million from 1936 to 1954. Even back in 1936, "bicycles and animals" combined accounted for just 938 of the more than 7 million total crossings (1 out of every 7,462). By the mid-1950s, cyclists no longer had to pay a toll. And no one bothered to count them anymore.[64]

At this point, the Triborough Bridge and Tunnel Authority, the Department of Public Works, and the Port Authority had collectively banned bicycles from three East River bridges; the Bronx-Whitestone, Marine Parkway, and Henry Hudson bridges; and the Queens-Midtown, Brooklyn-Battery, Holland, and Lincoln tunnels. Other major bridges built around the country in the period, like the Delaware Memorial Bridge and the Walt Whitman Bridge, also had no space for cyclists.

Neither did the new interstate highways, born from the Federal-Aid Highway Act of 1956, which were, as historian James Longhurst put it, "the first legally segregated public" roads. Bicycles and other vehicles that could not achieve highway speeds were prohibited. Bridges were less likely to include pedestrian, cycling, rail, and public transit facilities as well. In 1961, when the Throgs Neck Bridge linked the Bronx to Queens, it had no bike/pedestrian paths either. While cyclists could still ride on a few bridges and push their bicycles across pedestrian paths on others, it had become rare to see a New Yorker bicycling between the boroughs.[65]

Thus, in 1955, when Moses published renderings for the not-yet-named Verrazano Bridge (which, like the Triborough and the George Washington, was designed by Moses's favorite engineer, the slender, Swiss-born, bespectacled Othmar Ammann), he offered a public explanation for the lack of subway and rail cars (the cost and the likely "adverse effect on" neighboring properties). But the drawings, which showed passenger cars dotting the majestic span framed by a view of the Manhattan skyline and Lady Liberty, were also missing pedestrian and bicycle paths. Moses said nothing about the omission. It was hardly something that needed to be defended.[66]

At least most of the time. Early in 1964, a group of 150 protestors—one on a high-wheeler and a father and son wearing taped-on mustaches and "Gay Nineties" apparel—biked from Manhattan over the Queensboro Bridge to the World's Fair to raise awareness about the lack of bike lanes on the interborough bridges. And after the Verrazano Bridge opened, a Manhattan man named Louis Rosenberg complained to Moses that the bridge had no bicycle and pedestrian facilities. Moses replied that the issue "was carefully considered." If it was, Ammann and Moses must have made that decision very early on, because the initial drawings never included a path.[67]

Years after the bridge had been built, Moses claimed that cost—$3.5 million if built originally and considerably more if added later—was the primary deterrent. What he did not mention was that the $3.5 million represented only about one percent of the total construction cost. Moses also noted that existing bridge paths had proven more trouble than they were worth, as pedestrians threw things into the water below and "youngsters" made a habit of climbing the bridge trusses. Rumors then and later also suggested that engineers worried about suicides.[68]

That the spectacular new bridge—it boasted a record-setting 4,260-foot span, 12 lanes, and two separate decks for motor traffic (the lower level sat unused for years)—lacked something as ordinary as a pedestrian/bicycle path irritated bicycle advocates when it was built and still does so today. For critics, the Verrazano is the poster child of Moses's autocentric planning. But the truth is that the decision not to include paths was hardly unusual. Most major new bridges served only motor vehicles.[69]

In terms of promoting and integrating automobiles into the city, Moses was ahead of his time. By the time the Verrazano opened in 1964, the rest of the country had caught up.

In 1939, the *New York Times* described Moses as a "cooperative proponent" of the cyclists' cause. Rarely was (still grumpy) Moses praised for cooperating; he amassed power so that he would not have to cooperate. Singularly, the unelected bureaucrat shaped New York more than any elected official ever has.[70]

While Moses was not alone in promoting an autocentric city, what differentiated him was the scale of his successes and failures. The same holds true for his bicycle-infrastructure campaigns. His 58-plus-mile plan proposed building paths at a pace largely unimagined—then, before, or after—by city builders anywhere in the country. Had the New Deal money kept flowing, the paths likely would have too. Instead, Moses's interest ceased when the spigots turned off. New Yorkers felt the same way. Although the persistent kept on lobbying and riding, the bicycling boom of the late 1930s changed shape in the years during and following World War II.

And so we are left to ponder the irony that Moses, the man who proposed one of the most ambitious bicycle programs, was hardly a bicycle advocate. He wanted bicycle paths in every borough, but also a network of roads that prioritized cars. He promoted the bicycle, but in a way that helped to delegitimize it as a serious tool for transportation. In Moses's philosophy, bicycles were purely for recreation, and the city he built reflected this belief.

Moses's decisions cast long shadows. He was responsible for building the many highways that made cycling more difficult in the decades to follow. From the perspective of a cyclist, he disintegrated the city.

CHAPTER FOUR

THE BAN

In the summer of 1987, Randi Taylor-Habib was living on Norfolk Street on the Lower East Side. She shared an apartment with "Big Charlie," the bouncer at the punk rock bar CBGB, and a couple of "junkies." She slept on a cot, tucked beneath an exposed pipe. Over in the corner sat a beat-up Bianchi frame left behind by a former tenant. There, Taylor-Habib saw an opportunity. She was not interested in exercising or commuting; she was looking for a way to survive, a way to make money. Scooping ice cream at Häagen-Dazs had not worked out. It was time to try something else: being a bike messenger.[1]

It did not take long for Taylor-Habib to get her name on the roster at Chick Chack, one of the many courier firms that welcomed job seekers. Basically, all anyone needed was a bike, bag, and lock. Taylor-Habib's regular twelve-hour days began with a morning call to the Chick Chack office for the specifics of her first delivery, which would kick off a day of stuffing legal contracts, modeling portfolios, and blueprints into her oversized postal bag. She learned to dodge trucks, hop curbs, lock her bicycle in seconds, and scarf down dollar slices of pizza. When one delivery was done, she got her next by calling back in to the dispatcher from a nearby pay phone. Sometimes, like many of her colleagues, she used wooden slugs instead of real quarters. The small infraction hardly made her a serious criminal.[2]

Yet Mayor Ed Koch, who saw in the bicycle the promise of a cleaner, healthier, and more navigable New York, saw in the mostly nonwhite messengers a group of outlaws adding to the chaos of a city that desperately needed to catch its breath. There was a crack cocaine epidemic, an AIDS crisis, racial unrest, and charges of government corruption. To Koch and others, the bike messengers symbolized the lawlessness unfolding on Gotham's streets. They were dangerous. And they needed to be put in their place.[3]

Within weeks of Habib-Taylor's first day on the job, the city announced a drastic plan. One surefire way to get rid of bike messengers was to ban the one thing they needed to do their job. In 1987, bikes would be banned from the streets of midtown.

One year after the Verrazano Bridge opened, New Yorkers headed to the polls to elect their 103rd mayor. It was 1965, and the prospects of biking in the city were looking up. Literally.

Mayoral candidate and famous conservative William F. Buckley Jr. proposed building an elevated bicycle highway on Second Avenue, running from 125th to First Street. Standing 20 feet above the ground, stretching 20 feet across, and with 6 spurs heading crosstown, the bikeway could solve the traffic riddle below and, for just a 15-cent toll, offer a healthy and speedy way to commute. "To go back to the age of the bicycle," an amused Buckley told reporters, might be "ultra-reactionary," but it sure would be fun. Buckley lost the election (he came in a distant third) and his elevated bikeway never got off the ground.[4]

Nevertheless, Buckley's proposal for a bicycle commuter highway was an early sign of an important shift in how New Yorkers saw bicycles. No longer just toys for fun (though they would remain that too), bicycles in the coming decades would be increasingly understood as vehicles to get *to* work and as vehicles *for* work.

The ultimate winner of the 1965 race, John Lindsay, also offered cyclists hope. Though not as bold as Buckley, Lindsay, in the summer of 1966, delivered on a long-sought request: car-free hours in Central Park. Moses's long stranglehold over the park was finally over. First on Sundays (from 6:00 a.m. to 3:00 p.m. and later expanded to 8:00 p.m.) and

FIGURE 4.1 Cyclists enjoy periods of a car-free Central Park during the Lindsay administration, ca. 1970.

then on certain Saturdays as well, the "bicycle be-in" afforded recreational riders the chance to pedal in peace. Racers no longer had to start before sunup to avoid competing against cars. Tall and with an athletic build, the mayor easily circled the 6.1-mile Central Park loop that had transformed into a de facto weekend bicycle path. He may have been the only New York mayor to actually look comfortable riding a bike.[5]

Still, Lindsay, like most New Yorkers, continued to think of the bike as more of a toy than a tool. When the mayor signed a bill requiring that all substantial city parks include designated bike paths, the purpose was to provide safe spaces for children to enjoy this "wholesome" activity. Endorsing recreational cycling in the parks was one thing. Promoting utilitarian cycling with infrastructure on the streets was far more controversial. But Lindsay seemed every bit the bike advocate, especially after winning a second term. (In the mayoral primaries that year, writer Norman Mailer unsuccessfully ran on a wide-ranging platform that included banning private cars from Manhattan.)[6]

On April 22, 1970, New Yorkers celebrated the very first Earth Day. There were rallies, teach-ins, concerts, come clean up the park campaigns, and a giant carbon monoxide detector parked on the streets. The "blue mobile laboratory" was there to measure the effect of the day's main attraction: two hours of a car-free Fifth Avenue. New Yorkers walked and biked along the legendary thoroughfare on a day when people around the country helped forge the modern environmentalist movement and build an "eco-infrastructure" that "inspired a decade of far reaching legislation," as one historian put it. In particular, the new environmentalists were worried about air pollution and transportation; cars were increasingly seen as the culprits.[7]

When Mayor Lindsay temporarily barred automobiles from Fifth Avenue, he praised the bicycle as an alternative and "non-polluting mode of transportation." Months later, in one of the many aftershocks of Earth Day, the mayor joined 1,000 riders—reported as a mix of "Wall Street executives, hippies, housewives, and labor leaders"—who pedaled down Fifth Avenue on a day when one traffic lane was momentarily converted into a bike lane. "Bike for a Better City Day" appeared to demonstrate that there was a real demand for commuting by bicycle if only the city encouraged it. Lindsay pledged to keep doing exactly that. Probably on

Fifth Avenue and perhaps on the East River bridges as well, the administration said, bike lanes would be coming.[8]

Lindsay's promise was a bold one, especially considering how rare bike infrastructure was in the United States at the time. The 1967 bike lanes laid in the college town of Davis, California, are often cited as America's first. Although people forget about the on-street bike lanes (the asphalt ribbons) in 1890s New York, it is true that New York and almost every other American city had not seen any kind of bike lanes since the nineteenth century. Even off-road bicycle paths, like the kind Moses had championed, were not common. For now, the Bronx claimed just 5.1 miles of paths, which included some measly (.1 or .25-mile) stretches that went nowhere. Staten Island was no better. Even inside Manhattan, almost all of the path mileage was contained within Central Park. But at least Central Park was open to bikes; all of the major bridges (save the Brooklyn Bridge) prohibited them. Subways and buses did not permit them on board either.[9]

Fifth Avenue business owners wanted nothing to do with bikes and resisted the plan for lanes. They worried that the bicycles would deter people from stepping into their stores and ridiculed the idea that their customers might prefer to come by two wheels. "Sure," the executive vice president of the Fifth Avenue Association joked, "I can see those matronly women coming to Bergdorf's on a bicycle." Bike advocates, meanwhile, cheered. They implored the mayor to stick to his promise and promote the "healthy, quiet, convenient, inexpensive and energy-conserving" bicycle by building bike lanes and thereby freeing riders from "driver harassment" and "fear of our lives." Then Congressman Ed Koch chimed in too. "The only way to insure safety for the many thousands of New Yorkers who want to bicycle," he averred, "is to designate official and exclusive bike lanes."[10]

Bowing to the pressure of business owners and the difficulty (politically and designwise) of finding a permanent place for bicycles on roads clogged by cars, Lindsay called off the bike lane plan. Instead, he touted the city's effort to build an extensive network of bicycle routes known as bikeways. The bikeway program did not require altering the street, or any serious investment at all. Posted signs merely designated roadways as preferred bicycle routes and reminded motorists to share the road.[11]

Bikeways were bike lanes in name only and offered, as the President of the New York Cycle Club protested, "no protection whatsoever to the cyclist." And protection the cyclists needed, for "when a New Yorker gets behind the wheel of a car he becomes a demon. He seems to develop a strange sense of power when any trace of decency leaves him. To all intents and purposes he becomes a monster."[12]

The "monsters" had advantages on the cyclists, including numbers. But in the early 1970s the balance started to shift. In 1972 Americans bought more bicycles than cars, roughly three times as many bikes as they had in 1960, and 30 percent more than the prior year. In 1973, the year of the oil crisis, a record 15 million bicycles were sold in the United States. The budding environmental movement and rise of flower power mentality certainly attracted some of the new riders. Increased gas prices also gave Americans a renewed chance to consider the bicycle as a substitute for the car.[13]

These new riders joined the small but devoted group of New Yorkers who, just like Arthur Hyde in the 1890s, found the bicycle the fastest, easiest, and most pleasant way to commute and run errands. Why, they wondered, did so few other New Yorkers, typically keen on practicality and independence, follow suit?

In 1971, *New Yorker* writer Calvin Trillin described his experience riding on a Moulton, an English bicycle with no top bar, small wheels, and a light frame. It was a far cry from the "Schwinn fat-wheel," a "rotund machine that weighed slightly less than the medium-priced Pontiac" that the "genius of American advertising" once suckered him into wanting and his parents into buying. The Moulton was a practical city bike: easy to get on and off, light enough for walk-up buildings, and small enough for New York-sized apartments.[14]

For Trillin, the bicycle easily beat the alternatives. Millions rode the subways, "most of them," he quipped, "quivering from anger at the experience." The buses, and the calculus involved in figuring out where they stopped, where they were headed, and which numbers corresponded to which routes, were an "uncrackable code." Taxis needed to be found and hailed, were increasingly expensive, and worst of all, were driven by editorializing cabbies. "I ride my Moulton. While I'm on it, nobody yammers at me about how that movie star Lindsay is giving away everything to the blacks," Trillin wrote. "Some people look at me and smile, and some bus drivers try to run over me, but I can handle that sort of thing. People who ride bikes in New York tend to be particularly independent."[15]

Even though New Yorkers bought bicycles in record numbers, far from everyone took part. A 1973 New York City Transportation Administration report found that cycling was "fashionable with middle and upper income classes. Lower income people, to whom a car is often an important status symbol, would probably consider it a serious slight and official insensitivity if they were asked to use a bicycle for anything besides recreation." It was true that many of the new cyclists enjoyed the privileges that came with discretionary income and leisure time. Bike shops opened in impressive numbers but tended to be concentrated in Manhattan's more moneyed neighborhoods. Lindsay supporters, once derided by a mayoral opponent as "limousine liberals," might have instead been described, according to Trillin, as "Raleigh Three-Speed liberals." But while those in the middle and upper classes might have taken the bike as a lifestyle choice, the working class also had reason to opt for a bike instead of a car.[16]

Whether out of a drive for independence, economic necessity, environmental concern, or a mix of the three, with the new wave of bikes came new frustration at the limitations of New York City bike infrastructure. Built to channel this frustration were the bicycle advocacy groups.

The most important player was Transportation Alternatives (TA). TA would become the leading voice in the campaign to demonstrate that bikes could be used for more than just a joy ride; they offered the best, healthiest, and cleanest way to navigate the dense, overly trafficked, polluted city. Formed in 1973, TA evolved from Action Against Automobiles (the *other* Triple A) and the activists who participated in its bicycle protest rides. In 1972, the 150 "bicycle freaks, environmental activists, and various other unaffiliated car haters," as the *Village Voice* called them, paraded through the city shouting "Cars Must Go!" and booed as they rode past the New York Coliseum, which was hosting the Greater New York Automobile Show. The organizer of the ride and TA cofounder, David Gurin, was an anticar evangelist who worried about the destructive effect of cars on the quality of the air and, à la Jane Jacobs, on the quality and character of urban life.[17]

Working out of the Cathedral of Saint John the Divine's basement, TA wasted no time making its presence known. On April 7, 1973, TA hosted its first "bike-in," encouraging riders from each of the boroughs to "Ride & Rally" from Central Park to Washington Square, the park that Jane Jacobs had saved from Robert Moses. A poster advertising the event featured a hand-drawn cavalcade of goofy-looking cyclists, a special invitation to Spanish-speaking New Yorkers, and a promise that folk singer Pete Seeger, an early supporter of the organization, would perform. More than 2,000 people attended, calling on the city to build a dedicated network of bicycle lanes. Many came back the following year for a similar event, including Congressman Ed Koch.[18]

TA was not alone. Bike for a Better City agitated for bike lanes and bike parking and provided the muscle behind the famous Lindsay-led bike demonstrations. American Youth Hostels (AYH) promoted bicycles as a means for its young clientele to affordably travel the country. The League of American Wheelmen, while not as important as it once had been, also maintained a New York presence and a powerful local advocate, Roger Herz. Then there were the Bicycle Commuters of New York, The New York Cycle Club, the Staten Island Bicycling Association, and the Bring Back the Bicycle Committee, whose title was a reminder that bicycles were once and could again be a major force in the city. It included an impressive list of New York power brokers, congressmen, borough presidents, assemblymen, state senators, and celebrities, Koch among them.[19]

The number of advocates grew in tandem with the number of new riders—as did the number of crashes and the number of people who saw bicycles as dangerous, even deadly (deaths by bicycle had more than doubled from 1962 to 1972) and demanded they be regulated. But what kind of regulations were needed?[20]

Much of the problem stemmed from the complicated way New Yorkers and Americans at large understood bicycles. As a municipal report described in unusually existential terms, how could the city plan for the bicycle, "this step-child of the transportation world," unless it was "firmly anchored conceptually"? Was the bicycle more like a pedestrian and thus in need of a separate space, or was it more like a car that belonged on the road? "It is unlikely that the bicycle can successfully straddle this dichotomy, no matter how nimble it may be." Because of its interrupted history and the changing ways it was most popularly used, the bicycle still did not have a conceptual grounding.[21]

FIGURE 4.2 A group of about 7,500 cyclists ride up Church Street in Lower Manhattan as part of the thirty-six-mile Five Boro Bike Tour in 1979. With safety vests donated by Citibank, police escorts, the National Guard standing by to aid exhausted riders, and for just a $1 registration fee, New Yorkers got to experience the feeling of cycling on streets that belonged to them for the day. The New York affiliates of American Youth Hostels started these annual rides (not a race, they emphasized) in 1977. The event, now organized by Bike New York, remains popular today.

Photo by Steve Faust

To make cycling safer and less intimidating, the city floated a number of measures, including dedicated bicycle lanes, off-street bicycle paths, and license requirements. They thought, for a moment, about putting out free bikes for people to share before they concluded that they would likely be stolen. City staff even reconsidered Buckley's elevated bike superhighway, but reasoned that while it would solve some problems, it would create others: liability, shadows, and justifying its cost, to name a few.[22]

Although they did not get a new elevated path, opportunistic cyclists seized on the next best thing: repurposing the elevated West Side Highway after it was closed to automobiles in 1973 (following its partial collapse when a dump truck loaded with asphalt, ironically on its way to repair the very same highway, proved too heavy for the aging road). The "reclaimed" and only partly destroyed roadway offered more than just a speedy route from midtown to downtown. As one rider remembered it, the highway was a "utopian space" enjoyed by cyclists, pedestrians, roller skaters, and picnickers.[23]

For now, serendipitous reuse of infrastructure was the best New York cyclists could hope for, because by the mid-1970s, New York had started to crumble. The fiscal crisis brought the city to its knees. President Ford essentially told the city on the brink of bankruptcy, and the mayor who succeeded Lindsay, Abraham Beame, to "Drop Dead." But once the eye of the storm passed, the debates about bicycles would return—with higher stakes than ever before.[24]

Enter Edward Irving Koch, the bald, Jewish, colorful, smiley, unpredictable Democratic congressman. In 1977 he won the first of three consecutive mayoral races. The summer before the election, there had been a citywide blackout. It only added to the chaos and the feeling that New York was a sinking ship.[25]

To his inauguration, on a frigid January 1, 1978, Koch rode the bus. He probably did not see many and almost certainly was not thinking about bicycles. But the issue of what to do with them would come up over and over again during his twelve years in office.[26]

And it did not take long. During his first summer as mayor, Koch announced that he would do what Lindsay would not: build on-street bike lanes. Long an advocate for this kind of infrastructure, Koch followed through quickly. For the first time in eighty years, the city, through infrastructure, actively encouraged New Yorkers to see the bike as a tool for commuting. One lane stretched from Central Park South, on Broadway to Madison Square and then down Fifth Avenue, to Washington Square Park and its signature marble arch (designed by Stanford White, whose wife was a cyclist in the 1890s and pedaled alongside Violet Ward). The other lane ran north on Sixth Avenue, also from one park to the other. The four-foot-wide paths took space from parking lanes; the moving traffic lanes remained untouched. Nevertheless, opponents predicted that the bike lanes would exacerbate traffic problems. The mayor asked

FIGURE 4.3 A commuter rides in one of the new bike lanes on Sixth Avenue.

Photo by Vernon Shibla/New York Post Archives/© NYP Holdings, Inc. via Getty Images, July 6, 1978

everyone to be patient. If the lanes worked, there would be more coming, he said, many more—some 500 miles of lanes spanning all of the boroughs.[27]

Whether or not they were successful depended on who you asked. In just a couple of weeks, the avenues with the lanes experienced a more than threefold increase in bicycle traffic. City officials were encouraged. As David Gurin, the TA cofounder, now the Deputy Commissioner of the Department of Transportation (DOT), put it: "We want to make people realize that bicycle riding is a serious business, a valid way of getting around the city." The benefits of having an advocate working inside City Hall were already showing. Yet there were obstacles blocking the lanes, including cyclists riding the wrong way. And in at least one section and only six months after the lanes were inaugurated, some of the paint had literally disappeared. A group of activists repainted it themselves. Koch did not seem to be paying much attention one way or the other. But his enthusiasm for bike lanes would soon return.[28]

In February 1980, in the third year of his first term, Koch visited China. He was smitten with the food, the people, and their bicycles. Struck by the absence of cars in Tiananmen Square and what seemed like a "million people on bikes," Koch thought, "Isn't this marvelous? All these people on bikes. I gotta do something about that in New York City." When he returned home, he told his Commissioner of Transportation, Tony Ameruso, that he wanted two protected bicycle lanes (separated from cars by more than just paint), one on Sixth and another on Seventh Avenue. He did not want to spend a fortune. And he did not want to wait long.[29]

The transit strike later that spring only added to the mayor's conviction that New York could become a cycling city. When 34,000 members of the Transport Workers Union threatened to stop driving buses and subways should the city fail to meet their demands, Koch urged everyone to bike: "We'd like to see New York City look like Peking in the mornings." The city and the union could not come to terms, and on April 1, 1980, the strike began.[30]

While they came nowhere near the million riders Koch had hoped to see, the group of commuters who biked to work during the springtime strike did include tens of thousands of people who had never done so before. (Before the strike, one New Yorker remembered that there were so few cyclists on the streets that when riders saw each other, they felt compelled to wave.) The number of cyclists entering and exiting Manhattan's central business district increased tenfold. Among the new commuters were many who did not own a bicycle. In a city defined by business, eager entrepreneurs wasted no time setting up shop, renting out bicycles and selling T-shirts that read "I survived the 1980 Transit Strike."[31]

Bike advocacy groups could hardly contain their enthusiasm. The AYH set up daily "bike caravans," leading novice riders from the outer boroughs into Manhattan. Volunteers helped direct bicycle traffic and even set up a "Bike Hot Line" for cyclists looking for advice or traffic updates.[32]

Some kept biking even after the eleven-day strike ended—enough, in fact, to double the number of regular bicycle commuters. With the increase in ridership came more complaints about cyclists, and for good reason; in the first few months following the strike, three pedestrians were killed in bicycle-related crashes. The DOT, police department, and city

FIGURE 4.4

Bike advocacy groups set up specially marked bike lanes and telephone hotlines to help new cyclists navigate the city during the transit strike.

Photo by Harry Hamburg/NY Daily News Archive via Getty Images, April 1, 1980

council again considered requiring cyclists to register and license their bicycles, in order to use the registration fees to fund bicycle safety campaigns. Licensing and registering bikes might also, city staff reasoned, reduce theft, which had long been a deterrent to becoming a cyclist. Although thefts had actually been on the decline since the mid-1970s, by 1979 there were still more than 10,000 bikes reported stolen each year, and the actual number was surely much higher. But after consulting with American Youth Hostels, the New York Cycle Club, Transportation Alternatives, the Staten Island Bicycle Association, and a handful of other local bike advocacy groups (which generally opposed the idea of registration) and the editorial divisions of television stations and newspapers (which were split), the city decided not to move forward.[33]

Even without registration fees to support it, the city launched a major campaign aimed at increasing traffic safety and improving the relationship between cyclists and noncyclists. Funded by a federal highway safety grant, the campaign included public service announcements on television and the radio, detailed brochures, and ads in the subways and on the scoreboard at Yankee Stadium. There were messages for every constituency. Posters reminded cyclists that their bikes needed to have reflectors and bells and that the rules of the road applied to them too. One public service announcement featured a "born again cyclist" who learned to "kick the red light habit." Stopping at red lights not only was safe but also could be meditative, offering "rare moments of relaxation." Children watched an eleven-minute film about bike safety, read free copies of the "Sprocketman Talks Road Sense" comic book, heard safety tips from "Mike the Talking Bike," and attended bicycle safety camp. Police cadets received updated training manuals, detailing how to interact with cyclists. Drivers were reminded that many cyclists were new and that they should be aware of this "welcome phenomenon" on the streets. Motorists were also invited to take a fairly obvious quiz about road safety. Question #6 asked if drivers should "consider bicycles a toy that don't belong on the road" or if they should "respect bicycles." (The wrong answer had been Robert Moses's answer.)[34]

Beyond teaching New Yorkers how to behave, Koch believed that he needed to change the streets themselves. In particular, New York needed bike lanes, better ones. Unlike in 1978, when the city painted white lanes, the new bike lanes would be protected, physically shielded by concrete-curbed, asphalt-filled islands. The segregated bicycles would have an eight-foot swath of roadway supposedly all to themselves.

By late August 1980, Sam Schwartz, then an Assistant Commissioner at the DOT who designed some of the city's most memorable traffic signs (e.g., "NO PARKING, NO STANDING, NO STOPPING, NO KIDDING") and coined the term "gridlock," prepared the signs that would adorn the new bike lanes. The top portion reminded cyclists to stop at red lights; the bottom panel warned them not to take the lanes for granted: "Bike Lanes. Use Them or Lose Them."[35]

In October, Ed Koch, wearing a helmet and a personalized reflective vest, clumsily rode along Sixth Avenue to officially inaugurate the new lanes that had already been open to traffic for a month. The two lanes ran over almost exactly the same terrain as the 1978 painted versions, which started and stopped at Washington Square Park and Central Park. As Schwartz's sign suggested, the lanes were still a trial; Koch said he would monitor use and determine the following spring if the lanes were working.[36]

FIGURE 4.5
The protected bike lanes along Sixth Avenue suggested, rather explicitly, that bicycles were not vehicles. The remnants of the earlier bike lane, painted in 1978 with white lines and diamond markings, are still visible.

Fred R Conrad/The New York Times/ Redux, September 24, 1980

FIGURE 4.6
Although Koch celebrated the new bike lanes with an inaugural ride, he was hardly a cyclist. In fact, he did not even know how to ride a bike. Having never learned as a child and so as not to embarrass himself in front of the media, Koch practiced pedaling up and down the driveway at Gracie Mansion. He managed to stay upright for the short ride.

Mayor Edward I. Koch on a Bike at a Press Conference Announcing the Official Opening of New Bike Lanes, photograph, October 15, 1980. Courtesy NYC Municipal Archives

Although pieces of the two lanes remained incomplete (a group of business owners who feared "more danger with the bike lanes" sued the city, temporarily preventing completion), early traffic counts showed an impressive increase in bike traffic on those avenues, roughly 50 percent, from the year prior. The crash rate dropped too—not surprising, given that riders no longer had to focus their attention on avoiding the cars and trucks they had previously shared a road with.[37]

Yet criticism of the lanes began immediately. Business owners griped about squandering city resources (it was widely advertised that the lanes cost $290,000 to build) on such wrong-headed infrastructure. Filling potholes would be a much better use of money, so the Fifth Avenue Merchants Association calculated. A group of black New Yorkers also challenged the mayor's priorities. Instead of spending hundreds of thousands of dollars building bike lanes, asked a writer for the *New York Amsterdam News*, why not spend the money on rehabilitating housing in black neighborhoods like Harlem or Bedford-Stuyvesant? Other ill-timed press reports did not help. "I only hit people when they are walking out in front of me," a twenty-year-old bike messenger was quoted as saying in the *New York Times*.[38]

Koch began to waver. Publicly, he leaned on the rhetoric displayed on the Schwartz-designed traffic signs, arguing that cyclists simply were not using them. "My own gut" the waffling mayor announced on November 11, "tells me they're not working." He recounted seeing only two cyclists in the lanes on a recent Sunday, and one of them was riding the wrong way. There was some evidence that ridership had, in fact, begun to decrease, with daily counts of roughly 3,000 users in September dropping to about 1,700 in November. But decreased ridership in colder weather was no surprise, and there had been some particularly foul-weathered days around the time of the November traffic count.[39]

Motorists kept pressuring the mayor to rip up the lanes, noting that evening rush hour traffic on Sixth Avenue had worsened. Exaggerated media reports of "perpetual traffic jams" did not help the cyclists' cause. Even the cyclists were complaining. Some lamented being pushed off the main road and therefore delegitimized. Others pointed out that joggers, skaters, pedestrians, and pushcarts regularly obstructed the so-called bicycle lanes. (The same was true even for cyclists' favorite haunts, including Central Park. In a humorous, hand-drawn cycling map of the park, riders are warned to beware of the "dancing roller-skaters," joggers running four abreast, and teetering pedestrians in the "Hearing Impaired Walkman Area.") One telling photograph of Sixth Avenue features a lone cyclist riding alongside auto traffic on the main road, while two briefcase-toting pedestrians in suits walk (the wrong way no less) down the middle of the adjacent bike lane.[40]

The death knell sounded shortly after one particularly uncomfortable ride—not on a bike, but in a limousine with three prominent Democrats: Mayor Koch, Governor of New York Hugh Carey, and President Jimmy Carter. As they were driving along Sixth Avenue, Carey turned to the president, gestured to the mostly vacant bike lanes, and jabbed the mayor, "See how Ed's pissing away your money?" Carey then told of how he had been nearly run over by a cyclist. In a final blow, he chastised Koch's interest in bicycles as a "fetish."[41]

On the 14th, just three days after the mayor suggested he was thinking about ripping up the lanes and in spite of his promise to leave them in place until at least spring, construction crews began to dismantle them. Protestors threw themselves in front of the bulldozers. But it was no use. By the Thanksgiving Day Parade, the lanes were a relic of history.[42]

Once the lanes were removed, Koch wrote a memo to his staff insisting that he remained committed to cycling: "I believe that bicycles offer a valuable transportation option. . . . Cycling should be encouraged in all parts of the City, including the avenues where marked bike lanes have been restored in place of the physical barriers." Koch was not throwing in the towel completely. The DOT installed its first bicycle traffic signal on Thirty-Third Street and Herald Square. The department hired a full-time staffer devoted to bicycle planning, allowed cycling commuters to park their bicycles in a couple of city-owned buildings, and installed "bicycle-safe" sewer grates that would prevent cyclists from getting their wheels caught and "fly[ing] over the handlebars." Koch's administration also won a battle with preservationists to replace stairs with ramps on the access to the Brooklyn Bridge promenade. Stairs were not just a nuisance for riders; having to stop and dismount also increased the likelihood of being mugged. "They were holding the Brooklyn Bridge, it was theirs for three or four hours," reported a cyclist who had been "held prisoner" in 1980.[43]

Nor was Koch just bowing to the automobile interests. The same year the protected bike lanes went in and out, he irked motorists by pushing a plan to ban cars with a single occupant from using any of the East River bridges during the morning rush. Later he backed a proposal to toll midtown drivers.

But for now, he convinced himself that the bike lanes had been a mistake. Instead of building infrastructure to promote cycling, he began thinking about how to control cycling. The rules of the road were not being enforced. And the most egregious offenders were the bike messengers.

New Yorkers cycling for commercial purposes was nothing new. Starting in the nineteenth century, boys on bicycles delivered telegraph messages. In 1938, Robert Moses complained about the bicycle "delivery boys who weave in and out of traffic or steal a tow on the rear of fast-moving vehicles and trolley cars." And during World War II, nurses on wheels made house calls.[44]

While bicycles had been used for commercial purposes on and off for the better part of a century, the modern bike messengers, first seen in the early 1970s and popularized in the mid-1980s, were of a different sort. "Part Horatio Alger and part hippie" is how the president of Can Carriers Messenger Service described the new breed.[45]

For one thing, they were fast. It soon became clear that bike messengers could tote a can of film, architectural drawings, contracts, or anything else that would fit in the soon-to-become trademark canvas sacks (Can Carriers messengers used blue bags and the other early courier companies each had a unique color) faster than anyone else—certainly faster than the already popular foot messengers. Messengers were most useful where congestion was the greatest and where businesses needed things quickly. Manhattan, with its extraordinary density and street traffic, and its legion of advertisers, film and television producers, lawyers, modeling agencies, and design firms, was the natural center of a messenger world that spread well beyond the Empire State. Whether in New York or another big city, struggling artists, immigrants, "renegades," and those on the "fringe of society" could easily find work. Firms were happy to give rookies a chance since they were typically paid by the piece and not put on the payroll. Newbies often lasted less than two weeks, but those who stayed in the job became part of a close community that fostered a specialized skill set.[46]

To be successful, speed was not enough. As for the city's taxi drivers, the job required an encyclopedic knowledge of Manhattan's grid. A first-rate messenger could take an address and know exactly where it was and the fastest path there. That involved memorizing not just the layout of the streets, traffic patterns, and blocks of addresses but also smaller details like the best spot to ride on a given street or even within a given lane.

They also had to navigate the labyrinths of office buildings. Doormen, security guards, and receptionists led couriers through hidden mazes and back doors. The less conspicuous, the better. Delivering a package to Trump Tower on Fifth Avenue, which messengers ranked as the second least welcoming building in the city, involved side entrances, freight elevators, and a "cavernous sub-chamber." (Only Tiffany & Co., which in the 1890s was all-in on bikes and even had its own bicycle club, was ranked worse.)[47]

In most buildings, couriers had to sign in before heading upstairs. Sometimes there were metal detectors and escorts. Over the course of a week, hours could be squandered dealing with receptionists, scanning office directories, or waiting for elevators. Top messengers learned the quickest ways to get in and out. When twenty-five-year-old Mark DiSalvo made deliveries to the fifteenth floor of an eighteen-story building, he made sure to hit the elevator buttons for floors 16 and 17 before getting off on 15. That way, after a quick drop-off and signature, he could get back on the very same elevator without having to wait for another. Picking up seconds here and minutes there, messengers took pride in mastering the game of delivery.[48]

Racing through buildings with sweat soaking through T-shirts and tank tops and often with headbands holding back a sea of hair, the army of young messengers were rarely confused with the Wall Streeters and Madison Avenue admen they served. One well-known messenger had an affinity for riding around in a Speedo bathing suit and army boots. To prevent such unsightly messengers from disturbing tasteful lobbies, one company found a niche by promising clients that its couriers would arrive well groomed, even donning neckties. While Tiffany & Co., Trump, banks, and other building owners sought to protect their brands by keeping messengers out of public view, there was also a widely held belief that corporations applied their policies unevenly, discriminating against messengers of color.[49]

Whether black, brown, or white, messengers did not earn a lot of money. They made about $5 per delivery or about half of the firm's fee, which was calculated based on the distance of the run and the requested speed of delivery (rush, double rush, etc.). Large or awkward-to-carry parcels cost extra. On a fairly good day, a rider might have netted around $100, which equals about $25,000 a year on the assumption they worked five days a week, ten hours a day, and never took any time off. Bike advocates, using different calculations but the same unrealistic assumptions, cited average yearly earnings of only $13,500.[50]

By either measure, messengers were not rich. In addition, they had to foot the bill for their own bicycles and pay to maintain them. The job came without benefits—no medical insurance and no paid leave, despite the fact that injury occurred at unusually high rates compared to other industries. And even though many of the courier company owners and dispatchers were themselves former messengers, the prospects for moving into management, earning salary increases, or maintaining a stable career were slim.

But the job did come with some perks, notably independence. "You basically don't have to answer to anyone," one messenger remarked. Some hardly felt it was a job at all. "I can't believe they're actually paying me to do this," said a courier who appreciated not having to "work for a living." What messengers did during the day when not making a delivery was largely up to them.[51]

And there was a sense of fellowship among those who remained in the job. Couriers traveling to other cities had no problem finding a place to stay or comrades with whom to talk shop. The bonds could be so tight that messengers sometimes had difficulty leaving the profession, fearing they would lose the community. Some reported that they, like the broader cycling community, were part of a group within a group, because messengers broadly were a group within the larger cycling world. One worker described her messenger company as home to three types: punk rockers, Jamaicans, and "the sport boys." Rockers from the punk-infused Lower East Side and the Jamaicans from hip-hop's birthplace in the South Bronx shared an enthusiasm for music and the need to make money. A number of musicians did work as messengers in New York, including punk rocker Marky Ramone of the Ramones, Rob Zombie of the heavy metal band White Zombie, and GZA of the Staten Island-born hip-hop group the Wu-Tang Clan. Meanwhile, the sporty types saw the job as a means to train and as a game to play—a competition to see who could make the most deliveries in a day.[52]

The sense of community stemmed in part from possessing a shared skill set. Messengers were required to ride in an environment filled with hazards: jaywalkers, swerving cabbies, double-parked vehicles, a minefield of potholes, car doors swung open, and pavement slick with rain or frosted with snow. Riding safely through the gauntlet required physical skill and the intuition to anticipate movement. Is the taxi about to change lanes? Is the pedestrian about to step off the curb? Success required being in harmony with the rhythms of the city.

It also required being in harmony with the bike. No wonder, then, that messengers eschewed the bikes so popular with many of the new riders of the 1970s and '80s—the European-style models that typically featured drop handlebars, lighter frames, and modern derailleurs for shifting gears (sometimes ten, hence "ten-speed"). Designed for the road, racing, and recreation, ten-speeds made pedaling up Central Park's hills or over the Palisades a bit easier, although the handlebars tempted riders to drop into a racing position—not a great vantage point from which to navigate New York traffic.

Messengers, on the other hand, preferred fixed-gear bicycles. With only a single gear fixed to the rear wheel, these bicycles were light and easy to maintain but difficult to ride, since pedals spun in tandem with the wheels, making coasting impossible. Often they had no brakes. Track bikes, a special kind of fixed-gear designed for use on velodromes but popular among messengers, never had brakes. In order to stop, riders locked their legs, exerting backward pressure on the pedals, forcing the bike to skid. Whether on a track bike or an ordinary fixed-gear, messengers who had "an almost spiritual relationship with their bicycles" preferred the smooth handling and more intimate relationship between rider and machine. These simpler, leaner bicycles felt like an extension of the cyclist. Plus, not everyone was capable of riding them. Mastering a fixed-gear was "like the black belt of bicycle riding," one messenger described in 1986.[53]

The challenge of being a messenger was certainly part of the appeal. The "romance of danger," as one anthropologist cum bike messenger observed, lured a certain kind of person, one who preferred adventure and independence to the tired routine and hierarchies that dominated the culture of the offices where couriers picked up and dropped off deliveries.[54]

While some New Yorkers loathed messengers for their recklessness, others worshiped them. "Despised as bicycle messengers may be (by all but their employers) and dangerous as they are, they are fast becoming folk heroes—the pony-express riders of the eighties," wrote Dinitia Smith in a 1986 *New York Magazine* essay. "The bicycle messenger who speeds through Manhattan might be regarded as the ultimate urban man—tough, resourceful, riding against the odds the city stacks against everybody."[55]

That the messenger was seen as the "ultimate urban man" was no accident. Smith estimated that only 3 or 4 percent of messengers were women. And they knowingly adopted a profession that was characterized by hypermasculinity. "There is macho involved," said the vice president of an early courier company. The machismo culture was visible in the bikes themselves, which rarely had brakes and never had baskets, even though they were always hauling cargo.[56]

None of that bothered Catherine Potter. An aspiring model, she moved to New York City from the small town of Denton, Texas, when she was twenty-six. She was immediately attracted to the bold style and work of the messengers and decided to tackle her fear of riding a bike in traffic in order to become a "member of the elite." Soon enough, she was. Other than the fact that she applied lipstick and eyeliner before tucking her short, bleached-blond hair into a blue Campagnolo cap, Potter did not stand out from her all-male colleagues. Like many in the business, Potter became better known by a nickname, Soviet (because she was "always rushin' ").[57]

Soviet loved the sense of power that came with riding beneath the skyscrapers. "You can't help but feel superior," she confessed, having delighted in the feeling of "rul[ing] the city." Looking for the next pickup, she and her Lightspeed colleagues would call one of the handful of all-male dispatchers who worked the phones, studied giant maps of the city, moved thumbtacks to chart the locations of the couriers, and barked orders loudly and quickly. One of the dispatchers described himself as a "general" trying to orchestrate "guerilla warfare." Unlike on actual battlefields, women were allowed to ride alongside men. Soviet loved it.[58]

Although Soviet and other messengers spent more time on bikes than almost anyone else, they did not fit neatly within the larger cycling community. A coherent cycling community was itself a fraught concept or, as one advocate put it, "oxymoronic." Other than the messengers—who of course had their differences—children continued to pedal in playgrounds and along sidewalks. Recreationalists caught up in a fitness boom biked too. A small but committed number of environmentalists also rode, including George Bliss, who built cargo tricycles and pedicabs, delivering newspapers and people in hopes of replacing trucks and taxis. Many of these ecocentric riders (some self-identified as Yippies) shared an interest in recycling, community gardens, animal rights, etc. And there were those who commuted for environmental, personal health, practical, and other reasons.[59]

And yet bicycles also became a symbol of the new wave of young urban professionals known as Yuppies. When *Newsweek* magazine declared 1984 the "Year of the Yuppie," a cartoonish man in a suit, riding his bike over a bridge in Central Park, presumably on his way to work, was on the cover. Later in the decade, Spike Lee's masterpiece *Do the Right Thing* teased the very real tensions of gentrification through a scene in which a white gentrifier literally scuffs up a black man's Air Jordan sneakers and metaphorically ruins his Brooklyn neighborhood. The clumsy white guy is wearing a Boston Celtics jersey and has a bicycle, both symbols that he does not belong. At the same time, across the East River poor blacks worked as messengers. That bicycles belonged to yuppies and yippies, gentrifiers and messengers, was proof that the cycling ecosystem was not a monoculture.[60]

It also made the job of political organizing more difficult, especially in terms of crossing the divide between the recreational and the increasing number and increasingly diverse group of utilitarian cyclists. When one bike activist recruited would-be members at a local club, the response was less than enthusiastic: "You out of your fucking mind? We don't ride our bikes in New York City." More interested in touring, recreational riders navigated the city's potholes via Volvos (with bikes on the roof) and headed out to the country for long rides. Other advocates saw the sporty cyclists, stooped over on racing bikes, as endangering the welfare of the pro-bike campaign. Racers made cycling seem exotic, expensive, and dangerous instead of a viable means of transportation, "the human and humane alternative to automobiles."[61]

Even more than road racing bikes, the increasing prevalence of mountain bikes and BMX bikes furthered the notion that cycling was aggressive, dangerous, and extreme. Between the messengers, children on regular bicycles, kids (and some adults) on BMX bikes, and mountain bikes, a segment of advocates worried that bike culture was "stuck in adolescence." As long as the bicycle was seen as a toy, it would be difficult to push for infrastructure on the streets.[62]

Even within the group of commercial cyclists there were sharp divisions. Delivering food by bicycle in 1980s New York was a much rarer activity than it became in subsequent decades (all the way back in the 1890s, oysters, pastries, and other goodies came by bicycle), but there was still a regular flow of bicycles shuttling food between restaurants and apartments. Never were these cyclists, who often illegally traversed the sidewalks, confused with the "messengers." "There was no connection. It was a completely different animal," one courier company boss said. Even TA at the time failed to see people delivering food by bikes—often Asians toting Chinese food—as cyclists or in need of advocacy. That New Yorkers might not conceive of someone delivering food by bicycle as a messenger, or even as a cyclist, had much to do with perceptions of culture, race, and ethnicity. The term "messenger" became shorthand for a certain kind of bike, attitude, and look.[63]

The philosophical challenges of thinking about cyclists as a whole made it all the more difficult to find consensus in terms of regulation. But with messengers the most visible riders in the city, lawmakers focused on them. And some, like Councilwoman Carol Greitzer, had had enough. At the corner of Sixth Avenue and Thirteenth Street, a bike messenger sped through a red light and came barreling toward the politician. Greitzer stuck out her arm like a shield, stopping the rider just in time. She took a good look at him. And then she smacked him.[64]

Greitzer's near-crash prompted her to sponsor a commercial bicycle bill requiring messengers to carry special identification cards and wear and affix to their bicycles a tag bearing a three-digit number. Cyclists, at that point, did not have to carry identification, which meant traffic cops had no power to detain riders and could not issue a summons unless they volunteered their name and address. Keeping track of the number of summonses issued, the sites of infractions, and fines paid and unpaid was also exceedingly difficult since the computerized system that kept track of traffic violations was designed for motor vehicles with registration numbers and drivers with licenses.

Greitzer's bill aimed to solve this problem through compulsory identification, which would make it easier to issue tickets for infractions like running red lights, riding the wrong direction, or violating any of the other rules of the road that applied to all vehicles, bicycles included. The bill won the support of the mayor, nearly every city council member, the *Times*, ordinary citizens ("KILLER BICYCLES" needed to be regulated, one New Yorker shouted to her councilwoman), and even an assortment of bike advocates who "mildly" endorsed the bill. A group representing the messengers did protest, describing the requirement to "ride with a huge three-digit number on their backs" as humiliating and "Orwellian."[65]

Nonetheless, the bill (Local Law 47) passed in 1984 and was implemented the following year. Tickets came pouring down. After just six months, 514 summonses had been issued, but no one had been arrested and only about 5 percent of messengers who received a summons actually showed up in court.[66]

While the police fruitlessly issued summonses, the DOT tried to figure out how many messengers were actually complying with Local Law

47. Relatively few (27.7 percent) displayed the required identification. But the DOT claimed that not all was lost. Messengers were behaving better. Over the course of a two-day period in the summer of 1985, counters observed only 3.64 percent of cyclists riding against traffic, about a third the number witnessed the previous summer. The bill targeted only messengers, although in truth they were not the only cyclists flouting the laws. A survey conducted earlier in the decade revealed that 93 percent of all cyclists rode through red lights.[67]

The debates about bike messengers intensified the following year thanks to a popular movie that painted an idealistic portrait of messenger life. *Quicksilver*, starring Kevin Bacon as Jack, a stock trader turned bicycle messenger, debuted in February 1986. The movie opens with Jack sitting in the backseat of a cab, watching in awe as the driver vainly tries to keep pace with a messenger weaving in and out of traffic. That on-screen messenger was a real, former New York City messenger named Nelson "The Cheetah" Vails, who won a silver medal in bicycle track racing at the 1984 Olympics. Later, when Jack loses a fortune, he chooses not to return to the tumultuous pits of market capitalism and instead becomes a messenger, delighting in riding fast, ignoring traffic laws, and enjoying the freedom of the streets. Jack and his new messenger friends, doing tricks atop their wheels, were cool. And the girls liked them to boot.[68]

In the aftermath of *Quicksilver*, a new crop of messengers hit the streets in San Francisco, where the movie was set, and in Toronto, New York, and elsewhere. Despite an escalating number of summonses, the problems with messengers only seemed to intensify. In the winter of 1986, a seventeen-year-old messenger struck and killed a pedestrian. In response, demonstrators lined Park Avenue as *Newsday* proclaimed that the "Anti-Bicyclist Movement Gets Rolling." Of course, it had long been rolling—rolling, stopping, and rolling again since 1819. Councilwoman Greitzer admitted that Local Law 47 was a failure, and in a *New York Post* article in April 1987, she lambasted Mayor Koch and the police for failing to do more. Within days of the article, Koch wrote to his then deputy and future Police Commissioner Richard Condon, asking about the merits of the critiques and potential solutions.[69]

The police department went to work. In the beginning of July, staff delivered a twenty-plus-page report. Filled with statistics, maps, and historical context, the report referenced cyclists of all varieties but designated messengers as "flagrant bicycle riding violators." While the review purported to demonstrate that the current education and enforcement programs were not working, it contained data showing that the number of bicycle-pedestrian crashes had actually declined in the wake of the commercial bike bill by roughly 9 percent from 1985 to 1986, and bicycle-motor vehicle crashes had dropped by a whopping 45 percent. Inversely, the number of cycling-related summonses, which had been rising steadily from 1981 to 1985, nearly tripled to over 19,000 by 1986.[70]

Two years does not a pattern make, but there nevertheless was a plausible correlation between more enforcement and fewer crashes. And the focus was on the danger from cyclists, not the danger to them, even though, in 1985, bicycle-motor vehicle crashes resulted in twenty-four fatalities, compared to two deaths from bicycle-pedestrian crashes. Cyclists were about as likely to be stabbed to death while riding as they were to send a pedestrian to the morgue, and pedestrians had about as much reason to fear death by bicycle as death by falling air conditioner. Yet the report authors concluded that cycling was a real danger, that the messengers were the source of the problem, and that current legislation and enforcement was insufficient.[71]

The internal report offered a number of recommendations, including working with the city council to develop legislation that would require messenger firms and messengers to carry insurance, mandate regular safety inspections (e.g., making sure that the messengers rode bicycles that actually had brakes), and grant the police the power to seize bicycles from unlawful cyclists. But the boldest proposal circumvented the city council and the legislative process altogether. It would become known as the Midtown Bike Ban.[72]

The news came on the front page of the *New York Times* on July 23, 1987: "New York to Ban Bicycles on 3 Major Avenues."[73]

Not everywhere and not all day, but as part of a three-month experiment, the city planned to ban bicycles from the midtown chunks of Fifth, Madison, and Park avenues on weekdays starting in late August. The prohibition included children who dared to ride through the urban jungle and adults zigzagging their way to work, but there was no mistaking the real intention: to restrict the thousands of bike messengers who zoomed along midtown Manhattan's streets. The time restrictions were intended to allow those who cycled *to* (before 10:00 a.m.) and *from* (after 4:00 p.m.) work to continue to do so while banning those who cycled *for* work. In the news conference announcing the ban, Koch, standing in front of City Hall, described the problem bluntly. Messengers "imperil the lives of New Yorkers every day." They rode where they did not belong. They dashed through red lights. Violators of the ban, Koch said, would be subject to fines between $40 and $60.[74]

Despite the certainty of Koch's assertion about the danger of messengers and the need for the ban, one of the reasons it was framed as an experiment was precisely that there were so many unknowns. First and foremost, the administration confessed that it had no idea how many messengers currently crisscrossed midtown. Although they were now required to register with the police, thousands of couriers never did. There were 3,000 known, registered messengers plus another 2,000 or so unregistered, so the city guessed. Further unknown was what effect the ban would have on the local businesses that relied on messengers. City staff did promise to begin collecting relevant data before deciding whether to make the ban permanent and whether to expand the forbidden zone.[75]

The Bike Ban area was determined from data that supposedly showed a concentration of cycling violations in the midtown district. Yet a DOT report indicated that in 1986 only 77 of the 640 bicycle-pedestrian crashes citywide occurred within the Bike Ban zone, and only 39 of those occurred between 10:00 a.m. and 4:00 p.m. Other statistics, not widely advertised at the time, revealed that pedestrians were most likely to be hit by a bike after 4:00 p.m. Considering the volume of traffic (bicycle, pedestrian, and otherwise), the fact that 39 of 640 crashes (6 percent) occurred during the day, during the week, and within a 58-square-block chunk in the heart of Manhattan did not seem all that remarkable. In other words, there was reason to think the Bike Ban would not work because the problem was overinflated to begin with.[76]

Uncertainties and all, the ban was coming. Koch did offer cyclists one concession: freshly painted bicycle lanes on portions of Broadway and on Sixth Avenue, the same spots where painted bike lanes appeared in 1978 and protected ones in 1980. The mayor hoped that would prevent any protests.

He was wrong. Within days of his announcement, marchers on wheels lined the streets, shouting "Fifth! Park! And Madison!" as the messenger workday ended each evening. They paraded up Sixth Avenue at a crawling pace that intentionally caught them at every red light where they stopped, bringing the traffic behind them to a halt. The protests grew in intensity and size, with some attracting over 1,000 people riding across several lanes of traffic, sometimes the entire width of the avenue. Participants hoisted signs ("BAN LIMOS, NOT BIKES," "Cycle and Recycle," etc.) and occasionally stopped to thrust their bikes toward the sky. Some pedestrians took part too, joining in the street or cheering from the sidelines.[77]

With the stakes as they were, many messengers not only participated in the protests but also pledged to disregard the forthcoming ban. Others promised to follow the law, but to find new ways of creating havoc atop skateboards, roller skates, or motorized bikes. No longer allowed on the avenues, messengers would have to walk their bikes for at least part of their trips on the already crowded sidewalks. As a sign of what could come, a group of 100 protesters slowly walked their bicycles up and down a stretch of sidewalk, purposely aggravating crowds of midtown pedestrians along the way.[78]

Even if messengers stayed on their bicycles and complied with the new restrictions, they argued, life in midtown would not be more tranquil. In fact, things would only get worse. The overall number of messengers would actually rise, since restricting cyclists to the side streets would lead to more circuitous routes and thus, longer delivery times and higher accident rates. Before the ban, for example, a delivery from the Tiffany & Co. building on Fifth Avenue between Fifty-Sixth and Fifty-Seventh streets to the limestone-faced B. Altman & Co. department store on Fifth Avenue between Thirty-Fourth and Thirty-Fifth streets (now the Graduate Center, City University of New York) would have been extraordinarily easy. A swift messenger who made (or rode through) all of the traffic lights could traverse the 22 blocks (1.1 miles) in just a few minutes and without having to make a single turn. Under the ban, the same messenger would have to walk to the corner of Fifty-Seventh Street, then ride across to Seventh Avenue or Lexington (since Sixth Avenue runs northward), then head south to Thirty-Fourth Street, then ride back over to Fifth, and then walk from the corner to the mid-block, column-studded entrance. The same delivery would now cover 1.8 miles, extending the length of the trip by more than 60 percent and the total time, considering the added lights, turns, and walking, by even more. When applied to all messengers and all deliveries, the result would be thousands of extra miles and minutes.[79]

Yet the city pressed on. And the animosity was palpable. At least one taxi crumpled a protestor's bike. From the sidewalk abutting one of the street protests, a middle-aged man wearing a thick mustache and tan suit made his feelings clear: "I think you're all fucking assholes." One woman wondered aloud if the couriers were delivering messages sent by communists. At one point, eggs came shooting out of a car window.[80]

Those eggs happened to land on Steve Athineos, a thirty-one-year-old white messenger (sometimes called Steve "The Greek") who became the most prominent face of the Bike Ban opposition and de facto spokesmen for the mostly nonwhite messengers. Cleaning up the egg on his face, Athineos mocked the notion that it was the messengers who needed to behave themselves. He enjoined his followers not to mimic such behavior for fear of developing a "bad image" (it was way too late for that). Nor should they "engage in civil disobedience" (it was too late for that too). With a heavy New York accent and in his loud but by now hoarse voice, Athineos warned that the police were looking for a reason to ticket messengers. Indeed, the police began handing out dozens of summonses to protestors and on at least one occasion, arrested several participants.[81]

FIGURE 4.7 Steve Athineos doles out instructions to fellow messengers alongside Sixth Avenue near Houston Street.

Photo by Carl Hultberg, July 1987, from the *Garden of Eden* book series

Athineos, whose dark wavy hair fell beneath the shoulders of his neon-colored tank tops, began regularly appearing on television and the radio, representing the messengers on a host of issues. He considered and rejected the idea of forming a messenger union. And while more than a few New Yorkers once again suggested building protected bike lanes (the short-lived 1980 bike lane experiment already seemed like ancient history), Athineos insisted that cyclists had a right to the road itself. Riding on the side, he explained, was "sui*side*."[82]

On the streets, gripping his handlebars with black fingerless gloves, Athineos led his comrades in a call and answer chant: "What do we want? Our streets back. When do we want it? Now." Despite the festival atmosphere, the messengers understood the gravity of the situation. "This is no party," a black female messenger reminded everyone who huddled around and awaited the latest news and protest instructions. "This is politics," she

FIGURE 4.8 Athineos leads a protest against the impending bike ban.

Photo by Carl Hultberg, July 1987, from the *Garden of Eden* book series

continued. "We're talking money." As fax machines loomed on the hori-
zon, there seemed to be a sense that the days of messengering, at least as
they knew them, were numbered.[83]

While many nonmessenger cyclists were behind Athineos, one important group was slow to declare a position: the bike advocates. Whether
or not they should stand with the messengers had long been a subject of
debate. As Steve Stollman, a radical newspaper distributor whose storefront became a messenger hangout, said, the conventional bike advocates
thought that messengers "were a bad thing because they were besmirch-
ing the name of goody good bicyclists." And Charles Komanoff, an
energy policy whiz who had become president of Transportation Alternatives in 1986, recalled that there was a "war going on in my head." The
cycling community was "fractious," and there was "pressure" to avoid
backing the messengers.[84]

Komanoff's friend, partner, and mentor, Carl Hultberg, argued that
TA needed to bring the messengers into the fold to both "reform them

as well as organize for them." So in 1986, Hultberg and Komanoff began manning a lemonade stand set up for messengers on Broadway in Greenwich Village. As the messengers sipped free lemonade, Hultberg handed them a copy of the "safety code," encouraging them to "never threaten pedestrians" and "show respect." The hope was that messengers would behave better and that the broader community would, in turn, develop respect for them. While those goals were not immediately met, the stand did nurture a relationship between TA and the messengers that would soon prove powerful—a combination of tough messengers armed with heavy locks and policy wonks/community organizers armed with data, lobbying skills, and Ivy League vocabularies.[85]

Because of his experience at the lemonade stand and as a consequence of Carl Hultberg and other colleagues' input, Komanoff, by the time of the 1987 Bike Ban, had begun to see messenger work as a "sweatshop of the streets." And he believed that there was a broader, "common cause" to be fought; while the messengers would be on the front lines, the other cyclists—commuters, racers, and recreational riders—also stood to gain from victory. He soon realized that the messengers were the ideal group to back. They gave the battle a "personality" and a "currency" that other cyclists could not. For better and worse, they were also more vulnerable than other cyclists. Their lives and their livelihood depended on the right to ride.[86]

The advocates began attacking the ban on legal, logical, and moral grounds. Why were messengers being singled out? Pedestrians and drivers broke the laws too. As one messenger put it: "We were scapegoats for the chronic failure of the city government to control its rampant traffic disorder." Charlie McCorkell, a former director of TA and then owner of a well-known bike shop who generously paid part of Athineos's salary so that he could spend less time messengering and more time organizing, spread the blame around to include the pedestrians who crossed the streets on a whim, the motorists who parked their cars illegally, and the taxi drivers who notoriously violated the rules of the road. McCorkell thought it was obvious that lightweight bicycles were much less of a threat than automobiles. He did acknowledge that there was a problem of perception caused by too many "close calls." Pedestrians were scared of cyclists, but the danger was exaggerated.[87]

Or was it? One New York journalist sought to find out for himself. As the fights over the Bike Ban intensified, *New York Post* columnist Tim McDarrah took a week off from his desk job to experience life as a New York City messenger. It was not pretty. One woman spat on him. Others yelled. More than a few drivers cut him off. And despite trying to follow the law, the police served up tickets. McDarrah's experience taught him that messengers were—for the most part—the victims, not the assailants. But it was true that messengers confessed to purposefully scaring pedestrians as they briskly rode by.[88]

Some businesses also saw themselves as likely victims of the ban: the courier companies, most obviously, but also the many Manhattan design firms, advertising agencies, banks, law firms, and fashion houses that relied on the five thousand or so messengers for speedy delivery. Yet messengers behaving badly might scare off window-shopping pedestrians and render the streets, the lobbies of corporate buildings, and the city in general less attractive. In that spirit, the New York Chamber of Commerce backed stricter regulations to curb the cycling "scofflaw." *Crain's New York Business* publicly supported the ban, asking the city to go one step further by seizing serial offenders' bikes. "Wild messengers" needed to be tamed.[89]

Media outlets in and outside of New York chimed in too. The *Village Voice* publicly litigated the mayor, underscoring the financial burdens that the ban would place on messengers by asking Koch how it was "that bicycles were the most dangerous vehicles." Was it instead that the messengers were just the "least capable of fighting" back? *Time* magazine saw it differently, declaring in a headline—borrowed from New York City Police Commissioner Benjamin Ward—that messengers were "Scaring the Public to Death." The *Daily News* endorsed the ban as well, expecting that it would "help control the scourge of wild-eyed messengers who think nothing of—maybe even *enjoy*—barreling down a crowded street, scattering terrified pedestrians right and left."[90]

One of the reasons messengers appeared so frightening, according to their defenders, was not simply the way they rode, but rather because "many of them belong to a subgroup which frightens many people whether on a train, bus, city street, or park." This was as much about race as anything else, they insisted. McCorkell pointed out that it was no accident that under the Bike Ban the largely white cyclists who commuted to work could continue to do so, but the predominantly black and Latino messengers (roughly 75 percent of the total number of couriers, by his estimates) could not. To him the message was clear: nonwhite cyclists were "not welcome on the most affluent streets of New York City." Supporters of the messengers increasingly framed the ban as an unfair attack on a group that consisted primarily of nonwhites who earned little money and had few resources to fight back. With more than just traffic working against them, the messengers were trying hard (and often failing) to earn a good living and pursue "the American dream." Read this way, the Bike Ban was less about bikes and messengers and more about controlling a population perceived to be dangerous. Not only did the ban restrict the messengers' movement, but it also offered the occasion to stop, and perhaps even search, those violating the ban. City officials responded to the allegations as "not worth a response" and reasserted that the rationale for the ninety-day experiment was to increase safety for all.[91]

The black press was not buying it. In a stinging editorial, the *New York Amsterdam News* wrote that "Koch was waxing in the glow of having socked it to the bike riders, mostly black and Hispanic messengers trying to make a living by working rather than availing themselves of criminal opportunities." Instead of paying police officers to punish messengers of color, the mayor, so the paper argued, should figure out how to deliver food to the hungry and shelter to the homeless. Ron, a twenty-three-year-old messenger known as the "Loan Shark," agreed. "Most of us cannot read or write," he confessed, before explaining the hypocrisy emanating from City Hall. How could the city talk about high rates of criminality among young black males and then, in the same breath, do something that made it harder for them to earn an honest living? Beyond just misusing city resources, the *Amsterdam News* suggested that the mayor was stoking racism. Koch's "racist" rhetoric, the paper alleged, was responsible for a *Daily News* headline that referred to messengers as "Pit Bulls." The *Amsterdam News* even called for Koch's resignation.[92]

FIGURE 4.9 A press conference featuring the key bike advocates fighting against the Bike Ban, including Charles Komanoff (front, center), Steve Athineos (front, right), Roger Herz (back, right), Mary Frances Dunham (back, center), and Charlie McCorkell (back, second from left).

Photo by Carl Hultberg, August 1987, from the *Garden of Eden* book series

Nevertheless, on Monday, August 24, the Midtown Bike Ban came into effect. The city announced that during the first week of the ban—and only the first week—officers would issue warnings. After that, fines would be coming. Dozens of officers doled out pink warning slips to the many messengers who refused to comply with the new regulations.[93]

But not for long. Just before the actual fines were to take effect, the bike advocates took their case to court. Together, Transportation Alternatives, the League of American Wheelmen, an association of courier companies, Steve Athineos, and a handful of other cyclists sued the city. Pending the outcome, the ban was temporarily put on hold.[94]

The case rested on the question of whether the city had the legal authority to ban bikes—in particular, whether the DOT had the right to promulgate the restrictions, whether the process complied with environmental review requirements, and whether state laws prohibited the city from taking such action. The current law governing traffic was merely an updated version of the same nineteenth-century law that prevented the city from prohibiting bicycles on any street that allowed "other pleasure carriages." The remnants of the 1890s cycling city suddenly mattered again. Were automobiles pleasure carriages? City attorneys were not sure. But they aimed to get around the law, claiming that more recent statutes superseded and "impliedly repeal[ed]" the provision about prohibiting bicycles.[95]

Earlier in Koch's mayoralty, the DOT had had internal debates about whether it could legally ban bicycles from certain streets. DOT staff ultimately reasoned that so long as they provided cyclists with an alternative network of bicycle lanes (even if not exactly adjacent to the roadways) they could legally ban bicycles from the roads. (Brooklyn park commissioners in the 1890s came to the same conclusion when they built the Coney Island Cycle Path and banned bikes on the parallel Ocean Parkway.) But absent a reasonable network of bike paths, they lacked the authority to do so. That was in 1980. By 1987, that stipulation quietly disappeared.[96]

The answers to the central legal questions would have to wait. When State Supreme Court Justice Edward Lehner issued his opinion about the Bike Ban on September 8, 1987, there was no clear verdict as to whether the city had the right to ban bikes. Instead, Justice Lehner decided that the city had violated matters of process (mostly the need to give the public adequate notice and allow for comment). The ban was tabled. An irate Koch called the loss "short-lived and foolish" and promised to clear the regulatory hurdles and restart the ban in due time.[97]

The stock market crash in October offered an opportunity to quietly forget about the messengers. Instead Koch doubled down. He promoted new legislation to beef up Local Law 47. He wanted stricter penalties for repeat offenders (e.g., allowing the police to confiscate their bicycles) and to require employers (not just riders) to maintain a license. At the same time, he promised that the required public hearings for the Bike Ban were forthcoming. But while Koch kept on pushing, it was also clear that he was growing tired. Privately, he complained of "constantly" having to deal with the bike advocates, and asked his staff to prepare him a list of talking points to ward off the attacks.[98]

Criticisms of the mayor were being lobbed from new directions, in a sign that the organized protests were working. One argument in particular gained traction within the business community: Bike Ban = higher delivery prices. In the fall, hundreds of letters flooded City Hall from businesses that depended on messenger work. Once a supporter of the ban, *Crain's New York Business* now changed its tune, calling the plan "ill advised" and proposing more modest regulations for the "hard pressed messengers." By December, *Crain's* asked why the mayor was being so "stubborn." Koch himself would soon begin talking about the importance of not compromising the messengers' ability to make a living.[99]

By the end of 1987, support within and outside City Hall had dissolved. The debates that played out in the media and on the streets had softened the perceptions of messengers. Openly criticizing them was made more difficult. Instead of diabolic, messengers were now viewed as vulnerable. Both sitting senators, Daniel Patrick Moynihan and Al D'Amato, came out against the ban. David Dinkins, the Manhattan Borough President and the man who would ultimately succeed Koch as mayor, had once supported the ban; now he opposed it. The Municipal Art Society, the Women's City Club of New York, and other civic groups came to the defense of the messengers as well. And although environmental groups were initially unwilling to endorse the protests, the Sierra Club and the National Resources Defense Council eventually panned the Bike Ban once it became more politically acceptable to do so.[100]

The protests had worked. The tide had turned, and in March 1988, the city council adopted a formal resolution calling for the "overboard" and "extreme" Bike Ban to be withdrawn. It passed with unanimous support. The battle was over.[101]

In the summer of 1989, the biggest buzz in the local cycling world surrounded not bike lanes or bike messengers, but a ten-stage bicycle race, the Tour de Trump. Standing in front of his namesake hotel, signing copies of his book, and distributing flyers and advertisements for his

Atlantic City hotel and casino ("facilities nonpareil," with the "incredible Trump touch"), Donald Trump fired the starter's pistol signaling the 110 riders to get moving. (Nobody was better at getting his name in the papers, Governor Cuomo remarked that day, suggesting that every politician could learn something from future President Trump.)[102]

That same summer and in the wake of the Central Park jogger attack, Koch entertained the idea of allowing automobiles to use one of the park's bike lanes, reasoning that twinkling headlights would make the park brighter and therefore less appealing to criminals. The mayor was ready to sign off on the measure, but Parks Commissioner Henry Stern convinced him otherwise, pointing out that pedestrians and cyclists, not motorists speeding by, were most likely to notice unscrupulous activity.[103]

In September, Koch lost to David Dinkins in the Democratic primary, ending his bid for yet another term as mayor. Cycling was far from a central campaign issue, but it did come up. That Koch "established and then abandoned bicycle lanes," Sam Roberts reported in the *Times*, was a prime example of Koch's tendency to waver. A Dinkins spokesperson echoed the criticism: "How many times has Ed Koch shot from the hip on everything from bicycle lanes to Bernhard Goetz and then reversed himself?" Dinkins made the same point himself in a televised debate (no matter that he too had wavered on bicycles, first supporting and later opposing the Bike Ban). The issue was not bicycles per se; they were a footnote in the larger narrative of Koch's mercuriality.[104]

After Koch lost, perhaps thinking of his legacy, he thought about expanding the bike lanes in the park. "Would it make sense, and is it possible, to have a bike lane that goes through the entire park?" he asked Parks Commissioner Stern. Stern proposed extending the current lane to the southern loop of the main drive. Koch approved, but insisted that the work be done "expeditiously." With two months left in his term, he was determined to announce the new bike lane "before I leave."[105]

To say that Koch was of two minds about cycling would be an understatement. Sitting at the imaginary kitchen table inside his brain were at least four or five versions of the bald mayor, each arguing with the others. Where did bicycles belong in the city? What kind of infrastructure worked best? What kind of legislation was needed? What was politically expedient? Koch, who before he was mayor ridiculed politicians for failing to build better bike infrastructure and as mayor managed to get long-talked-about bike lanes built before deciding it was a terrible idea, could never figure out the answers. Frankly, neither could anyone else. The bicycle was an odd device that proved difficult to categorize. Fitting cyclists neatly, safely, and happily onto the city map remained a puzzle. Conflicting ideas each had merit; good ideas turned bad at the speed of a Dwight Gooden fastball.

Long after defeating Koch's Bike Ban, messengers continued to pedal through midtown. But in the years to come, they would never again number so many. By the early 1990s fax machines were commonplace. Then there was email. Still, certain packages needed to be delivered in a flash, some documents needed to be signed by hand, and not every print could be digitized. Messengers remained visible in other ways too. Alley Cat Races on July 4, Halloween, and other special occasions invited couriers to see who could navigate the city the fastest and fostered a sense of camaraderie among the subset of riders most invested in being a messenger through and through. Messenger bags even became fashionable accessories for people who never rode bicycles. And a group of New Yorkers continued to complain about messengers—and they still worried about getting run over.[106]

But there is no mistaking the more recent messengers for those back in the summer of '87, perhaps the heyday of the bike messenger. It was the only period in which messengers were the predominant face of the cycling community, even if, to Koch and others, cyclists and messengers were two different species.

The story of the Bike Ban is also a story of coming together. The protests did not completely bridge the gap, but disparate groups of cyclists eventually joined the fight that ended in victory. Together, they helped lawmakers and New Yorkers at large come to understand the bike's place, not only as a vehicle of pleasure but also for work. And more New Yorkers—whether because of a transit strike, a dislike for cars, a wish for cleaner air, or the (brief) experience of riding in a bike lane—were beginning to see the bicycle as a vehicle to get to work.

Eventually, the city would come to recognize not only that bicycles belong on the streets but also that the streets should be remade with them in mind.

CHAPTER FIVE

BLOOMBERG

The victors in the 1987 battle of the Bike Ban had good reason to feel optimistic. Even so, they never imagined that in a couple of decades, New York would earn a spot as one of the most bike-friendly cities in the country. Nor did anyone think that when Michael Bloomberg was voted into office in the fall of 2001 that his administration would someday be remembered for promoting the bicycle. But, like the city itself, the streets and the bicycle's place on them changed dramatically over the course of his twelve years as mayor, and especially over the course of Janette Sadik-Khan's nearly seven years as Commissioner of the Department of Transportation (DOT).

To be sure, the city was no bicycle heaven. New York was still famous for lurching cabs, impatient pedestrians, and potholes galore. Compared to Copenhagen or Amsterdam, New York was in the minor leagues and even within the United States, cycling was more popular, per capita, in cities like Portland, Oregon, and Minneapolis. Not all of the bike projects in New York were a success, and even those that were spurred renewed calls to put the bicycle back in its place. And the same old questions about where bicycles belonged, how cyclists ought to behave, and what the bicycle stood for played out once again.

But things were also different. New Yorkers increasingly embraced the bicycle as a utilitarian tool, a notion reinforced by the bike advocates and bike messengers who had defeated Koch and his ban. Now, city leaders, Sadik-Khan chief among them, argued that bicycles had real practical value and deserved real space on the streets. The city came to reflect that vision.

In early November 2001, New Yorkers headed to the polls to elect their 108th mayor. Ashes from the September 11th terrorist attack still dusted Lower Manhattan. The 107th mayor, Republican Rudy Giuliani, was wildly popular, but term limits prevented him from running again. Those same limits would not stop his successor, the billionaire Democrat turned Republican (and later Independent) king of Wall Street, Michael Bloomberg.

With the Bloomberg data terminal a fixture of the trading desk from the 1980s on, Bloomberg earned money no matter which way the market moved. A degree in engineering and a first career in equities trading made Bloomberg's foray into the world of financial information technology natural; his transition to politics was anything but. Although smart and ambitious, and with a resume that appealed to voters looking for a CEO at a moment when New York's seat as the financial capital of the world appeared up for grabs, Bloomberg was not a natural politician.

He lacked charisma, delivered workmanlike speeches, and was ridiculed for efforts to connect to common New Yorkers like riding the subway and speaking (nonfluent) Spanish at press conferences. But with Giuliani's endorsement and by running as a Republican to avoid the crowded Democratic primary, Bloomberg squeaked into Gracie Mansion. (Although he never actually moved in; he already lived in a nicer mansion.)[1]

Early in his administration, Bloomberg viewed bicycles as pests, in large part because of the growing popularity of group bicycle rides known as Critical Mass. Begun in 1992 in San Francisco, Critical Mass looked a lot like the 1987 messenger protests in New York when Steve Athineos and his army of cyclists halted traffic. Originally the rides were called the "Commute Clot"; the eventual name, Critical Mass, had New York roots too. George Bliss, the New York activist and pedicab designer, had visited Guangzhou and recounted (for a niche documentary film called *The Return of the Scorcher*) how Chinese cyclists waited for a "critical mass" before crossing the street as a group. There was strength in numbers. The name stuck.[2]

From San Francisco, rides spread across the country, reaching New York within a year. On the last Friday of each month, riders congregated at Union Square (initially they launched from Washington Square Park and later the Astor Place Cube before moving to this more spacious site) for an evening parade through the streets. As one participant described, the purpose was "to celebrate the bicycle and to dominate the streets for a change. To experience what it's like to be in the majority, to experience what it's like to feel safe and feel surrounded by fellow cyclists." For many participants and onlookers, Critical Mass was a protest, *for* bicycles and *against* cars. Yet since Critical Mass was without any official leadership or defined purpose, massers could characterize their involvement as they saw fit. The catchphrases (e.g., "Still We Ride," "Reclaim Our Streets," "Kill Your Car Before It Kills You," "Off Your Ass, Ride a Bike"), drawings, and caricatures found on Critical Mass flyers, leaflets, stickers, buttons, and in e-mail messages varied from city to city, week to week, and author to author.[3]

For this part protest, part carnival, part street theater, part show of force, and part joyride, riders often dressed up to reinforce a particular message. Cyclists disguised as plants, for example, railed against the

Giuliani-led effort to sell community gardens to private developers. From the beginning, there had been clear overlaps between environmentalists and massers. An environmental group known as Time's Up was the leading local organizer of New York City's Critical Mass. It was founded in 1987 (the same year as Mayor Koch's Bike Ban) and called Steve Stollman's shop on East Houston Street home (the same storefront that was the de facto headquarters for bike messengers).[4]

During the monthly events, packs of riders who seemed to be in no hurry and headed to no particular place rolled through red lights as drivers waited at green ones. The cyclists were unapologetic: "We aren't blocking traffic, we *are* traffic!" became the group's unofficial motto (deliberately, nothing about Critical Mass was "official").

Early on, the police occasionally intervened, but only occasionally. Sometimes bicycle cops even helped out by "corking," the practice of blocking automobile traffic from the side roads to keep the cyclists together. But things changed dramatically in 2004.[5]

On August 30, the Republican National Committee (RNC) kicked off its nominating convention at Madison Square Garden, despite the fact that New Yorkers had overwhelmingly voted against George W. Bush back in 2000 and would do so again in November. The Friday before the convention and at the usual six o'clock hour, a larger-than-normal, 5,000-strong group assembled for what would be one of the most infamous rides in Critical Mass history. By the end of the night, hundreds of cyclists would be arrested. The relationship between the "massers" and the city would never be the same.[6]

The police department had predicted trouble and, wanting to set the tone early, started issuing warnings in the days and weeks leading up to the convention. Officers reminded the public that it was illegal to block traffic and to parade without a permit. Though neither law was new, the promise to enforce them was. Unfazed, protestors on wheels snaked up and down Manhattan's grid, blocking traffic as usual, this time chanting "No more Bush!" as they homed in on Madison Square Garden. Outside the cylindrical arena, adrenalized massers hurled insults into the thick summer air and lifted their bicycles toward the sky. Helmeted officers on motorcycles stood by and watched.[7]

Then word came down. The officers swarmed in, handcuffing the protestors and packing them and their bicycles into white passenger vans. In all, 264 were arrested—so many that the police took them to a makeshift holding pen at Pier 57, so as not to inundate local precincts.[8]

The event further associated Critical Mass, and to some degree cyclists as a whole, with radicalism and the political left. Partisan views of cyclists only grew more entrenched: bikes were either symbols of progressive change or tools to break the law. That a Texas oilman lived in the White House and was coming to New York to extend his stay unsurprisingly drew the ire of progressives on bikes.

The 2004 battle between police and Critical Mass marked the beginning of war, with fights on the street and inside courtrooms. The police argued that the demonstrators reveled in breaking the law; the cyclists charged officers with violence, harassment, discrimination, and wasting time and money, on the order of "547 officers, 81 sergeants, 29 lieutenants . . . a helicopter . . . more than 100 scooters and bicycles," and nearly two dozen buses in preparation for the October 2004 ride. In the two years following the RNC, the city spent more than $1.3 million policing Critical Mass, nearly double what it spent on bicycle lanes. The city would spend even more money settling lawsuits for officers captured on video, throwing riders from their bikes in 2007 and 2008. Although the legal challenges would continue over the coming years, much of the uproar died down. Fewer riders showed up. Perhaps the police crackdown had worked.[9]

Regardless, Critical Mass was an important marker in the long campaign to improve the cyclists' place in the city. Whether or not the rides helped or hurt bike advocacy was an open question, widely debated among the participants themselves. On the one hand, like the messengers of the 1980s, massers rankled the police and politicians and tested the conventions of what cycling and cyclists looked like. Yet, Critical Mass served as a kind of cultural link between the messengers of the 1980s and twenty-first-century riders as the events eventually began attracting librarians and lawyers, professional types who sensed that a "real alternative" to the automobile existed. Perhaps the experience of

FIGURE 5.1 A Critical Mass ride through Times Square in 2006 highlights just how much the city was about to change. The streets here would soon look much different. And the plea, as spelled out on the back of the masser's T-shirt (center), that the city needed to "Legalize Bicycling" would soon seem outdated. Instead, protestors of a different sort would argue that the city had gone too far in its effort to promote the bicycle.

Photo by Brian McGloin, September 29, 2006

riding on the streets could always be so pleasurable. Members of the administration began wondering the same thing.[10]

On Earth Day in 2007, Bloomberg announced his plan for New York in the year 2030. *PlaNYC: A Greener, Greater New York* called for a larger (the city population was projected to grow by a million people) but more sustainable city. In 2006, the hit documentary *An Inconvenient Truth*—essentially a lecture by Al Gore—convinced millions of people, Bloomberg and his Deputy Mayor Dan Doctoroff among them, that global warming was real and the danger profound. Doctoroff told DOT bigwigs that it was time to start thinking more boldly about how New York could become a global leader in the fight against climate change.[11]

For Bloomberg, environmental stewardship was tied to notions of economic development, prosperity, and "competitive advantage." In a new age of governance, presciently labeled by urban theorist David Harvey as "entrepreneurialism," "quality of life" became a competitive metric. If New York could become a sustainable and "livable" city, economic benefits would follow.[12]

The mayor of the country's largest city also recognized that he was in a position to shape, by example, the agenda of other cities. New York was a giant laboratory, and city levers could be pulled more easily than state or national ones. To be sure, the days of master builder Robert Moses were long gone—bureaucracy could and still did snare visionary projects. But Bloomberg did not have to wait for assemblymen or congressmen to sign off.

The unusually long-term plan set ambitious targets. There needed to be more housing, and it needed to be more affordable and built more sustainably. Public transit would have to be expanded and modernized. Green space should multiply and the air should be cleaner. Spearheading the effort to set and achieve *PlaNYC*'s goals was Rohit (Rit) Aggarwala, a smart, affable historian by training, who wrote his dissertation about the rivalry between New York and Philadelphia in the Early Republic. New York had won, and Aggarwala, "the brains behind *PlaNYC*," was charged with making sure it won again in the twenty-first century.[13]

PlaNYC envisioned the bicycle as the solution to a number of problems: overcrowded subways, streets clogged with cars, poor access to mass transit facilities, and terribly long commute times. At the same time, the report noted, bikes were relatively inexpensive, took up little city space, and were a way of getting around that did not exacerbate air pollution or contribute to global warming: "Nothing is as low-polluting as the human-powered bicycle, which can give many New Yorkers an alternative to the auto for short trips." *PlaNYC* declared the bicycle a perfect little light, efficient vehicle for a too crowded and too polluted city.[14]

When *PlaNYC* was unveiled, the bicycle was still a tiny piece of the commuting puzzle—well under one percent of workers commuted by bike. In hopes of increasing those numbers, city officials planned to publish and disseminate bicycle maps, push legislation to require that all commercial buildings have bike parking, and introduce bicycle safety campaigns. *PlaNYC* also called for installing 1,200 new bike racks, adding 304 miles of separate paths, and building 1,076 miles of lanes with green paint or dotted with symbols reminding everyone to share the road. Adding more than 1,300 miles of bike paths/lanes to a network that totaled roughly 400 miles at the time was certainly ambitious.

Compared to what would come, the proposals were hardly radical. The report said nothing about innovative street design or bikesharing. The proposals leaned heavily in the direction of adding on-street, non-separated bike lanes. By simply painting "sharrows" (a bicycle symbol with two arrows pointing in the direction of traffic) on roads, the city could fulfill most of its promises without seriously improving the cyclescape. Progressive? Yes. Revolutionary? No. That was because Janette Sadik-Khan had not yet arrived.[15]

Sadik-Khan was not Bloomberg's first transportation commissioner, but she is the one people remember. Over the course of her six-plus years on the job she garnered fame and contempt on a scale that few other city bureaucrats have ever known. Her name was a fixture in news headlines. Her determined brown eyes regularly fixed on television cameras broadcasting to locales near and far. After she left the job, she wrote a best-selling memoir. Rarely does the general public care what a transportation commissioner has to say, let alone a retired one.[16]

But Sadik-Khan, like the mayor who hired her, was unusually ambitious. Born in San Francisco, raised in Greenwich, Connecticut, and with a law degree from Columbia and a father who had climbed to the top of the business world, Sadik-Khan could very well have gone into a lucrative Wall Street career. But in 1989 she waded into politics, signing on to the mayoral campaign of David Dinkins. Having backed him early on, Sadik-Khan was ready to accept a post in the new administration. Her mother, a journalist, suggested that if she wanted to really make an impact and affect all New Yorkers she had only two choices: the trash or the streets. She chose the streets, taking a position as transportation advisor, and then served in the same role for President Clinton.[17]

Years later, in the spring of 2007, Mayor Bloomberg summoned Sadik-Khan for an interview. There was a vacancy at the head of the DOT. When asked why she wanted the job of *traffic* commissioner, she corrected the mayor, insisting that she was interested in becoming *transportation* commissioner, not a meaningless distinction even if the commissioner had no responsibility for the subways. The job offer came with a draft of *PlaNYC*. It would be up to her to meet the benchmarks assigned to the DOT.[18]

It did not take long for Sadik-Khan to start checking off boxes. *PlaNYC*'s once seemingly lofty objectives soon appeared too modest. As she charged through and beyond them, both friends and enemies of the bicycle were seriously wounded.

Sadik-Khan began on the streets. As her mother had realized, the stakes were enormous. The streets accounted for roughly one quarter of all New York City real estate, and almost all of that space was understood to serve as a traffic corridor for motor vehicles. Influenced by the teachings of Jane Jacobs and inspired by alternative models employed in some European cities, Sadik-Khan proposed that there was a better use for such valuable land. That the streets should be more than just arteries of transportation, should serve more than just motorists, and ought to function (like they had before the popularization of the automobile) as public, active, and social spaces seemed obvious to the commissioner—so much so that she often struggled to empathize with her opponents and anticipate their frustration.[19]

Sadik-Khan wasted little time. Shortly after she assumed the commissionership in 2007, the DOT announced plans to reshape a section of Ninth Avenue in Manhattan's Chelsea neighborhood. It would become home to the city's first protected bike lane since Ed Koch's infamous 1980 experiment and the country's very first on-street bike lane "protected" by a row of parked cars and controlled by traffic signals designed to keep traffic flowing and prevent accidents. What was once four lanes of motor traffic slimmed to three, while the sidewalk and a line of parked cars flanked an eight-foot-wide path for cyclists.[20]

Would it work? The fire department worried about access. Taxi drivers and passengers worried about pickups. Everyone worried about safety.

FIGURES 5.2 Once DOT leaders were satisfied that the Ninth Avenue model worked, they lengthened the lane and adopted the design on other avenues across the city. Here is a 2010 photograph of the protected bike lane on Eighth Avenue and Twenty-Fourth Street. The healthy buffer between the parked cars and the bike lane afforded cyclists enough room to avoid being "doored" by people exiting the driver's side of vehicles (notice the open car door near the bottom).

Courtesy of the NYC DOT, June 2, 2010

But it did not take long for the DOT to judge the lane a success. Ninth Avenue attracted 63 percent more cyclists than before and managed to do so while reducing the number of crashes. Numbers aside, by the bike lane's first winter, Ryan Russo, the DOT Director of Bicycle Programs, saw something that made it clear the lane was a triumph: an eight-year-old rode along the lane with her mother by her side. That a mother and child could feel safe biking on a Manhattan avenue was "really powerful." Ninth Avenue would become the DOT model for turning old-fashioned streets into "complete" ones.[21]

In the process of working on Ninth Avenue, DOT staff realized just how dated and uninspired the federal road design guidelines were. Two important handbooks, the *Manual on Uniform Traffic Control Devices* and *A Policy on Geometric Design of Highways and Streets* (also known as the Green Book), explained how roads should be built, what the signs should look like, how bicycle lanes should be marked, etc. But as Sadik-Khan noted, some of the science and recommendations dated "from the era of Moses." The kinds of protected lanes being pioneered in New York were "nowhere to be found" in the thousands of pages of guidelines. Actually, they did show up in the more specialized *Guide for the Development of Bicycle Facilities* put out by the American Association of State Highway and Transportation Officials (AASHTO) as an example of what not to do: "bike lanes should never be placed between the parking lane and curb lane" because that would create "poor visibility at intersections." But Sadik-Khan and her team had found that discrete traffic signal phases for cyclists and turning motorists could solve the problem.[22]

Not everyone was willing to take such risks and go against the seemingly sacrosanct wisdom found in the guidebooks, so Sadik-Khan and the DOT began to rewrite the rules. A trained lawyer who had also worked at an engineering firm, Sadik-Khan understood the power of regulations as well as anyone. In 2009, the city published its first ever *Street Design Manual*, a 232-page guide on how to build "world-class streets." Sadik-Khan wanted to take what her team had done on Ninth Avenue and institutionalize it, to make what was now novel into part of ordinary street building and redesign—and not just in New York. Many of New York's innovations later became codified in the *Urban Bikeway Design Guide*, put out by the National Association of City Transportation Officials, an organization that Sadik-Khan led as president.[23]

The city's *Street Design Manual* spelled out preferred design principles, including an intent to "prioritize walking, bicycling, and transit." Complete streets also needed trees, benches, and ideally even tables and chairs. Transforming thoroughfares into plazas would become a hallmark of the Sadik-Khan era; Times Square was the poster child. What was once a dizzying intersection of honking traffic morphed into a (still dizzying) stretch of reclaimed open space, filled with lunchtime diners, tourists, and hucksters—sometimes dressed as Disney characters and sometimes hardly dressed at all. Whether it was the pedestrian playground in Times Square or the redesign of Ninth Avenue, cabbies fumed over lost traffic lanes, truck drivers grumbled about impossible deliveries, and motorists complained about vanishing parking spots (the DOT called it "repurposing").[24]

Undaunted, Sadik-Khan marched on and with an increasing number of allies. The bicycle advocacy group Transportation Alternatives (TA), which had lost some of its sway after the 1987 Bike Ban, grew in terms of the number of staff (from 4 in 2004, the year of Critical Mass's largest protest ride, to 24 in 2011), members (some 8,000 by 2011), and influence, influence that permeated the walls of City Hall as Sadik-Khan invited former TA staff members and advocates to join her team.

At the helm of this more cooperative TA was Paul Steely White, a likeable Brooklynite who seemed to know when and, more importantly, when not to stir the pot. Though he later adopted hipster dress—mustache and jean-jacket vest—White was corporate and cool, a middle-aged white male professional who looked like he could probably ride to work in a tie without breaking a sweat. He hardly resembled the protesting messengers of the 1980s famous for big hair and loud voices, the face of bicycle advocacy in the previous generation. White and Sadik-Khan, both comfortable biking in the streets and sitting in boardrooms, found much in common.[25]

The media landscape was also changing. Starting in 2006, Streetsblog and its sister site Streetfilms attracted internet audiences by chronicling frustrated cyclists and pedestrians, poorly designed roads and intersections, and avoidable traffic crashes. One of Streetfilms's first features was a thirty-second video of a cab sitting still in a pedestrian crosswalk. Another three-minute piece starred histrionic cyclists dressed as clowns doling out fake tickets to those obstructing a bike lane. Though their posts were critical and sometimes silly, Streetsblog and Streetfilms joined TA and the DOT in pushing for a reconceptualization of the street.[26]

Ideas also came from outside the United States. One example was Ciclovía, a weekly event in Bogotá that turned streets generally reserved for motor traffic into open spaces for walkers, cyclists, and the public at large. In 2008, the DOT experimented with its own version known as Summer Streets. On three Saturdays in August from 7:00 a.m. to 1:00 p.m., the city closed a continuous seven-mile stretch of roadway, extending from Seventy-Second Street down to City Hall, opening Park Avenue and other streets to people on foot, bicycles, and skates. With a festival-like atmosphere, the event grew in popularity. By 2013, more than 300,000 people participated. Like the Critical Mass rides, Summer Streets allowed New Yorkers to imagine another use for the ocean of asphalt.[27]

European cities offered much to admire as well. It was on a trip to Copenhagen early in her tenure that Sadik-Khan observed the separated bike lanes (protected by parked cars) that would serve as the basis for the Ninth Avenue design. In Copenhagen, Amsterdam, and elsewhere, an impressive array of infrastructure prioritized bicycling and walking. But could such feats be duplicated in the United States? In New York, for example, parking-protected bike lanes would be shielded by more than just compact cars; Americans' taste for husky SUVs complicated issues of visibility. And in Amsterdam, bicycles had been used for commuting for decades, by a substantial portion of the population; in New York City, they were used only by a dedicated few.[28]

Beyond the obvious and deep-rooted dependency on automobiles, there were also unanswered questions about the community of cyclists. As a group, cyclists in the twenty-first century still defied easy categorization. There were the occasional cyclists who played the part, like those who once casually joined Critical Mass rides or participated in the Five Boro Bike Tour but otherwise rarely rode on the streets. There were the hipsters (some of whom had been committed massers) on their fixed-gear machines—"fixies," as they were affectionately dubbed. There were the students pedaling to class on colorful, beat-up 1970s European bikes. Messengers still floated up and down the avenues, if much less visibly than before. Spandex-clad racers (including training triathletes, one third of the time) zoomed around Central Park's long loop, up Riverside Drive, and over the George Washington Bridge. Delivery cyclists shuttled stacks of steaming-hot pizzas across town. There was a growing number of riders clad in suit and tie (sometimes on folding bikes) on their way to work. They were all part of a cycling community that still rarely communed.

While New York was home to many different types of cyclists, not all were equally represented. Women were a decided minority, accounting for only 21.1 percent of all cyclists (in the same 2013 study, not a single commercial cyclist was identified as female). Women rode differently than men too. They were much more likely to obey traffic laws and to wear helmets. And while commuters were still far outnumbered by the recreationalists riding on the recently expanded greenways and elsewhere, the balance was shifting. New Yorkers began to see the streets, or at least a piece of them, as rightly belonging to them too.[29]

Not everyone and not every neighborhood was so welcoming.

Fights over bike lanes and paths were not new to Gotham. When plans for the Coney Island Cycle Path surfaced in the 1890s, cyclists themselves split into two camps: one arguing that the majestic, exclusive pathway was exactly the kind of infrastructure needed, the other that separating bicycles on pleasure paths would lead to cyclists ultimately losing their right to the road. Later, kids and adults wrote to Robert Moses complaining about the lack of paths. And the Koch debacle of 1980—building then hastily ripping out bike lanes—was not yet ancient history. But the twenty-first-century fights riled more New Yorkers than ever before.[30]

The first Bloomberg-era bike lane tempest swirled around the Williamsburg section of Brooklyn. Running alongside the East River, Kent Avenue hugged the edge of north Brooklyn. (It might very well have been called New Brooklyn, considering its rapid development and gentrification.) In 2008, the DOT sought approval from the local community board to transform Kent Avenue into a piece of a larger waterfront greenway. With permission secured, the DOT prepared to pave a two-way "bike superhighway."[31]

There was the usual grumbling that it would cut into road space and parking spots, but the particular demographics of the neighborhood presented another concern. The area was home to over 70,000 Hasidic Jews, loath to have men, and more importantly women, cruising by in clothes—or not enough clothes—that religious community members found immodest. They were already upset about an existing bike lane on Bedford Avenue, a few streets inland. With the lane on Bedford and the proposed lanes on Kent, locals feared that the neighborhood they called home was headed toward ruin. While cultural invasion was not entirely a new threat (cash-rich patrons from faraway places had long been stopping for steaks at Peter Luger's), cyclists and their outfits posed a new kind of danger.

New Yorkers had long argued about women's cycling garb, and the issue of cyclists' dress came up again, this time filtered through the twenty-first-century media. Columnists and bloggers delighted in pitting Hasidic Jews, typically draped in black, conservative attire, against the unorthodox cyclists. It was, *New York Magazine* reported, "Hipsters" versus "Hasids" in the "Clash of the Bearded Ones." Dress was not the only issue, or even the real issue, according to Isaac Abraham, a leading voice of the antibike lane coalition. Echoing complaints widely heard, Abraham argued that cyclists were reckless, immature, law-breaking road hazards. Moreover, he claimed that the DOT had overreached in forcing its agenda on a neighborhood uninterested in such changes (and a neighborhood already a victim of gentrification). This was obvious, he said, to everyone but the "bunch of morons" over at the DOT.[32]

Name calling was commonplace, especially in the comments sections at the bottom of online news stories, blogs, and videos, where angry New Yorkers weighed in. They labeled cyclists as "arrogant" "radical" "attention-seeking whiners," "trustfunders," "idiot hipster[s]," and "gentrifying yuppies." Bike lanes were "boondoggles" for riders who broke the law. "Anyone running a red light is fair game if you ask me," threatened "Snoopy." Taunting back, "Billdozer" said: "I would gladly bring a chain lock to your windshield." Online the bike wars were palpable—even more so than on the streets.[33]

Amid the rancor, Sadik-Khan strategized about how to move forward. Ultimately, she agreed to sacrifice the existing bike lane on Bedford Avenue in order to score what she saw as the bigger victory of installing new lanes on Kent Avenue. Not everyone was impressed with the trade-off. Transportation Alternatives lamented the precedent of sandblasting a bike lane. Others viewed it as a ploy to win over a small but politically important group of Hasidic voters. Church (in this case synagogue) had infiltrated the state. One female bike messenger (the "topless protestor," as the journalists dubbed her) planned a "scantily clad women" parade down Bedford Avenue, which even though its bike lane had been removed could, like other ordinary city streets, still be legally biked upon. (In the end, the scores of protestors who took part on a cold December day were fully clothed.)[34]

Not all Hasidic Jews opposed the new two-way bike lanes on Kent Avenue or the fourteen-block lane on Bedford; some even joined a protest repainting the Bedford lane after it had been removed. But the fight in Williamsburg would ultimately seem tame and short-lived compared to the battle brewing a few miles south.[35]

It was the summer of 2010. Sadik-Khan was three years into her job and had added about 100 miles to the on-street bike network and overseen the construction of 13 miles of protected bike lanes. The DOT had just finished installing a new bicycle lane alongside Prospect Park West (PPW). The local community board had requested it and plans had been in the works for years. Sadik-Khan probably expected a thank you card. Instead, she was sued.

In one corner stood Sadik-Khan, the increasingly recognizable transportation commissioner. In the other corner were some equally high-profile figures: Marty Markowitz, the punchy Brooklyn borough president; Iris Weinshall, Sadik-Khan's less bike-happy predecessor at the DOT and wife of powerful U.S. Senator Chuck Schumer (the couple lived on Prospect Park West); Norman Steisel, a former Deputy Mayor; Anthony Weiner, the (ultimately disgraced) congressman and aspiring mayor who once thumped to Bloomberg, "When I become mayor, you know what I'm going to spend my first year doing? I'm going to have a bunch of ribbon-cuttings tearing out your fucking bike lanes"; and Gibson Dunn LLP, the white-shoe law firm that worked pro bono to squash Sadik-Khan, her bike lane along the Park, and her larger vision for the city.[36]

In order to build the eight-foot wide, protected, bidirectional, green-painted bike lane that lined Prospect Park's nearly one-mile western edge, three lanes of motor traffic shrank to two and six parking spots disappeared. By October 2010, demonstrators armed with megaphones were marching on the streets. "It's insane, move this lane," they jeered before police inserted themselves between shouting protestors and counterprotesters. The lane, opponents alleged, was unsafe and unwelcome, and the setup was "extraordinarily ugly" and a mark of "vandalism" on a venerable neighborhood.[37]

FIGURES 5.3 The redesign of Prospect Park West included shrinking the number of driving lanes and adding a floating parking lane and a three-foot buffer to create a two-way bicycle lane.

Courtesy of the NYC DOT, March 15, 2012

The fight over the Propect Park West lane made one thing certain: the "bikelash" was in full effect. Residents across the boroughs began protesting against bike lanes—in Fort Greene, Brooklyn, on Columbus Avenue in Manhattan, and on Father Capodanno Boulevard in Staten Island, for example—more vehemently.[38]

In the face of mounting criticism, onetime allies of the DOT began to distance themselves. Weinshall announced her opposition via a letter published in the *Times* ("She's apparently decided to throw caution to the wind," a neighbor wrote in an email, now that Schumer had made "good progress in the Senate battles"). Weinshall, Steisel, and Louise Hainline, a PPW resident and Brooklyn College dean, signed the letter, arguing that the lane would result in more accidents and that, according to their "own videotapes," the "lanes are used by half the number of riders the D.O.T. says, and that cyclists are not riding to commute as originally contemplated." Bill de Blasio, then public advocate, called Sadik-Khan's approach "alienating." Others in City Hall attacked her for being too aggressive and difficult, charges not uncommonly heaped on women in power. Outside of City Hall, the name-calling was worse. Marty Markowitz said she was a "zealot." Others referred to her as "Chaka Khan" (a reference to the 1970s funk singer) or the "wacko nutso bike commissioner."[39]

Escalating the fight, Park Slope residents organized two new community groups, Seniors for Safety and Neighbors for Better Bike Lanes. Working together, they filed a lawsuit in March 2011 claiming that the DOT and Sadik-Khan had engaged in a "scheme" premised on "misleading, selective, and unsound data." Moreover, the suit alleged that the DOT secretly "colluded with radical . . . lobbyists" (bike advocates) to squash opposition and "wage personal attacks, via internet postings" on innocent neighbors with legitimate safety concerns, namely that the new design made it more difficult for pedestrians (especially senior citizens) to cross the street. Further, the suit referenced DOT "bare-knuckled tactics," which included egging on a blogger who defamed critics of the bike lane as "shameless, selfish pigs," "complete f'ing troglodytes" and "the worst of what the baby boom generation has to offer." The bike-hating elderly, so the writer further teased, should "move to Florida."[40]

The 85 members of Seniors for Safety and the 130-person strong Neighbors for Better Bike Lanes were not amused. Their suit against the DOT painted Sadik-Khan as an extremist who ignored federal guidelines; fudged data to make it seem as if the lane resulted in more cyclists, fewer crashes, and improved motor traffic flow; and promised that this novel lane (PPW and Kent Avenue were the only two-way protected bike lanes in all of New York City) was merely a pilot project and that any decisions about its permanence would be based on a close examination of data and community input.[41]

The case garnered international attention. In England, the *Guardian* wondered "How One New York Bike Lane Could Affect the Future of Cycling Worldwide."[42] In New York, the lawsuit was front-page news, and the subject of a feature story in the *New Yorker* in which staff writer John Cassidy described the bike lane as "a classic case of regulatory capture by a small faddist minority intent on foisting its bipedalist views on a disinterested or actively reluctant populace." The piece elicited so strong a reaction that Cassidy wrote a follow-up the next day, "Bike Lanes II: The Condemned Motorist Speaks." In it he tried to defend himself from reader comments (never a good idea): "Thanks to the commenters in general for providing me with a handy guide to the cultural politics of the twenty-first century. I'll keep a copy of it in my walnut glove compartment:"

Bicyclist = Urbane, enlightened, sophisticate.
Car Driver = Suburban, reactionary, moron.

The following day he wrote yet another piece, "Bike Lanes III: A Closing Word." It was hardly the last word.[43]

New York Magazine also ran a piece, subtitled "Is New York too New York for bike lanes?" Writer Matthew Shaer profiled some of the key players behind the suit, including Louise Hainline. "They really think they're doing work for the environment if, instead of taking the car a block, they take the bike to go to the food co-op," Hainline jabbed. "That's touching, and it's in the right direction. But it's silly." The long-time Park Slope resident worried about aesthetics, safety, and convenience. Double-parking may have been illegal, but it was an expected reality of New York living. Getting furniture, groceries, or dry cleaning delivered would be more of a hassle than ever, even if the DOT did include designated "loading zones."[44]

While most Brooklynites supported the bike lanes, those who lived directly on Prospect Park West were much less enthusiastic. Only 31 percent of them wanted to keep the lanes as they were. Polls also revealed that bicycles had young liberal supporters and older conservative foes; citywide, voters between the ages of eighteen and forty-nine supported the lanes much more than older voters (although even older New Yorkers favored the lanes overall) and registered Republicans also opposed the lanes more than Democrats. In general, the polls made one thing clear: those who liked the lanes really liked them, and those who did not like them really did not like them.[45]

Though not opposed to bike lanes in general, Hainline really did not like this particular one. She noted the proximity to the adjacent park and the fact that the PPW lanes were not an integral piece of some larger bike lane network. And she argued that the local community board that had requested the project was, like other such institutions, far from "democratic" and "invisible to most citizens." (Admittedly, Brooklyn Community Board 6, like most other community boards, did not always command the neighborhood's attention. At its June 2010 meeting, for example, in the same month that the bike lane was installed, the chairperson began the proceedings with an award ceremony for the four board members who had earned "Perfect Attendance Awards." Then there was a long round of applause for a board member who had recently celebrated his twenty-fifth wedding anniversary.)[46]

Hainline, a Harvard-trained psychologist well versed in collecting and analyzing data, was determined to prove that the DOT was "cherry-picking" data to suit its agenda. From her neighbor's apartment and with cameras turned on, she counted the cyclists rolling by and used the data to challenge the larger narrative that the new bike lanes were well used, much needed, and safer for cyclists, pedestrians, and motorists. For instance, in a January 2011 presentation designed to highlight the benefits of the infant-aged path, DOT staff noted that weekday cycling along Prospect Park West had "nearly tripled"; they failed to mention that the baseline, pre-bike lane traffic count was taken on a day of drenching rain and high wind, and that it rained just .09 inches over the course of the four days of post-bike lane traffic counts.[47]

Although irritated by the DOT's process and use of data, Hainline was, relatively, a voice of moderation. At one community board meeting she suggested that a compromise might be in order. Attendees booed, hissed, and instructed her to "sit down." There were certainly extremists. "When it comes to cyclists, the danger is infinite," one warned. "Cyclists can be anywhere, at any time. . . . It is homegrown terrorism. The cumulative effect is equivalent to what happened on 9/11." Few others were willing to equate cyclists with terrorists, but animosity was real and widespread.[48]

The ubiquitous media coverage forced the mayor's office to weigh in more strongly. On March 21, 2011—the day after *New York* ran its story on the "newest urban culture war"—Deputy Mayor Howard Wolfson issued a memorandum with a list of talking points. He cited favorable poll numbers for bike lanes, emphasized that safety was a priority, noted that most new bike lanes did not necessitate closing lanes to motorists or eliminating parking spots, and highlighted the fact that bike lanes were still relatively small potatoes (there were six thousand miles of streets, after all). On Twitter, he reminded the *Wall Street Journal*, which had just run its own article, "New York Liberals Battle a Bike Lane," that the PPW bike lane had been requested by the community. Wolfson also wrote a piece for the *Huffington Post* lamenting that the bike lanes had erroneously come to "symbolize the 'nanny state' run amok." "To paraphrase the great cyclist Sigmund Freud, sometimes a bike lane is just a bike lane." (The lawsuit against the DOT was ultimately dropped, but not until 2016.)[49]

That bicycles were part of a liberal agenda and a symbol of "nanny-state politics" fit with a larger narrative about government overreach in the Bloomberg administration, dating back to 2002 when the mayor announced he would prohibit smoking in all bars and restaurants. In the years after, New Yorkers complained that banning trans fats made for less tasty french fries—as did requiring restaurants to publish the disturbing number of calories therein. Those measures would soon be adopted nationally, but at the time they were tinged with controversy. Be it bike paths and lanes, congestion pricing, smoking, or trans fats, critics said the government was going too far in telling its citizens how they ought to live.[50]

Yet Bloomberg was hardly afraid to back policies that were new to the United States and unpopular with certain, even vocal, local constituencies. New kinds of street designs were no different. The administration had Sadik-Khan's back. And while the city did shelve a few bicycle-related projects, in large part they pressed on. In fact, they were already laying the groundwork for one of the largest bikesharing systems on Earth.[51]

In the spring of 2013, as Sadik-Khan's tenure as commissioner was winding down and the mayor's third and final term was ending, Citi Bike was born. With thousands of cobalt-blue bicycles and hundreds of docking

FIGURE 5.4 In the wake of the Prospect Park West bike lane hullaballoo, artist and humorist Bruce McCall captured the spirit of the "bikelash" and the growing perception of a "nanny-state" run amok. In this Op-Art, McCall depicts "Bloomberg's dream of a vehicle-free paradise." Motorists have to park on the sidewalks, which is both required and illegal. The roadway is divided into seven lanes. Lane A is a "traffic agent lane" on which officers can stroll and dole out tickets. Lane E is a "prohibited lane" with "no purpose except to slap the unwary with a $95 fine." In addition to lanes reserved for horses, runners, skateboards/scooters/Segways, and baby strollers, bicycles were invited to use Lane G. "As many as seven cyclists per hour are expected to exploit this lane."

"Shakedown Street," *New York Times*, December 18, 2010. Courtesy of Bruce McCall

stations across the lower half of Manhattan and western Brooklyn, the bikeshare system became the most visible marker of the administration's cycling initiatives. Citi Bike was designed for short trips and commutes in particular, appropriate in a city where roughly half of all commutes were less than three miles. Members could use the bikes, park them at any station (94 percent of which were within ½ mile of a subway entrance), and not have to pay anything beyond the $95 yearly fee so long as they rode for forty-five minutes or less per trip. The plan had been in the works for years and announced back in 2010, when the city had promised that a private company would pay for and maintain the system, costing New Yorkers not a penny.[52]

Bikeshare was not a new idea. Back in the 1960s, a group of Dutch revolutionaries painted bicycles white and left them scattered around Amsterdam (the program was short-lived, as the police quickly seized the bikes). Small bikeshare programs came and went in the subsequent decades but gained steam at the end of the twentieth and beginning of the twenty-first century. In the mid-1990s, Copenhagen started a program. In 2005, Lyon, France, launched Vélo'v, and in 2007 Paris offered thousands of bicycles as part of Vélib'. Barcelona began its bikeshare system the same year. Cities in Canada, Mexico, China, Australia, and Argentina followed suit. Even in the United States, Denver, Washington,

FIGURE 5.5
In September 2011, to celebrate the announcement that Alta Bike Share had been selected to manage New York's system, ultimately to be known as Citi Bike, Janette Sadik-Khan and other officials took a spin on bikes used in different bikeshare programs around the world. She is riding a "Boris Bike" from London.

Courtesy of the NYC DOT, September 14, 2011

DC, and Minneapolis beat New York to the punch, launching programs in 2010.[53]

Still, it was not clear that bikesharing could work in New York. This was America, not Europe. And Denver, Minneapolis, and Washington, DC, had many fewer people (and taxicabs) than New York. Criticism and protests stirred. The city comptroller warned about lawsuits from an expected increase in crashes. A restauranteur in Tribeca, concerned about a new station opening outside his bistro, staged a one-man sit-in. The board of a co-op building on Bank Street sued the city, arguing that nearby docks would "severely endanger the health and safety" of its residents. Neighbors of the United Nations predicted that the bikes and the stations could be used to abet terrorists. Many Citi Bike opponents went out of their way to say that they were for bikes and even bikesharing generally, but that a particular station in their backyard was misplaced, or that the way the administration rolled out the program—not enough warning, not enough foresight—was dictatorial. One critic went so far as to compare the Bloomberg administration to the Taliban.[54]

No protestor drew more attention than political commentator Dorothy Rabinowitz. In a *Wall Street Journal* editorial video titled "Death by Bicycle," Rabinowitz railed against the "all powerful bike lobby" and the "autocratic mayor" who "begrimed" the city's "best neighborhoods" with "blazing blue Citibank bikes." Cycling was, she said, "the most important danger in the city." Her editorial drew quite a response, including from comedian Jon Stewart, who poked fun at Rabinowitz and her like-minded New Yorkers on a *Daily Show* segment. After airing a clip of the Rabinowitz interview, a perplexed Stewart said, "They're just fucking bikes, lady." *Daily Show* correspondents then hit the streets to interview unwary New Yorkers, mocking those who feared lost parking spots and lower real estate values. A brownstone, one woman moped, might now only fetch $21 million instead of $22 million.[55]

Although pessimists predicted that theft and vandalism would be pervasive and that the system would fail, Citi Bike had a strong launch; within four months of the May 2013 start date, more than 3.5 million trips had been taken and more than 80,000 New Yorkers had signed up for an annual membership to ride the 5,130 bicycles parked at 322 stations. But there were also some major setbacks. Hurricane Sandy destroyed roughly 1,000 bicycles stored at the Brooklyn Navy Yard. The electric locks that were supposed to ward off thieves but allow users to quickly access bicycles proved unreliable—and so did the bicycles. In the first full month, there were 1,428 instances in which bicycles needed to be fixed or maintained. There were also 55 cases of vandalism. And there was chronic imbalance, with some stations too full for cyclists to dock bikes and others completely empty. Users were not happy: 55,271 telephone calls came in during the opening quarter.[56]

Critics also questioned the station locations. Was Citi Bike designed for wealthy whites? If not, why were there so few stations in neighborhoods where immigrants, nonwhites, and the less than affluent tended to live? Jon Stewart's *Daily Show* piece on Citi Bike included a lighthearted but pointed interview with a Bedford-Stuyvesant resident who argued that "we need the bikes" more than the "motherfuckers in Clinton Hill [who] own houses and [can] afford cars." Others expressed concern about a perceived shift in priorities. They saw the thousands of Citi Bikes as reminders of how the city favored bicycles at the expense of cars and trucks. In the eyes of detractors, the 322 stations were 322 monuments to Sadik-Khan's blurred vision of a cycling utopia, monuments erected on sacred ground—areas that had once been home to gathering spots and parking spaces.[57]

Even some of those who promoted cycling voiced concern. A former bike messenger, now in his fifties and living in Battery Park City, complained that a Citi Bike station replaced an ordinary bike rack, the place where his son had parked his wheels and a site where families had congregated. Bike shop owners added to the chorus of boos, predicting that they would lose a share of the tourist rental business and that local residents would opt to share, rather than buy, a bike.[58]

Over time, however, the controversy ebbed and the system improved. The number of members, riders, and stations grew. Vandalism became less of an issue. Fewer calls came in. And system operators became more adept at "balancing" bicycles, shifting the bikes from less to more popular stations. By August 2014, Citi Bikes had traversed more than 20 million miles, and by September 2017 New Yorkers took an average of 62,605

FIGURE 5.6
A Citi Bike station on the cover
of *The New Yorker*.

Urban Cycles, Marcellus Hall,
The New Yorker, June 3, 2013.
Courtesy of Marcellus Hall/
The New Yorker © Conde Nast

trips each day. The typical Citi Bike was unlocked, ridden, and locked
again at one of the now 622 stations more than six times each day.[59]

Citi Bike provided not only a new means to navigate the city but also
a treasure trove of data made available to the public. Number crunchers
asked and answered questions about how New Yorkers used bikeshare.
Were Citi Bikes used to commute? Definitely. Stations in residential-heavy
neighborhoods like Fort Greene and the East Village, for example,
emptied out in the morning and refilled in the evening; stations in the
Financial District, SoHo, and midtown were flooded with bicycles in the
morning that cascaded out during the evening rush. How did weather
affect usage? Fewer New Yorkers rode when the temperature rose above
80 degrees or below 60, when the wind speed reached 17 miles per hour,
and when it was raining (though it had to be more than a drizzle).
Were women using Citi Bike? Yes and no. Over the course of Citi Bike's
first six months, women accounted for just 23.7 percent of all trips.
In the particularly dense areas of Manhattan, the percentage was even

smaller. At the station on West Forty-Fifth Street and Seventh Avenue, for example, 85 percent of users were men. In the leafier (albeit not that leafy) sections of Brooklyn like Fort Greene, women accounted for a higher, but still minority percentage (roughly one-third). How old were Citi Bike riders? Thirty-one-year-olds logged the most miles. Data even allowed media outlets and individuals to create movement graphs, showing a day, or a week, or a month in the life of Citi Bike.[60]

Although Citi Bikes were not available for everyone and were not a perfect proxy to understand the cycling population as a whole, never was so much data available about who rode and where they went. Anyone, including the DOT, could see which stations had the most traffic and, at least implicitly, the places where infrastructure was most needed. Not every problem had an easy fix. For example, one surprising detail buried in the heap of data was that users were more likely to ride downtown than uptown. Why? One Citi Bike official theorized that New Yorkers instinctively thought of riding uptown as *up*hill and downtown as *down*hill. A new bike lane would not solve that problem.[61]

Despite all of the success, Citi Bike was bleeding money. In December 2013, the final month of the Sadik-Khan era, operators boasted about gross revenues, including more than $13 million from membership fees since Citi Bike's inception earlier that year. With sponsorships and over-age charges (when users rode for more than the allotted time) tacked on, total revenues neared $26 million. There was no mention of any losses or fears thereof. In the spring of 2014, when de Blasio was mayor, news outlets began reporting a different story. Despite having 100,000 annual members, Citi Bike was struggling. The manager of the private company that operated Citi Bike stepped down, and the company that furnished the bicycles filed for bankruptcy.[62]

By October 2014 investors had stabilized Citi Bike with a new $30 million commitment. It came with a pledge to increase the number of bicycles and stations and to expand the system's geographic reach. The investor group included Jeff Blau, CEO of the behemoth real estate development firm Related Companies. As it turned out, Bloomberg was not the only one who saw the link between sustainability, bike infrastructure, and rising real estate values. Indeed, the privately owned, data-driven bikesharing model fit perfectly with Bloomberg's larger vision for the city. The bikes were a kind of urban amenity, and real estate agents began advertising proximity to Citi Bike stations as a perk.[63]

That bike lanes, Citi Bike, and other bike-friendly infrastructure could be viewed positively by developers and Bloomberg-esque civic leaders was a sign of a cultural change. Throughout New York's history, the typical cyclist had often been portrayed as young, male, and aggressive. In the 1890s it was the reckless scorchers, even if women rode (and were criticized for it). The 1980s were famous for young messengers, many black and brown, often depicted as unruly. In the mid-2010s *the* cyclist still conjured up images of a young man, but this time he tended to be white, clean-cut (even if many had beards), and well heeled—and in reality, New York cyclists were, compared to the general city population, whiter, more likely to be college-educated, and more likely to live in Manhattan (and to a lesser extent Brooklyn).[64]

Policies and the location of infrastructure were certainly factors in the demographics; activists raised concerns in New York and across the country that public officials and bike advocacy groups catered to wealthier and whiter cyclists at the expense of poorer nonwhites who stood to gain the most from improved mobility. Of course, cyclists were still a varied group. Women rode, albeit in disproportionately small numbers, as did commercial cyclists—some now on electric bikes—who accounted for 18.4 percent of total bicycle traffic and still shouldered complaints about reckless riding and not-hot-enough Chinese food.[65]

While cyclists were still a diverse group and nonwhite riders continued to be disparaged, many critics reoriented their attacks, now perceiving cyclists as an "entitled, smug, and affected minority." Those lamenting the casualties of gentrification, including Jeremiah Moss in his book *Vanishing New York*, cast blame not just on the influx of chain stores and luxury residences but also on the new breed of cyclists. According to Moss, the essence of the new soul-less "entitlement" at the heart of Gotham's demise could be found in "the Citi Bike rider who dings his bell at a slow-moving old lady as he blows through a red light." The new cyclists, often on Citi Bikes, were actually better behaved than their predecessors—less likely to run through red lights, "salmon" down the street against the flow of traffic, and flout other traffic laws. As for all those new bike lanes, Moss labeled them a "tool of hyper-gentrification," "green veins that stream gentrifiers into low-income neighborhoods." Now bicyclists and developers appeared to be on the same team.[66]

A bike lane was not just a bike lane. A Citi Bike was not just a Citi Bike. A bicycle was not just a bicycle. A cyclist was not just a cyclist. What exactly they symbolized depended on the moment and person in question; they usefully served as metaphors, ways to talk indirectly about (and argue about) politics, class, and culture; critique an ever-changing city; and coalesce around a perceived threat to the neighborhood, whether immigrant commercial cyclists run amok or white gentrifying cycling commuters. Both kinds of riders indicated that New York was home, even if not a completely welcoming one, to more practical cyclists than ever before.

In 2009, *New York Magazine* described Janette Sadik-Khan as "equal parts Jane Jacobs and Robert Moses," and in 2016, Bloomberg wrote: "Janette Sadik-Khan is like the child that Robert Moses and Jane Jacobs never had." They recognized that Sadik-Khan's style included a dash of Jacobs-like vision and a dollop of Moses-like efficiency.[67]

Jacobs and Sadik-Khan both lived in the West Village, biked to work, advocated for what they saw as common-sense policy, and never shied away from challenging the status quo. They shared ideas about the purpose, value, and meaning of city space and understood that improving conditions for cycling and pedestrians was one piece of a larger project. As Jacobs remarked in 1985, "a city good for cycling is also a city good for walking, strolling, running, playing, window-shopping, and listening to bullfrogs if listening for bullfrogs is your thing."[68]

And Sadik-Khan shared traits with Moses too. Allies and opponents marveled at how fast she worked. She was able to turn car lanes into bike lanes and streets into public cafés seemingly (and sometimes actually) overnight. Sadik-Khan and Moses both understood that transportation was the lifeblood of the city, that what the streets looked like and how they functioned was fundamental to the character of urban life. They were both unelected bureaucrats who reshaped the physical landscape.

"I am basically the largest real-estate developer in New York City," Sadik-Khan liked to say. One could imagine Moses saying the same.[69]

Sadik-Khan often evoked Jacobs, a demigod to bicycle and pedestrian advocates. But Moses also served as a useful reminder. As Sadik-Khan historicized, reclaiming portions of roads once dedicated to cars was "Jane Jacobs's revenge on Robert Moses." In her own time, she faced no single Moses-like adversary, but she and Bloomberg did have plenty of foes, and sometimes the foes won. Public protest killed congestion pricing, a New York City Olympic bid, a ban on giant sodas, and a bike lane on Bedford Avenue.[70]

But opposition could not rewind Bloomberg and Sadik-Khan's agenda. More people biked to work in New York than in any other American city. The rate of growth, especially from 2010 onward, was much higher than that experienced in widely recognized bike-friendly cities like Portland, Oregon, Minneapolis, and Seattle. From 2006 to 2013, the number of bike commuters and the number of total cycling trips per year doubled to 139 million. Hundreds of thousands more New Yorkers now biked "at least several times a month." And the number of crashes resulting in "serious injury" fell by 73 percent over Bloomberg's three terms in office.[71]

The DOT had built the infrastructure and the cyclists had come. During Sadik-Khan's nearly seven-year run, the city averaged 55.9 miles of new lanes a year, almost the same amount, in bicycle paths, that Robert Moses had once falsely promised. Some of the new lanes, those protected by parked cars, blurred the distinction between on-street bike lanes and off-road bike paths. There were no protected bike lanes when Sadik-Khan assumed the commissionership, but by the time she left office, New York City was home to 36.4 miles, or roughly one-quarter of all protected bike lane mileage in the entire country. And that was despite a financial crisis, a recession, protests, and lawsuits. There was a dip in bike lane construction in 2011 in the wake of the PPW lane debate, but as Sadik-Khan later noted, the bike wars were ending—and she, and the bicycles, had won.[72]

Indeed, in August 2012, a *New York Times* poll found that city dwellers preferred bike lanes by a 66 to 27 percent margin. The percentage of those who supported Citi Bike was even higher. Of course, people continued to complain—as they always had—that the city spent too much money on and allotted too much space to cyclists whose numbers were too few and whose behavior was too reckless.[773]

In their final year on the job, Bloomberg and Sadik-Khan oversaw 40 new bike lane projects, totaling 73.5 miles. The frenzied pace may have reflected a worry that their priorities would fade in a future administration. But the new mayor and the new transportation commissioner promised to press on, vowing to build more bike lanes and to double the number of riders. That doing so seemed plausible instead of fantastic was an indication of just how much the culture had changed. And not just in New York. Officials in Chicago, Mexico City, Buenos Aires, and elsewhere began to copy Gotham's streets and bicycle paths.[74]

In 2014, *Bicycling Magazine* named New York the number one cycling city in the country. As recently as 1990, it had been ranked as the very worst place to ride a bike in all of America. By the time New York earned its top spot in the biennial survey, Bloomberg and Sadik-Khan had already left office. New DOT Commissioner Polly Trottenberg and new Mayor Bill de Blasio warmly accepted the honor, but everyone knew that it was their predecessors who had earned it.[75]

After Bloomberg's twelve years in office, his imprint on New York was hard to miss. Rectangular, glass-encrusted towers arranged cheek by jowl dotted neighborhoods filled with millionaires and billionaires. With soaring rents, the retail landscape consisted of repeating blocks of chain stores: CVS, Duane Reade, Starbucks, Subway, Metro PCS, and a (pick your favorite) big bank. Any doubt about New York's position as the capital of finance, fanned in the flames of 9/11, was dispelled. Despite rising prices, people kept coming to the city to visit, to work, to play, and to live. Bloomberg recognized that livability was a component of economic vitality. In that way, promoting cycling made sense. Car traffic was not only irritating but also bad for business. If New York was really going to be home to more than 9 million people by 2030, then the streets would have to change.

It is worth remembering that the mayor arrived at City Hall with no investment in cycling. And early in his tenure, he clashed with riders over Critical Mass. But as the years went by and the notion of sustainability came to the fore, Bloomberg warmed to the bicycle. His second transportation commissioner pushed him, her natural allies, and her many opponents to imagine an alternative vision for the streets, in which there were fewer lanes for motor traffic and more space for other uses. That the bicycle belonged on the street became an idea so entrenched that the streets began to look different. And those streets served to encourage New Yorkers to rethink the bicycle and to consider that it might actually be a good, cheap, clean, healthy, fun, and quick way to move around a city tangled by traffic jams, above and below ground.

EPILOGUE

In March 2018, I spent a day touring Manhattan and Brooklyn on a Citi Bike. Compared to the experiences of the small flock of commuters back in the early 1980s, the messengers later in the decade, or even cyclists at the beginning of the Bloomberg era, biking in New York has become much easier, much more pleasant, and much less lonely. On a one-day pass that limited me to 30 minutes per trip, I "dock-surfed" from neighborhood to neighborhood, checking my Citi Bike in and out every 28 minutes or so. The stations (now 739 of them) were so ubiquitous that it hardly required going out of the way. To be sure, there were plenty of obstacles, even in the dedicated bike lanes—impressively large potholes; construction cones; leftover piles of snow; idle delivery trucks, mail trucks, and police cars; vehicle exhaust; an oversized dumpster; cases of Poland Spring water bottles stacked five feet high; occasional hills; cyclists riding the wrong way; and tired legs. And there were some streets on which there was no obvious place to ride and a few cars that drove uncomfortably close. But a person casually riding around western Brooklyn and the bottom half of Manhattan in 2018 would find bike lanes galore, clear signage indicating preferred bike routes, Citi Bike stations all over the place, and plenty of other riders. Indeed, never have so many New Yorkers chosen the bike. And they have chosen it, now more than ever, as a practical way to get from A to B.

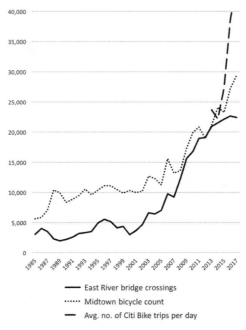

40,000

35,000

30,000

25,000

20,000

15,000

10,000

5,000

0

1985 1987 1989 1991 1993 1995 1997 1999 2001 2003 2005 2007 2009 2011 2013 2015 2017

——— East River bridge crossings
······ Midtown bicycle count
▬▬ Avg. no. of Citi Bike trips per day

FIGURE 6.1 The popularity of cycling in New York, 1985–2017. Over the same period, the population of New York City grew by 19.8 percent.

NYC DOT, "Cycling in the City: Cycling Trends in NYC," 2018, http://www.nyc.gov/html/dot /downloads/pdf/cycling-in-the-city.pdf; "Citi Bike System Data," https://www.citibikenyc.com /system-data

My ride was also a kind of New York cycling history tour. I began on Kent Avenue's protected bike lanes and then rode to Bedford Avenue, where a bike lane controversy pitted Hasidic against hipster Williamsburg in the twenty-first century; it was, back in 1869, a choice street for velocipedists. Next, I cycled along Prospect Park West and the bike lanes that had elicited shouting matches and lawsuits before grabbing some coffee and riding over the Manhattan Bridge, where cyclists asked Robert Moses for lanes of their own in 1940. In Lower Manhattan, I circled City Hall Park, where velocipedes first rolled about in 1819 and from which they were soon banned. Then I pedaled up to Chelsea along some of Arthur Hyde's preferred routes from the mid-1890s and rode along portions of the first Sadik-Khan-era protected bike lane on Ninth

FIGURES 6.2 (LEFT)
AND 6.3 (BELOW)
A Citi Bike and its rider/
photographer take a rest
along the Ed Koch
Queensboro Bridge
bike path.

Photographs by the author,
March 2018

Avenue. Then on Sixth Avenue, where messengers once stopped traffic in protest, and Fifth Avenue, where bikes were banned for a week in 1987. Finally I crossed the Ed Koch Queensboro Bridge—bicycle path and all—named in honor of the architect of the bike ban.

Among the many cyclists I saw was a crowd of bike messengers gathered on a Greenwich Village sidewalk. They were all dressed the same: black pants, neon green tops, and oversized, boxy knapsacks emblazoned with an avian-inspired corporate logo and a three-digit number. Like the majority of messengers decades before, most of these modern messengers were not white, but nothing about their helmeted, uniformed appearance radiated an affinity for danger or a distaste for corporate culture. Once upon a time messengers carried blueprints and film reels; today they tote beekeeping gloves and organic rutabagas that have been promised by local retailers to arrive the same day. Even if not quite the same, messengers persist and, like the bikes they ride, continue to be reconstructed in the public imagination.

Most of the couriers I saw were of a new generation, but some of the 1980s messengers can still be found biking today, though not as messengers. And many kept a footprint in the bike world long after giving up the job. Captain of the Bike Ban protest Steve Athineos was so invested in being a messenger that upon retiring from the streets he started his own courier firm. He even named his two children, Madison and Lexington, after the avenues targeted by the Bike Ban. (He died in 2015.) Catherine Potter ("Soviet") eventually moved to Charlottesville, Virginia, and opened her own bike shop before eventually getting into real estate financing. Her twenty-six-year-old self certainly would have been surprised, having then "felt sorry" for those who worked in an office. (She died in 2013.)[1]

The recent political leaders who championed the bicycle have also remained committed. Michael Bloomberg continues to donate millions to fight climate change and started a consulting firm, Bloomberg Associates, to help other cities follow the path he set in New York. One of its principals is Janette Sadik-Khan, who, through her writings, talks, and consulting practice, continues to spread the gospel of bicycling. To those who want to make their cities more bike-friendly, she is evoked and revered in an almost Jane Jacobsean way. Dan Doctoroff, Bloomberg's deputy mayor, who pushed sustainability to the top of the agenda, recently cofounded Sidewalk Labs, a subsidiary of Google's parent, Alphabet. One of its executives is Rit Aggarwala, the historian turned policy whiz who helped draft *PlaNYC*. The company's charge is to demonstrate how to build better cities through technology. Its first test is developing a Toronto waterfront neighborhood; in the conceptual drawings, streets are lined with autonomous buses, pods dangling from wires overhead, and "smart" traffic signals. Amid all this cutting-edge technology are plain old bicycles. Remarkably, the near-ancient bicycle features prominently in the city of the future.[2]

Bicycles are a unique combination of past, present, and future, viewed sometimes as tech-forward, sometimes as old-timey. The Citi Bike that I rode was a heavy machine that sported just three gears and a basic design established over a century ago. However, I used an app to unlock and lock the bike, view nearby stations and available docks, and track my number of calories burned and miles ridden. (Citi Bike users, my small bit included, logged 76,568 miles for the day.) Amid wandering Ubers and past parked Teslas, my Citi Bike seemed both out of place and right at home.

I didn't know what to think when men on electric bikes whizzed by me. Some of the so called "e-bikes" have a pedal assist to make riding easier, others a throttle that propels the bike without the need to pedal. Whether one or both types of e-bikes are in fact bicycles and whether the people riding them are in fact cyclists are the latest versions of age-old questions about the nature of bicycling and the bicycle. In October 2017, Mayor de Blasio promised to "step up enforcement" of a citywide prohibition on e-bikes, and the New York Police Department had already begun seizing e-bikes and doling out summonses and fines to riders, many of whom worked as commercial cyclists delivering food. Bike advocates fought back, drawing on rhetoric similar to that of the 1987 Bike Ban protests. They argued that the administration was unfairly attacking a vulnerable group—older, poorly paid immigrants who earned their living on a bike. By April 2018, the mayor budged, agreeing to permit the pedal-assist versions.[3]

Where e-bikes belong in New York is one of the still unsettled questions about the bicycle's place in the future of transportation. How can the city improve bike safety and eliminate bicycle-pedestrian crashes and bicycle-motor vehicle crashes (still a far too common, and even deadly, problem)? How can the city encourage more women and people of color to ride? Will a dockless bikeshare program, in which riders can pick up and drop off their wheels wherever they wish, work? How does the popularity of ridesharing affect the bicycle's place in the city?

This last question has become more urgent as rideshare vehicles have congested New York's streets more than ever. By the summer of 2017, Uber drivers chauffeured more New Yorkers than did cabbies. But Uber, Lyft, and the other rideshare companies did not displace taxis; they encouraged millions of people to get in the backseat of a car. One 2018 study found that without rideshare, roughly 60 percent of those trips would have instead been taken by subway, bike, or walking, or not taken at all.[4]

To complicate matters further, rideshare has now also come to mean bikeshare. In 2018, Uber purchased the electric bikeshare system operator Jump. Shortly thereafter and just weeks after New York became the first major American city to cap the number of new ride-hailing licenses, Uber's CEO announced that it would invest heavily in promoting bicycles, rather than cars, in dense urban centers. "It is very inefficient," he said, "for a one-ton hulk of metal to take one person 10 blocks." Sadik-Khan and the other brains behind Citi Bike already knew that.[5]

Yet, Citi Bike and its parent company, Motivate, have also been bought by another giant in the rideshare business, Lyft, which boasts more than a million drivers who take passengers on several hundred million rides each year. (On the streets of New York alone, Lyft, Uber, and the like added an extra 600 million miles of driving between 2013 and 2016.) Although Citi Bike and Lyft may seem like an unnatural pair, Lyft imagines an integrated fleet of cars, scooters, and bikes, all electric.[6]

On my regular, nonelectric, and perhaps soon to be vintage Citi Bike, I pedaled over to the High Line, one of a number of rails-to-trails projects across the country where defunct transportation corridors have morphed into inviting spaces for walkers, hikers, and cyclists. Bicycles are, however, not invited to tour New York's High Line. Those arriving by Citi

Bike have to dock their wheels before climbing a set of stairs. Despite calls for one (on and off since January 1869) there is still no elevated bicycle highway in Manhattan.

Perched a couple of stories off the ground and running over the west side of Manhattan, the High Line welcomes millions of visitors who amble between buildings and in their shadows, traversing a set of remnant elevated railroad tracks that have been handsomely woven into well-manicured gardens. What was once a site for transporting cargo, defined by smoke and deafening loudness, has become a space littered with gourmet food carts and carefully curated art installations (and too many visitors).

The crown jewel of the High Line is a descending amphitheater, which invites guests to sit on the oversized, wood-planked stairs and watch, through a series of glass panels, the street that lies beneath them. Like Parisians at a café, they watch the city breathe in and out. Taxis speed across the window. Pedestrians march up and down, left and right. Buses emerge from underneath before motoring uptown. Parked cars rest along stage right. It is from here that the city comes into view.

The park is also, in a sense, a museum—a reminder of New York's ability to transform itself. It is no accident that the defunct railroad tracks offer the perfect vantage point to reflect on the kinetic nature of city life, past and present. The streetcars that once ran along Gotham's streets and carried so many of its residents disappeared long ago. Horses began to look out of place by the time automobiles dotted the grid. The cars and buses that rode underfoot as I sat and caught my breath are also relatively new. The rattling of the subways is, likewise, little more than a century old. But bicycles have been rolling along New York's streets for two hundred years.

Over those two centuries, New Yorkers have struggled to define the bicycle, its purpose, and its place in the city. In Central Park, 137 years ago, three men broke the law by cycling through. Today, it is cars that are banned.

While many of the questions about bicycles and bicyclists have stayed the same, the answers—like the city that never sleeps—are always in motion.

ACKNOWLEDGMENTS

F or awarding me grants and providing institutional support; helping me find sources and make sense of them; sharing unpublished work; granting me access to private collections; offering me oatmeal and an (actually quite comfortable) air mattress on research trips; commenting on conference papers; talking shop and bicycle history; inviting me to guest lecture about this research-in-progress; expertly fulfilling the role of external reviewer; reading and critiquing the manuscript as a favor (you are wonderful colleagues, friends, and people); promoting my work at every opportunity; checking in regularly; granting me an interview; helping me conceive of this book and bringing me to Columbia University Press; cheering me and this project on; raising and supporting me; warmly welcoming me to the urban history crowd; reading this book; copyediting; helping with technical matters, small and significant; steering the book through the final stages; shaping me as a historian; editing like a wizard (a truly first-rate wizard); challenging me to games of Rummikub and soccer; giving welcome-home hugs and, along with your brother, reminding me what's important; and for giving me joy and love (and fresh-baked cookies), I wish to thank: the brains, hearts, and wallets behind the James Madison University Office of the Provost Faculty Development Awards, the James Madison University Program of Grants for Faculty Assistance, the College of Arts and Letters Alumni Legacy

Fund (especially Chris Arndt), and, as generous dean, Robert Aguirre, and, as generous department head, Gabrielle Lanier; Jonathan Cohen, Dylan Gottlieb, Jesse McDonough, Pat Nugent, Emily Westkaemper, and the archivists and librarians at the Brooklyn Historical Society, Brooklyn Public Library, JMU Libraries (especially the interlibrary loan folks), LaGuardia and Wagner Archives, New-York Historical Society, New York Public Library, MTA Bridges and Tunnels Archive (especially Nellie Hankins), Municipal Archives, Municipal Library, Museum of the City of New York Archives (also Donald Albrecht, Sarah Henry, and Susan Johnson), and the Tiffany & Co. Archives; Edward Albert; John Tomlinson; Gwynneth Malin and Katherine Marx; Rit Aggarwala, Martin Wachs, and Sandy Zipp; James Longhurst; Sonja Dümpelmann and the Harvard Graduate School of Design; Owen Gutfreund and the anonymous reviewers; Rebecca Brannon, Philip Herrington, and Andrew Witmer; Elaine Kaye and Nicole Wilson; Kevin Hegg; George Bliss, Joshua Freeman, Louise Hainline, Carl Hultberg, Charles Komanoff, Shelly Mossey, Ryan Russo, Steve Stollman, and Randi Taylor-Habib; Philip Leventhal; Ellen Cohen, Les Cohen, and all of my colleagues in the Department of History; Mom and Dad; Timothy Gilfoyle and Mark Rose; the reader; Leslie Kriesel; Christian Winting; Stephen Wesley; Thomas Kessner, Paul Naish, David Nasaw, and James Oakes; Bridget Flannery-McCoy; Miles Friss; Quincy Friss; and Amanda Cohen Friss.

NOTES

Introduction

1. Piet Mondrian, *Broadway Boogie Woogie*, 1942–1943, Oil on canvas, The Museum of Modern Art, New York.
2. New York City Transportation Administration, *Bicycles in New York City* (1973), 47.
3. Arthur P.S. Hyde Diaries, 1892–1896, vol. IV, 19–21, New-York Historical Society, New York.
4. For an excellent, anthropological take on how different people imbue bicycles with different meanings, see Luis A. Vivanco, *Reconsidering the Bicycle: An Anthropological Perspective on a New (Old) Thing* (New York: Routledge, 2013).
5. "Hobby Horses," *Ladies' Literary Cabinet*, May 29, 1819.
6. "Idiotic DOT Takes a Walk on the Wild Side," *New York Post*, November 13, 2008, https://nypost.com/2008/11/13/idiotic-dot-takes-a-walk-on-the-wild-side/; John Cassidy, "Battle of the Bike Lanes," *New Yorker*, March 8, 2011, https://www.newyorker.com/news/john-cassidy/battle-of-the-bike-lanes.
7. Arthur P.S. Hyde Diaries, 1892–1896, vol. III, 103, New-York Historical Society, New York.
8. Maria E. Ward, *The Common Sense of Bicycling: Bicycling for Ladies with Hints as to the Art of Wheeling—Advice to Beginners—Dress—Care of the Bicycle—Mechanics—Training—Exercise, Etc. Etc.* (New York: Brentano's, 1896), 1.
9. Joan Joy to Robert Moses, 26 November 1939, Box 102468, Folder 46, Records of the Department of Parks, Parks Commissioner and General Files, Municipal Archives, New York, NY; Marlene Sciascia to John Lindsay, 20 October 1966, Box 103295, Folder 53, Records of the Department of Parks, Parks Commissioner and General Files, Municipal Archives, New York, NY; Alan Goldman to Robert Wagner, 2

February 1958, Box 102957, Folder 21, Records of the Department of Parks, Parks
Commissioner and General Files, Municipal Archives, New York, NY; Neil Langley
to Robert Moses, 28 November 1939, Box 102412, Folder 17, Records of the Department of Parks, Parks Commissioner and General Files, Municipal Archives, New York,
NY; Alice M. Elting et al. to Robert Moses, 19 October 1939, Box 102467, Folder
90, Records of the Department of Parks, Parks Commissioner and General Files,
Municipal Archives, New York, NY; New York City Department of Parks, *Program
of Proposed Facilities for Bicycling* (New York, 1938).

10. As always, the historical record is far from complete. For some of the periods, I have
been forced to rely on newspapers and magazines more than I would have liked. For
most of the book, archival records complement, amplify, and correct the voluminous
contemporary media coverage.

11. There is already an excellent cycling history of Wisconsin: Jesse J. Gant and Nicho-
las J. Hoffman, *Wheel Fever: How Wisconsin Became a Great Bicycling State* (Madison: Wisconsin Historical Society Press, 2013). And Lorenz Finison's fine study of
another American city: *Boston's Cycling Craze, 1880–1900: A Story of Race, Sport,
and Society* (Amherst: University of Massachusetts Press, 2014).

12. With many thanks to the anonymous reviewer for making the toilet analogy for me.

1. Rough Start

1. "Velocipede," *New-York Columbian*, May 22, 1819; "Hobby Horses," *Ladies' Literary Cabinet*, May 29, 1819. For more on the prehistory of the bicycle, see Tony Hadland and Hans-Erhard Lessing, *Bicycle Design: An Illustrated History* (Cambridge,
MA: MIT Press, 2014), 8–28; David V. Herlihy, *Bicycle: The History* (New Haven: Yale
University Press, 2004), 15–71.

2. "Velocipede," *New-York Columbian*, May 22, 1819; "Velocipede," *New-York Colum-
bian*, May 25, 1819; "The Velocipede," *New-York Daily Advertiser*, May 22, 1819;
"The Velocipede," *New-York Evening Post*, May 21, 1819; "Velocipede," *New-York
Columbian*, June 15, 1819; "Velocipede," *New-York Columbian*, June 18, 1819.

3. "Velocipede Hoax," *Ladies' Literary Cabinet*, June 5, 1819, 32; "Ladies' Velocipede,"
Ladies' Literary Cabinet, July 31, 1819, 96; "A Velocipede of Fifty Years Ago," *Harper's Weekly*, March 6, 1859, 149.

4. The official minutes of the Common Council offer no rationale for the ban. *Minutes
of the Common Council of the City of New York: Volume X, September 7, 1818 to
February 28, 1820* (New York: The City of New York, 1917), 511; "A Law," (New York)
Commercial Advertiser, August 30, 1919. A similar law had already been passed in
Philadelphia. "Philadelphia; Velocipede," *New-York Daily Advertiser*, June 6, 1919.
The ban even made an appearance in the landmark Supreme Court case *Gibbons
v. Ogden*. One of the questions in the case was whether New York could regulate
steamboats, an invention patented by the federal government. The New York ban on
velocipedes was presented as an example of how New York can, in fact, regulate the
use of a federally patented device. *Gibbons v. Ogden* 22 U.S. 1 (1824); *Reports of*

Cases Argued and Adjudged in the Supreme Court of United States, February Term, 1824 (New York: Banks & Brothers Law Publishers, 1883), 151.

5. There were some children who used velocipedes in the interim, often with more than two wheels.

6. "Velocipede," *New-York Columbian*, May 25, 1819.

7. "Topics of To-Day," *Brooklyn Daily Eagle*, June 8, 1868.

8. Louis Kellner, Velocipede, US Patent 19,092, issued January 12, 1858.

9. For more on the invention and development of the bicycle, see Herlihy, *Bicycle*, 75–101; Hadland and Lessing, *Bicycle Design*, 37–53; Paul Smethurst, *The Bicycle—Towards a Global History* (Basingstoke: Palgrave Macmillan, 2015), 12–66.

10. For more on the creation of New York's grid, see *The Greatest Grid: The Master Plan of Manhattan 1811–2011*, ed. Hilary Ballon (New York: Columbia University Press, 2012); Gerard Koeppel, *City on a Grid: How New York Became New York* (Boston: Da Capo Press, 2015).

11. For more on the Erie Canal, see Peter L. Bernstein, *Wedding of the Waters: The Erie Canal and the Making of a Great Nation* (New York: Norton, 2006). For more on the development of New York during this period, see Edwin G. Burrows and Mike Wallace, *Gotham: A History of New York City to 1898* (New York: Oxford University Press, 1999), 429–905.

12. Francis Guy, *Winter Scene in Brooklyn*, circa 1819–1820, Oil on canvas, Brooklyn Museum.

13. "Topics of To-Day," *Brooklyn Daily Eagle*, June 8, 1868; "Topics of To-Day," *Brooklyn Daily Eagle*, September 21, 1868; "History of the Velocipede," *Velocipedist*, February 1869, 1–2; "Our Paper," *Velocipedist*, February 1869, 1; "General City News," *New York Times*, September 4, 1868; J. T. Goddard, *The Velocipede; Its History, Varieties, and Practice* (New York: Hurd and Houghton, 1869), iv.

14. "The Velocipede in a Medical Point of View," *Velocipedist*, February 1869, 6.

15. "Velocipedes," *Brooklyn Daily Eagle*, September 4, 1868; "Topics of To-Day," *Brooklyn Daily Eagle*, September 21, 1868; Hadland and Lessing, *Bicycle Design*, 63. Several historians cite the Boston Bicycle Club, which began in 1878, as the first bicycle club in the country. See, for example, Norman L. Dunham, "The Bicycle Era in American History" (PhD diss., Harvard University, 1956), 196.

16. "Our Paper," *Velocipedist*, February 1869, 1. For more on the competing designs of New York bike builders, see Hadland and Lessing, *Bicycle Design*, 68. For another example of a New Yorker designing a decidedly American version of the velocipede, see Gary W. Sanderson, "Velocipede-Mania in the USA (1868–1869), and the 'New American Improved Velocipede' by A. T. Demarest & Co. in New York City," in *Cycle History 19: Proceedings of the 19th International Cycling History Conference, Saint-Etienne, France, June 25–28 2008* (Cheltenham, UK: John Pinkerton Memorial Pub. Fund, 2010), 8–18.

17. "Correspondence," *Velocipedist*, March 1869, 3.

18. "Velocipede Riding Schools," *Velocipedist*, February 1869, 3; "Empire City Velocipedrome," *Velocipedist*, April 1869, 3; "Velocipedes," *New York Times*, January 27, 1869; "Velocipede Notes," *New York Times*, February 26, 1869; "The First Velocipede Reception in Brooklyn," *New York Times*, February 28, 1869; "Velocipede Items,"

New York Times, March 8, 1869; "Velocipedes" *New York Times*, March 9, 1869; "Velocipede Items," *New York Times*, March 20, 1869; "Velocipede Matters," *New York Times*, May 22, 1869; "Velocipede Matters," *New York Times*, June 1, 1869; Dunham, "The Bicycle Era in American History," 76, 82; "New Velocipede School," *Brooklyn Daily Eagle*, February 23, 1869; "New Velocipede School," *Brooklyn Daily Eagle*, March 20, 1869; "Schools," *Velocipedist*, March 1869, 4. Though the fees varied, one school advertised membership rates of $15 for the first month and $7.50 a month thereafter. Many schools did offer a discount for those who purchased a bicycle from them. "Velocipede Talk," *Brooklyn Daily Eagle*, February 19, 1869; "The First Gymnacyclidium," Printed Ephemera Collection, Lot 10632–3, Library of Congress, Washington, DC.

19. "Brick Pomery on a Velocipede," *Velocipedist*, April 1869, 7; "Velocipede Talk," *Brooklyn Daily Eagle*, March 2, 1869.

20. Dunham, "The Bicycle Era in American History," 105–8. For more on early racing, see Andrew Ritchie, *Quest for Speed: A History of Early Bicycle Racing 1868–1903* (El Cerrito, CA: Published by the author, 2011); Andrew Ritchie, "The Beginnings of Trans-Atlantic Bicycle Racing: Harry Etherington and the Anglo-French Team in America, 1879–80," *The International Journal of the History of Sport* 15, no. 3 (1998): 125–41.

21. "Velocipede Talk," *Brooklyn Daily Eagle*, March 1, 1869; "Velocipede Talk," *Brooklyn Daily Eagle*, February 9, 1869; "Velocipede Riding Schools," *Velocipedist*, February 1869, 3.

22. "The Future of the Bicycle," *Velocipedist*, February 1869, 2; "Velocipede Matters," *New York Times*, March 10, 1869.

23. "The First Gymnacyclidium," Printed Ephemera Collection, Lot 10632–3, Library of Congress, Washington, DC.

24. "Velocipede Talk," *Brooklyn Daily Eagle*, March 5, 1869; Advertisement, *Velocipedist*, February 1869, 7.

25. "Velocipedes for Ladies," *Velocipedist*, March 1869, 2; "Correspondence," *Velocipedist*, March 1869, 3.

26. "Velocipedes," *Brooklyn Daily Eagle*, January 20, 1869; "Velocipedes for Ladies," *Velocipedist*, March 1869, 2; "Velocipede Talk," *Brooklyn Daily Eagle*, March 30, 1869; "Velox," *Velocipedes, Bicycles, and Tricycles: How to Make and How to Use Them with a Sketch of their History, Invention, and Progress* (London: George Routledge and Sons, 1869), 59; "Velocipede Items," *New York Times*, March 8, 1869.

27. Caitlin S. Cohn, "Wheelwomen: Women's Dress in Transatlantic Cycling Culture, 1868–1900" (PhD diss., University of Minnesota, 2016), 64–68; "Velocipede Talk," *Brooklyn Daily Eagle*, February 18, 1869; "Velocipede Matters," *New York Times*, April 14, 1869.

28. Currier & Ives, *The Velocipede*, 1869, Museum of the City of New York, New York.

29. "The Velocipede Furor," *New York Times*, February 19, 1869; "A Velocipede Race," *New York Times*, March 28, 1869; "Velocipede Matters," *New York Times*, April 17, 1869; Dunham, "The Bicycle Era in American History," 121–22.

30. "Velocipede Talk," *Brooklyn Daily Eagle*, February 18, 1869. For excellent analyses of women and the city during this period, see Christine Stansell, *City of Women: Sex and Class in New York, 1789–1860* (Urbana: University of Illinois Press, 1987); Timothy

J. Gilfoyle, *City of Eros: New York City, Prostitution, and the Commercialization of Sex, 1790–1920* (New York: Norton, 1992); Mary P. Ryan, *Women in Public: Between Banners and Ballots, 1825–1880* (Baltimore: Johns Hopkins University Press, 1992).

31. "Velocipede Talk," *Brooklyn Daily Eagle*, February 22, 1869; "Notes on the Veloci-pede," *Scientific American*, January 30, 1869; "Topics of To-Day," *Brooklyn Daily Eagle*, December 1, 1868; "Miscellaneous," *Velocipedist*, March 1869, 6.

32. "Velocipede Talk," *Brooklyn Daily Eagle*, March 22, 1869.

33. "Velocipedes," *New York Times*, January 27, 1869; Hadland and Lessing, *Bicycle Design*, 69.

34. *Thirteenth Annual Report of the Board of Commissioners of the Central Park for the Year Ending December 31, 1869* (New York, 1870), 141.

35. "Notes on the Velocipede," *Scientific American*, January 30, 1869; "The Velocipede Furor," *New York Times*, February 15, 1869; Dunham, "The Bicycle Era in American History," 111–12; "Velocipede Matters," *New York Times*, April 14, 1869. For more on the early history of Central Park, see Roy Rosenzweig and Elizabeth Blackmar, *The Park and the People: A History of Central Park* (Ithaca: Cornell University Press, 1992).

36. *Minutes of Proceedings of the Board of Commissioners of the Central Park for the Year Ending April 30th, 1869* (New York: Evening Post Steam Presses, 1869), 71–79. See also Dunham, "The Bicycle Era in American History," 111–12; "Topics of To-Day," *Brooklyn Daily Eagle*, October 19, 1868; "Topics of To-Day," *Brooklyn Daily Eagle*, December 1, 1868; "The Velocipede," *Brooklyn Daily Eagle*, December 4, 1868; "Mis-cellaneous," *Velocipedist*, March, 1869, 6.

37. "The Velocipede in New-York Streets," *New York Times*, May 3, 1869.

38. "Velocipedes on the Sidewalks," *Brooklyn Daily Eagle*, April 14, 1869; "Velocipedes," *Brooklyn Daily Eagle*, April 20, 1869.

39. *Minutes of the Brooklyn Common Council* (New York, 1874), 1355–56; "Special Notices," *Brooklyn Daily Eagle*, January 10, 1874; "Current Events," *Brooklyn Daily Eagle*, June 19, 1876; "Velocipeding," *Brooklyn Daily Eagle*, May 21, 1873; "Veloci-pedes" *Brooklyn Daily Eagle*, June 11, 1873; "The Aldermen," *Brooklyn Daily Eagle*, June 10, 1873. There were scattered complaints about the new ordinance. In a letter to the editor, one rider complained that the aldermen were depriving users of "a great pleasure and splendid exercise" that was certainly safer than carriages. Another sug-gested that a speed limit, rather than a prohibition, was the answer and that a much bigger problem was "incompetent women driving horses." "Velocipedes: They Cause Fewer Accidents than Carriages" and "Regulate Their Speed—More Danger from Women Driving," *Brooklyn Daily Eagle*, June 18, 1873.

40. *Thirteenth Annual Report of the Board of Commissioners of the Central Park for the Year Ending December 31, 1869* (New York, 1870), 141; *Minutes of the Brooklyn Com-mon Council* (New York, 1874), 1355–56; "Velocipede Exhibition," *New York Times*, July 28, 1869; "The Velocipede," *Brooklyn Daily Eagle*, June 28, 1869; "Local Brevi-ties," *Brooklyn Daily Eagle*, May 24, 1873; "Questions Answered," *Brooklyn Daily Eagle*, May 6, 1877.

41. Dunham, "The Bicycle Era in American History," 123–39; "Velocipede Talk," *Brook-lyn Daily Eagle*, March 7, 1869; "A Velocipede Race," *New York Times*, March 28, 1869; "Bicycles," *New York Times*, November 1, 1872.

42. For more on the development of the high-wheeler, see Hadland and Lessing, *Bicycle Design*, 84–120; Herlihy, *Bicycle*, 159–71. For more on Albert Pope and the nascent American bicycle industry, see Stephen B. Goddard, *Colonel Albert Pope and His American Dream Machines: The Life and Times of a Bicycle Tycoon Turned Automotive Pioneer* (Jefferson, NC: McFarland, 2000); Bruce D. Epperson, *Peddling Bicycles to America: The Rise of an Industry* (Jefferson, NC: McFarland, 2010).

43. One of the other seats of American cycling culture was Boston. For more on that city's experience, see Lorenz J. Finison, *Boston's Cycling Craze, 1880–1900: A Story of Race, Sport, and Society* (Amherst: University of Massachusetts Press, 2014). For more on high-wheel track racing, see Dunham, "The Bicycle Era in American History," chapter 10.

44. Second Annual Dinner of the Citizens Bicycle Club Program, February 26, 1886, 42.250.3, Museum of the City of New York Archives; Dunham, "The Bicycle Era in American History," 253–54.

45. Mark Twain wrote memorably about his experience learning to ride a high-wheeler: "You do it in this way: you hop along behind it on your right foot, resting the other on the mounting-peg, and grasping the tiller with your hands. At the word, you rise on the peg, stiffen your left leg, hang your other one around in the air in a general and indefinite way, lean your stomach against the rear of the saddle, and then fall off, maybe on one side, maybe on the other; but you fall off. You get up and do it again; and once more; and then several times." Mark Twain, *The Complete Essays of Mark Twain* (New York: Da Capo Press, 2000), 553. For more on the development of tricycles in this era, see Herlihy, *Bicycle*, 208–14; Dunham, "The Bicycle Era in American History," chapter 7. For more on women, and women racers, on the high-wheelers, see M. Ann Hall, *Muscle on Wheels: Louise Armaindo and the High-Wheel Racers of Nineteenth-Century America* (Montreal: McGill-Queens University Press, 2018).

46. Some early riders may have been European immigrants who may not have been perceived as white at the time. For more on race, immigrants, and whiteness, see Matthew Frye Jacobson, *Whiteness of a Different Color: European Immigrants and the Alchemy of Race* (Cambridge, MA: Harvard University Press, 1998).

47. Dunham, "The Bicycle Era in American History," 181; "Wheelmen in New York," *Harper's Weekly*, July 17, 1886, 455.

48. "Bicycles—Ordinance in Relation to the Use of Bicycles," *Brooklyn Daily Eagle*, May 22, 1880; "The Aldermen," *Brooklyn Daily Eagle*, April 27, 1880.

49. "Very Sad," *Brooklyn Daily Eagle*, October 20, 1880.

50. "Bicycles," *Brooklyn Daily Eagle*, November 19, 1880.

51. *Supreme Court, City and County of New York, General Term. In the Matter of the Application of William M. Wright, S. Conant Foster and Henry H. Walker, to be Released from Custody on a Writ of Habeas Corpus* (New York: Evening Post Job Printing Office, 1882), 101–102; *Minutes and Documents of the Board of Commissioners of the Department of Public Parks for the year ending April 30th 1881* (New York: Martin B. Brown, 1881), 143–44, 321.

52. *Minutes and Documents of the Board of Commissioners of the Department of Public Parks for the year ending April 30th 1881* (New York: Martin B. Brown, 1881), 143–44, 321. For more on Andrew Haswell Green, see George Alexander Mazaraki,

"The Public Career of Andrew Haswell Green" (PhD diss., New York University, 1966).

53. Subject Files, Box 21, Folder Bicycling, 1880–1938, Kirk Munroe Papers, Manuscript Division, Library of Congress, Washington, DC; *Minutes and Documents of the Board of Commissioners of the Department of Public Parks for the year ending April 30th 1881* (New York: Martin B. Brown, 1881), 548–49, 605.

54. *Minutes and Documents of the Board of Commissioners of the Department of Public Parks for the year ending April 30th 1881* (New York: Martin B. Brown, 1881), 508, 519, 520; *Minutes and Documents of the Board of Commissioners of the Department of Public Parks for the year ending April 30th 1882* (New York: Martin B. Brown, 1882), 25, 184.

55. "Spokes," *Brentano's*, December 1880, 295–96.

56. *Supreme Court, City and County of New York, General Term*, 6–52.

57. *Supreme Court, City and County of New York, General Term*, 92, 98, 101–102, 152.

58. The defense went out of its way to underscore that bicycles were recreational, not practical or commercial vehicles. Lawyers for the city hoped to paint a different picture. On cross-examination, they asked if bicycles were sometimes used for business and whether or not riders ever used them to carry packages. *Supreme Court, City and County of New York, General Term*, v, 29, 52, 88.

59. *Supreme Court, City and County of New York, General Term*, 319. For more on the legal battles over the park, see Evan Friss, *The Cycling City: Bicycles and Urban America in the 1890s* (Chicago: University of Chicago Press, 2015), 66–69.

60. Friss, *The Cycling City*, 67–69; *Minutes and Documents of the Board of Commissioners of the Department of Public Parks for the year ending April 30th 1884* (New York: Martin B. Brown, 1884), 94, 128, 351; "Wheelmen in New York," *Harper's Weekly*, July 17, 1886, 455.

61. *Minutes and Documents of the Board of Commissioners of the Department of Public Parks for the year ending April 30th 1885* (New York: Martin B. Brown, 1885), 82; *Supreme Court, City and County of New York, General Term*, 54, 174.

62. *Twenty-Fourth Annual Report of the Brooklyn Park Commissioners for the Year 1884* (Brooklyn, 1885), 12.

63. Admission badges to Central Park would be honored at Prospect Park too. *Twenty-Fifth Annual Report of the Brooklyn Park Commissioners for the Year 1885* (Brooklyn, 1886), 38–41, 52.

64. *New York Laws*, chapter 704 (1887); *Minutes and Documents of the Board of Commissioners of the Department of Public Parks for the year ending April 30th 1888* (New York: The Evening Post Job Printing Office, 1888), 49–50, 78.

65. The Laws of New York (2018), Consolidated Laws, Highway, Article 11, Section 316.

2. Up and Down

1. See, for example, "Gossip of the Cyclers," *New York Times*, March 13, 1898, and "Mighty Army on Wheel," *Boston Globe*, July 5, 1896, in Newspaper Clippings

Related to Cycling and Cycling Clubs, New-York Historical Society, New York. For more on the cycling boom of the 1890s in the United States and elsewhere, see Evan Friss, *The Cycling City: Bicycles and Urban America in the 1890s* (Chicago: University of Chicago Press, 2015); Robert L. McCullough, *Old Wheelways: Traces of Bicycle History on the Land* (Cambridge, MA: MIT Press, 2015); David V. Herlihy, *Bicycle: The History* (New Haven, CT: Yale University Press, 2004), 225–305; Lorenz Finison, *Boston's Cycling Craze, 1880–1900: A Story of Race, Sport, and Society* (Amherst: University of Massachusetts Press, 2014); Glen Norcliffe, *The Ride to Modernity: The Bicycle in Canada, 1869–1900* (Toronto: University of Toronto Press, 2001); Paul Smethurst, *The Bicycle: Towards a Global History* (New York: Palgrave Macmillan, 2015); Anne-Katrin Ebert, "Cycling Towards the Nation: The Use of the Bicycle in Germany and the Netherlands, 1880–1940," *European Review of History* 11, no. 3 (Autumn 2004): 347–64.

2. *New York Bicycle Directory: A Hand-book of Manufacturers of Bicycles, Tires, Bells, Lamps, Saddles, Tools, and Accessories in New York City* (New York: New Bicycle Directory Publishing Co., 1896).

3. Arthur P.S. Hyde Diaries, 1892–1896, vol. I, 39–41, New-York Historical Society, New York.

4. For more on the development of the safety bicycle, see Herlihy, *Bicycle*, 225–54; Tony Hadland and Hans-Erhard Lessing, *Bicycle Design: An Illustrated History* (Cambridge, MA: MIT Press, 2014), chapter 5.

5. Hyde diaries, vol. I, 3, 39–41.

6. Hyde diaries, vol. I, 35, 37; vol. III, 71–72, 76; vol. IV, 19–21.

7. Hyde diaries, vol. I, 35, 37; vol. III, 71–72, 76; vol. IV, 19–21. For more on the rise of the bicycle industry, see Bruce D. Epperson, *Peddling Bicycles to America: The Rise of an Industry* (Jefferson, NC: McFarland, 2010).

8. *Social Register* (New York), November 1897, 194; "The Rev. Arthur P.S. Hyde Dies; Holyrood Rector and Ex-Colonel," *New York Herald Tribune*, December 28, 1943. In 1890, there were 639,943 immigrants in New York. By 1900 that number swelled to 1,270,080. For more on immigration, see Tyler Anbinder, *City of Dreams: The 400-Year Epic History of Immigrant New York* (Boston: Houghton Mifflin Harcourt, 2016).

9. U.S. Bureau of Labor, "July 1900: Bulletin of the United States Bureau of Labor, No. 29, Volume V," *Bulletin of the United States Bureau of Labor, Nos. 1–100* (July 1900); Leonora O'Reilly Papers, Reel 1, Cash Account Book in *Papers of the Women's Trade Union League and Its Principal Leaders* (Woodbridge, CT: Published for the Schlesinger Library, Radcliffe College by Research Publication, 1981); Brittany Sage Chevalier, "The Relationship of Transportation Technology to Women's Expanded Independence: The Case of the Bicycle and Subway in New York City, 1890 to World War I" (master's thesis, Sarah Lawrence College, 2013), 15–17. For more on the cost of bicycles at the time, see Friss, *The Cycling City*, 42–45.

10. Hyde diaries, vol. I, 8–16; vol. II, 19, 35; vol. III, 22, 79; vol. IV, 41; "Captain Hyde to Act as Aide" (New York) *Evening Telegram*, May 21, 1896. It is not entirely clear where Hyde would have parked at the Polo Grounds. He might have just camped out deep in center field where spectators, horses, and carriages lingered. Or he might have left his wheels somewhere outside the ballpark.

11. "Joseph A. Farley's New and Artistic Dwellings," *Real Estate Record and Builders' Guide*, November 5, 1898; "A New Departure in Apartment Houses," *Real Estate Record and Builders' Guide*, April 29, 1899, 763; "The Cherbourg," *Real Estate Record and Builders' Guide*, November 10, 1900, 619.

12. *Wheel and Cycle Trade Review*, May 15, 1896, 74.

13. Hyde diaries, vol. I, 36; vol. II, 58; vol. III, 61, 64.

14. Hyde diaries, vol. III, 82, 94, 103, 104, 135; vol. IV, 9, 67, 71, 75, 80–84, 97, 104; Department of Commerce—Bureau of the Census, *Sixteenth Census of the United States: 1940. Population Schedule.*

15. For more on the evolution of dating, see Beth L. Bailey's excellent book, *From the Front Porch to the Back Seat: Courtship in Twentieth-Century America* (Baltimore: Johns Hopkins University Press, 1988).

16. Having searched the *New York Times* and the *Brooklyn Daily Eagle* for references to bicycle clubs and having examined the *Brooklyn Daily Eagle Almanac* (Brooklyn: Press of Brooklyn Daily Eagle Book and Job Department, 1894, 1895, 1897, 1898) and the *New York Bicycle Directory*, I found mention of 221 different clubs. Although extensive, my investigation was hardly exhaustive; there were surely many more clubs. As of last count (in 2015) there were 252 Starbucks locations in Manhattan and Brooklyn. Center for an Urban Future, "State of the Chains, 2015," accessed July 21, 2017, https://nycfuture.org/pdf/State-of-the-Chains-2015-5.pdf.

17. "A Model Cyclers' Club," *New York Times*, June 10, 1894; "The Long Island Wheelmen," *New York Times*, October 29, 1887.

18. Tiffany & Co. Engagement Books, Tiffany & Co. Archives; Map of Asphalt and Macadam Roads in League of American Wheelmen, *Fifty Miles Around New York: A Book of Maps and Descriptions of the Best Roads, Streets and Routes for Cyclists and Horsemen* (New York: New York State Division of the League of American Wheelmen, 1896); Tiffany & Co. Archives, "Tiffany and Company Bicycles, 1885–1901: A Research Report by the Tiffany & Co. Archives," January 8, 1016; The Metropolitan Museum of Art, "The Magnolia Vase," accessed May 1, 2017, http://www.metmuseum.org/toah/works-of-art/99.2/; Sotheby's, "The Ptarmigan Vase," accessed May 1, 2017, http://www.sothebys.com/en/auctions/ecatalogue/2011/important-americana-including-american-stoneware-assembled-by-mr-and-mrs-edwin-hochberg-n08710/lot.114.html; "Wheeled Around the Island," *Brooklyn Daily Eagle*, August 10, 1895; "Run of the Tiffany Wheelmen," *New York Times*, June 9, 1895.

19. "L.A.W. Membership Report," *New York Times*, September 12, 1897; Philip P. Mason, "The League of American Wheelmen and the Good Roads Movement: 1880–1905" (PhD diss., University of Michigan, 1957), 50; "Observations of the Month," *LAW Magazine*, August 1900, 1.

20. Hyde diaries, vol. IV, 38, 40; "New York to West Point by Wheel," *The LAW Bulletin and Good Roads*, July 5, 1895, 19–21; Arthur P. Stanley-Hyde, "A Pleasant Run Across Long Island," *The LAW Bulletin and Good Roads*, July 26, 1895, 13–14; "A Tour of New York's Parks," *The LAW Bulletin and Good Roads*, August 16, 1895, 15–17; League of American Wheelmen, *Fifty Miles Around New York*. See also, "A Test of the Bicycle for Military Purposes," *The LAW Bulletin and Good Roads*, July 19, 1895, 13–15.

21. For more on bicycle paths, see Friss, *The Cycling City*, chapter 5.

22. For more on the Coney Island Cycle Path, the proposed Brooklyn Bridge path, and the bicycle's place on the newly opened Williamsburg Bridge, see McCullough, *Old Wheelways*, 220–32, 258–66.

23. "Thousands of Cyclists Out," *Brooklyn Daily Eagle*, June 15, 1895. Unlike the *Eagle*, a colonel commended Hyde on his fine work: "It was a task a great many men would have shrunk from." In his diary, Hyde teased back, "I think that's pretty strong language, don't you?" Hyde diaries, vol. III, 58–61.

24. "Big Parade on Wheels," *New York Times*, June 7, 1896; Hyde diaries, vol. IV, 90.

25. Hyde diaries, vol. IV, 105, 108–9.

26. "Wheelmen's Big Pageant," *New York Times*, June 6, 1896.

27. "News for the Wheelmen," *New York Times*, July 14, 1897.

28. Petter Joffre Nye, Jeff Froman, and Mark Tyson, *The Six-Day Bicycle Races* (San Francisco: Van der Plas Publications, Cycle Publishing, 2006), 28–29; Charles Meinert, "Single Sixes in Madison Square Garden," in *Cycle History: Proceedings of the 7th International Cycle History Conference, Buffalo, New York, September 4–6, 1996*, ed. Rob van der Plas (San Francisco: Van der Plas Publications, Cycle Publishing, 1997), 57–64.

29. Hyde diaries, vol. III, 92, 94–96, 133; "Captain Hyde to Act as Aide," (New York) *Evening Telegram*, May 21, 1896.

30. Hyde diaries, vol. III, 95; vol. IV, 51.

31. Hyde diaries, vol. I, 7–10; vol. II, 66; vol. III, 74; vol. IV, 31, 36; "Unsightly New York Statues," *New York Times*, May 7, 1899.

32. Hyde diaries, vol. IV, 64; vol. II, 36–37; "News for the Wheelmen," *New York Times*, July 18, 1897. For more on the good roads movement, see Michael R. Fein, *Paving the Way: New York Road Building and the American State, 1880–1956* (Lawrence: University Press of Kansas, 2008), 27; Mason, "The League of American Wheelmen and the Good Roads Movement."

33. "News for the Wheelmen," *New York Times*, July 18, 1897.

34. Thanks to Robert L. McCullough for, by way of his fine book, pointing me to this image of the "ribbons." McCullough, *Old Wheelways*, 249.

35. Hyde diaries, vol. I, 34, for example.

36. Hyde diaries, vol. III, 70–71, 76, 93, 94, 120, 130–31; vol. IV, 7. Even when the temperature dropped to 18 degrees Fahrenheit, Hyde still cycled. Hyde diaries, vol. IV, 17–18.

37. Hyde diaries, vol. IV, 13–15.

38. H. Paul Jeffers, *Commissioner Roosevelt: The Story of Theodore Roosevelt and the New York City Police, 1895–1897* (New York: Wiley, 1994), 207–8.

39. *Theodore Roosevelt: An Autobiography* (New York: Macmillan, 1913), 201–3.

40. Hyde diaries, vol. III, 31–32; vol. IV, 42–43.

41. Hyde diaries, vol. III, 26–28. For more on the Croton Aqueduct path, see McCullough, *Old Wheelways*, 251–54.

42. As quoted in Jeffers, *Commissioner Roosevelt*, 206.

43. *General Ordinances of the City of New York under the Greater New York Charter* (New York: Banks Law Publishing Co., 1902), 128–30; Friss, *The Cycling City*, 71–77.

Though there were cars in New York in the 1890s, they were rare. For more on the early period of motoring in cities and New York in particular, see Clay McShane, *Down the Asphalt Path: The Automobile and the American City* (New York: Columbia University Press, 1995); Mike Wallace, *Greater Gotham: A History of New York City from 1898 to 1919* (New York: Oxford University Press, 2017), 240–50.

44. Hyde diaries, vol. III, 98–99; vol. IV, 17–18.

45. Hyde diaries, vol. II, 59; vol. III, 41–43, 46–50, 68–69, 91–92, 102, 106, 130–31.

46. "Furnishings of 18-Room Ward Mansion, Landmark on Grymes Hill since 1867, Will be Sold at Auction," October 8, 1942, in Maria (Violet) Ward Clippings File, Staten Island Historical Society, NY; "Death List of a Day," *New York Times*, January 17, 1901; C. G. Hine, *History and Legend of Howard Avenue and the Serpentine Road, Grymes Hill, Staten Island* (New York: Hines Brothers Printer, 1914), 74–75. Violet was a descendent of three generations of men named Samuel Ward—the first, a governor of the Rhode Island colony; the second, a lieutenant colonel in the Revolutionary War; and a third, a wealthy banker in early nineteenth-century New York. Roger Williams, who founded Rhode Island and famously advocated for the separation of church and state, and Julia Ward Howe, the poet who penned "The Battle Hymn of the Republic," were also celebrated relatives. Violet's mother, whom she closely resembled, died in 1877, when Violet was fourteen. "Miss Maria E. M'K. Ward," *New York Times*, September 11, 1941; "Death List of a Day," *New York Times*, January 17, 1901.

47. Violet Ward Copy Books, 1878, Box MS 4, Folder 2, Ward Family Papers, Staten Island Historical Society, NY; Violet Ward Report Card, December 1880, Folder 11, Ward Family Papers, Staten Island Historical Society, NY; *Tenth Census of the United States: 1880*, Richmond Co., NY, schedule 1, p. 22, dwelling 178, family 204; "Incidents in Society," *New-York Tribune*, December 27, 1889; "Now for the Horse Show," *New-York Tribune*, November 8, 1896; "The Week in Society," *New-York Tribune*, March 27, 1898; "City and Suburban News," *New York Times*, May 12, 1884.

48. "Golf Title at Stake," *New-York Tribune*, May 26, 1908; "Golfing Favorites Come Through," *New-York Tribune*, May 28, 1908; Ward Sisters Club Cards, undated, Folder 21, Ward Family Papers, Staten Island Historical Society, NY; Pierre Jay to Violet Ward, 25 February 1899, Folder 4, Ward Family Papers, Staten Island Historical Society, NY.

49. Staten Island Bicycle Store to Isaac B. Potter, 18 October 1895, in Newspaper Clippings Related to Cycling and Cycling Clubs, New-York Historical Society, New York.

50. "The Gentle Arts of Taking on Muscle," *Illustrated American*, April 27, 1895, 542; "The Michaux Club's Opening," *New York Times*, November 12, 1895; "Society's Cycling Club," *New York Times*, December 10, 1894.

51. "The Gentle Arts of Taking on Muscle," *Illustrated American*, April 27, 1895, 542; "Society's Cycling Club," *New York Times*, December 10, 1894; A. H. Godfrey, "Cycling Clubs and their Spheres of Action," *Outing*, July 1897, 347–49; Kathleen Mathew, "The Bicycle in Society," *Peterson Magazine*, June 1895, 599–605. For more on the history of the High Bridge, see Gwynneth C. Malin, "The High Bridge," *Place Matters*, accessed December 2016, http://www.placematters.net/node/1926.

52. "Cycling," *Outing*, January 1895, 82; "The Wheel," *Godey's Magazine*, May 1895, 554; "Costumes at Michaux Club," *New York Times*, March 15, 1895.

53. "Mrs. Minor Won the Race," *New York Times*, January 18, 1895; "Nelson Won the Race," *New York Times*, January 12, 1896. For more on the history of women's racing during this period, see Roger Gilles, *Women on the Move: The Forgotten Era of Women's Bicycle Racing* (Lincoln: University of Nebraska Press, 2018).
54. "News for the Wheelmen," *New York Times*, November 9, 1897. See also "A Host of Century Rides," *New York Times*, April 26, 1897; "Waverly Century Run," *Brooklyn Daily Eagle*, June 6, 1896. The riders were ultimately not sanctioned, as the Chairman of the National League of American Wheelmen Racing Board acknowledged that road races could be held on Sunday and with men and women racing together, since the road races organized by local clubs were not under his jurisdiction. "News for the Wheelmen," *New York Times*, November 16, 1897.
55. "Gossip of the Cyclers," *New York Times*, March 13, 1898.
56. Andrew Ritchie, *Major Taylor: The Extraordinary Career of a Champion Bicycle Racer* (Baltimore: Johns Hopkins University Press, 1988), 59–68; Friss, *The Cycling City*, 59–60. For more on Taylor, see Conrad Kerber and Terry Kerber, *Major Taylor: The Inspiring Story of a Black Cyclist and the Men who Helped him Achieve Worldwide Fame* (New York: Skyhorse Publishing, 2014).
57. Currier & Ives, "The Darktown Bicycle Race—A Sudden Halt: 'I konwd we'd have busted de record if it hadn't bin for dis misforchin,'" 1895, Library of Congress Prints and Photographs Division; Currier & Ives, "The Darktown Bicycle Club—Knocked Out: 'Dar! I knowed dem odd fellers was a breedin mischief,'" 1892, Library of Congress Prints and Photographs Division; Currier & Ives, "The Darktown Bicycle Club—On Parade: 'hooray for de rumatic! Don't she glide lubly,'" 1892, Library of Congress Prints and Photographs Division.
58. "Simmons Wants to Race," *New York Times*, May 24, 1894; "Race Committee Resigned," *New York Times*, June 16, 1894; "Holiday Road Run," *New York Times*, July 1, 1894. For more on black manhood and athletics, see Louis Moore, *I Fight for a Living: Boxing and the Battle for Black Manhood, 1880–1915* (Urbana: University of Illinois Press, 2017).
59. Receipt of LAW Dues, 4 April 1896, in Newspaper Clippings Related to Cycling and Cycling Clubs, New-York Historical Society, New York; Staten Island Bicycle Store to Isaac B. Potter, 1 August 1895, in Newspaper Clippings Related to Cycling and Cycling Clubs, New-York Historical Society, New York; Isaac B. Potter to Miss V. M. E. Ward, 10 August 1895, in Newspaper Clippings Related to Cycling and Cycling Clubs, New-York Historical Society, New York; Abbott Bassett to M.V.E. Ward, 25 April 1895, in Newspaper Clippings Related to Cycling and Cycling Clubs, New-York Historical Society, New York; Isaac Potter to M.V.E. Ward, undated, in Newspaper Clippings Related to Cycling and Cycling Clubs, New-York Historical Society, New York. For an interesting account of a mixed-race cyclist and her relationship to the LAW, see Lorenz J. Finison, *Boston's Cycling Craze, 1880–1900: A Story of Race, Sport, and Society* (Amherst: University of Massachusetts Press, 2014), chapter 1.
60. "The Social World," *New York Times*, June 26, 1895; Staten Island Bicycle Club, 1 June 1895, Box 3, MS 228, Staten Island Historical Society, NY. Ward and the keeper of the clubhouse, R. M. Dunne, had a bitter fight about who actually held the lease to the headquarters. While Ward changed the locks on the door to keep Dunne out,

Dunne accused Ward of having failed to pay the rent. He would not be the only one to charge Ward with financial neglect. "In a State of Siege," *New-York Tribune*, April 3, 1896.

61. Staten Island Bicycle Store to Isaac B. Potter, 18 October 1895, in Newspaper Clippings Related to Cycling and Cycling Clubs, New-York Historical Society, New York.

62. Staten Island Bicycle Store to Isaac B. Potter, 18 October 1895, in Newspaper Clippings Related to Cycling and Cycling Clubs, New-York Historical Society, New York; Receipt, 1 December 1895, Box 5, Folder 3, Ward Family Papers, Staten Island Historical Society, NY; "Two Enterprising Women," *Richmond County Advance*, November 9, 1895; M. E. Ward to Unadilla Tire Co., 24 June 1895, Box MS 4, Folder 5, Ward Family Papers, Staten Island Historical Society, NY; Various Receipts, 1895, Box 5, Folder 3, Ward Family Papers, Staten Island Historical Society, NY; Friss, *The Cycling City*, 23–25.

63. Ann Novotny, *Alice's World: The Life and Photography of an American Original, Alice Austen, 1866–1952* (Old Greenwich, CT: Chatham Press, 1976), 73–74; Alice E. Austen, [Group apparatus], May 23, 1893, Alice Austen Photograph Collection, Staten Island Historical Society, NY.

64. Carroll Smith-Rosenberg, "The New Woman as Androgyne: Social Disorder and Gender Crisis, 1870–1936," in *Disorderly Conduct: Visions of Gender in Victorian America*, ed. Carroll Smith-Rosenberg (New York: Knopf, 1985), 245–96; Martha H. Patterson, *Beyond the Gibson Girl: Reimaging the American New Woman, 1895–1915* (Urbana: University of Illinois Press, 2005); Lillian Faderman, *Odd Girls and Twilight Lovers: A History of Lesbian Life in Twentieth-Century America* (New York: Columbia University Press, 1991), chapter 1; Carroll Smith-Rosenberg, "The Female World of Love and Ritual: Relations Between Women in Nineteenth-Century America," in *Disorderly Conduct: Visions of Gender in Victorian America*, ed. Carroll Smith-Rosenberg (New York: Knopf, 1985), 53–76; Elizabeth L. Block, "Respecting Hair: The Culture and Representation of American Women's Hairstyles, 1865–90" (PhD diss., The City University of New York, 2011), 143–60. Like many other New Women, Ward became involved in local reform efforts, working, for example, with the State Charities Aid Association to support needy children. State Charities Aid Association, *Seventeenth Annual Report* (New York: The Association, 1889), iv. Austen's most memorable and provocative photograph was self-taken in 1891 (at 11 p.m. in the bedroom of Gertrude, the daughter of a minister no less); Austen and "Trude" are seen standing in skirted, sleeveless underwear, with their hair down, and wearing masks. They are inches apart, nearly kissing, with cigarettes in their mouths. Society women were not supposed to smoke, let their hair down, or have their arms exposed. Alice Austen, *Trude & I*, August 6, 1891, Alice Austen House, Staten Island, New York. For more on Austen's photography, see Jessica L. Roscio, "Photographic Domesticity: The Home/Studios of Alice Austen, Catharine Wee Barnes Ward, and Frances Benjamin Johnston, 1885–1915" (PhD diss., Boston University, 2013), chapter 1; Roscio, "Photographic Domesticity," 27. For an example of later New Yorkers identifying Ward as a lesbian, see Penny and Liza, "Alice Austen—Photographs," *Dyke* 3 (1976): 34–43.

65. Maria E. Ward, *The Common Sense of Bicycling: Bicycling for Ladies with Hints as to the Art of Wheeling—Advice to Beginners—Dress—Care of the Bicycle—Mechanics—Training—Exercise, Etc. Etc.* (New York: Brentano's, 1896), ix. For more on how Ward's manual fit into the larger context of how women adopted and wrote about bicycles, see Sarah Hallenbeck, *Claiming the Bicycle: Women, Rhetoric, and Technology in Nineteenth-Century America* (Carbondale: Southern Illinois University Press, 2016), esp. chapter 3. Ward promised to deliver the final manuscript to her publisher by the summer of 1895. Despite having earned a 100 in punctuality in grade school, Ward was running late. But in 1896 *The Common Sense of Bicycling* finally appeared. Royalty Contract, 1895, Box 5, Folder 12, Ward Family Papers, Staten Island Historical Society, NY; Frank Allen to Miss Ward, 13 January 1895, Box MS 4, Folder 5, Ward Family Papers, Staten Island Historical Society, NY. It is ironic that Ward was once commended for her punctuality since as an adult, she was often dogged for failing to pay her bills on time. See, for example, Henry Romeike to M. E. Ward, 8 October 1896, Folder 5, Ward Family Papers, Staten Island Historical Society, NY; Harbour Hill Golf Club to Violet Ward, 14 August 1899, Folder 21, Ward Family Papers, Staten Island Historical Society, NY; Pierre Jay to Violet Ward, 25 February 1899, Folder 4, Ward Family Papers, Staten Island Historical Society, NY.

66. Ward, *The Common Sense of Bicycling*, 4, 8–9, 12, 16–18, 35, 107–8, 112, 114, 118–23, 127, 157; M.E.G. McK Ward, Bodkin, US Patent 510,943, issued December 19, 1893; M. E. Ward to John Shepherd, 20 May 1909, Box MS 4, Folder 6, Ward Family Papers, Staten Island Historical Society, NY; Golf Club Drawings, undated, Box MS 4, Ward Family Papers, Staten Island Historical Society, NY. For more on women and their relationship to technology in this era, see Julie Wosk, *Women and the Machine: Representations from the Spinning Wheel to the Electronic Age* (Baltimore: Johns Hopkins University Press, 2003), esp. chapter 4.

67. Ward, *The Common Sense of Bicycling*, 107–8.

68. Ward, *The Common Sense of Bicycling*, 12–13, 48–49.

69. Ward, *The Common Sense of Bicycling*, 12.

70. Mary P. Ryan, *Women in Public: Between Banners and Ballots, 1825–1880* (Baltimore: Johns Hopkins University Press, 1992), 86; Friss, *The Cycling City*, 179–82. For more on how women negotiated public, urban space in this era, see Sarah Deutsch, *Women and the City: Gender, Space, and Power in Boston, 1870–1940* (New York: Oxford University Press, 2000); Christine Stansell, *City of Women: Sex and Class in New York 1789–1860* (Urbana: University of Illinois Press, 1987); Emily A. Remus, "Tippling Ladies and the Making of Consumer Culture: Gender and Public Space in *Fin-de-Siècle* Chicago," *Journal of American History* 101, no. 3 (2014): 751–77; Jessica Ellen Sewell, *Women and the Everyday City: Public Space in San Francisco, 1890–1915* (Minneapolis: University of Minnesota Press, 2011); Deborah Epstein Nord, *Walking the Victorian Streets: Women, Representation, and the City* (Ithaca: Cornell University Press, 1995).

71. Ward, *The Common Sense of Bicycling*, 115, 170.

72. Ward, *The Common Sense of Bicycling*, 172. For more on health and cycling in the 1890s, see Friss, *The Cycling City*, chapter 6. For more on how advertisers sought to promote cycling as a healthy activity for women in particular, see Ellen Gruber

Garvey, "Reframing the Bicycle: Advertising-Supporting Magazines and Scorching Women," *American Quarterly* 47, no. 1 (March 1995): 66–101.

73. Ward, *The Common Sense of Bicycling*, 27–29, 93–95. Patricia Marks, *Bicycles, Bangs, and Bloomers* (Lexington: University Press of Kentucky, 1990), chapter 6. Ward does, however, point out that "the clothing should be of one color or of colors that look well together." For more on wheelwomen and clothing, see Caitlin S. Cohn, "Wheel-women: Women's Dress in Transatlantic Cycling Culture, 1868–1900" (PhD diss., University of Minnesota, 2016).

74. "Woman's Wheeling Dress," *New York Times*, December 23, 1894. For more on Mary Sargent Hopkins (the source of the quote), see Finison, *Boston's Cycling Craze, 1880–1900*, chapter 2.

75. Ward, *The Common Sense of Bicycling*, 68, 78–79, 104.

76. "Wheels in House Decorations," *Cincinnati Enquirer*, November 18, 1896, in Newspaper Clippings Related to Cycling and Cycling Clubs, New-York Historical Society, New York.

77. "Fair Ladies and the Wheel," *New York Herald*, May 3, 1896. See also "Bicycling for Ladies," *Literary News*, July 1896, 200 (reprinted from *Springfield Republican*); "The Art of Wheeling," *Book News*, July 1896, 540 (reprinted from *Hartford Post*); "How to Alight from a Cycle," "Many Bicycle Clubs Take Runs," "New Devices Never Cease," "Launching of the Double Quint," "Claremont Has Its Bicycle Tea," "Whose Wheel is This," *New York Herald*, May 3, 1896.

78. Advertising Manager of Pope Manufacturing Co. to Maria E. Ward, 23 June 1896, Box MS 4, Folder 5, Ward Family Papers, Staten Island Historical Society, NY; M. E. Ward, memorandum, ca. June 1896, Box MS 4, Folder 5, Ward Family Papers, Staten Island Historical Society, NY.

79. M. E. Ward to George Bancroft, 8 February 1896, Box MS 4, Folder 5, Ward Family Papers, Staten Island Historical Society, NY; John Pl. Lovell Arms. Co to M. E. Ward, 29 June 1896, Box MS 4, Folder 5, Ward Family Papers, Staten Island Historical Society, NY; Vice President of the Spencer Brake Co. to Miss Ward, 13 June 1896, Box MS 4, Folder 5, Ward Family Papers, Staten Island Historical Society, NY.

80. Ellen Gruber Garvey, *Writing with Scissors: American Scrapbooks from the Civil War to the Harlem Renaissance* (New York: Oxford University Press, 2013), esp. chapter 5; Newspaper Clippings Related to Cycling and Cycling Clubs, New-York Historical Society, New York; Henry Romeike to M. E. Ward, 13 June 1896, Box MS 4, Folder 5, Ward Family Papers, Staten Island Historical Society, NY; Henry Romeike to M. E. Ward, 8 September 1896, Box MS 4, Folder 5, Ward Family Papers, Staten Island Historical Society, NY. In order to compile the clippings from newspapers around the country, Ward hired a clippings service that claimed to be "The First Established and Most Complete Newspaper Cutting Bureau in the World." For more on cutting bureaus, see Garvey's fascinating *Writing with Scissors*, 236–50, which makes clear that scrapbooks are a unique genre of writing, editing, and archiving.

81. Newspaper Clippings Related to Cycling and Cycling Clubs, New-York Historical Society, New York.

82. *Annual Report and List of Members of the New-York Historical Society* (New York: New-York Historical Society, 1938); Maxine Friedman, "Shall We Go For a Ride? A

Conversation about the Role of the Staten Island Historical Society's Model T," *Journal of Museum Education* 36, no. 2 (2011): 147; "Furnishings of 18-Room Ward Mansion, Landmark on Grymes Hill since 1867, Will be Sold at Auction," October 8, 1942, in Maria (Violet) Ward Clippings File, Staten Island Historical Society, NY; *Twelfth Census of the United States: 1900*, New York, NY, schedule 1, p. 54, house number 357, dwelling 37, family 82.

83. "The Rev. Arthur P.S. Hyde Dies; Holyrood Rector and Ex-Colonel," *New York Tribune*, December 28, 1943.

3. Moses

1. Robert Caro's Pulitzer prize-winning book, *The Power Broker: Robert Moses and the Fall of New York* (New York: Vintage, 1975), remains the most popular account of the master builder's life. Caro's narrative about an insensitive man unusually obsessed with power has subsequently been challenged by a group of historians who have suggested that the book is plagued by inaccuracies, exaggerations, and a lack of perspective. Embracing a more sympathetic narrative, a 2007 exhibition spread across three New York City museums and its corresponding book, Hilary Ballon and Kenneth T. Jackson, eds., *Robert Moses and the Modern City: The Transformation of New York* (New York: Norton, 2007), sought to catalog the astonishing record of Moses's work and understand him as a product of his own time. For a powerful criticism of Moses, see Marshall Berman, *All That Is Solid Melts Into Air: The Experience of Modernity* (New York: Penguin, 1988), 290–312. For another perspective, in which Moses is seen as merely one player in a longer and broader campaign to redevelop the city, see Joel Schwartz, *The New York Approach: Robert Moses, Urban Liberals, and Redevelopment of the Inner City* (Columbus: Ohio State University Press, 1993).

2. For a perspective on how cycling infrastructure can be limited by earlier autocentric planning, see Martin Emanuel, "Monuments of Unsustainability: Planning, Path Dependence, and Cycling in Stockholm," in *Cycling and Recycling: Histories of Sustainable Practices*, ed. Ruth Oldenziel and Helmuth Trischler (New York: Berghahn Books, 2016), 101–21.

3. Caro, *The Power Broker*, 25–37; *New York Bicycle Directory for 1896* (New York: New York Bicycle Directory Publishing Co., 1896); New York State Division LAW, *Fifty Miles Around Brooklyn* (New York: New York State Division of the League of American Wheelmen, 1896).

4. Robert J. Turpin, "'Our Best Bet is the Boy': A Cultural History of Bicycle Marketing and Consumption in the United States, 1880–1960" (PhD diss., University of Kentucky, 2013), 7, 115–70. See also Robert J. Turpin, *First Taste of Freedom: A Cultural History of Bicycle Marketing in the United States* (Syracuse, NY: Syracuse University Press, 2018).

5. "City's Cyclists Hold Their Own," *New York Times*, October 28, 1928; "What are your Prospects for 1938?" (advertisement), *American Bicyclist and Motorcyclist*, January 1938, 12. While state law prohibited cyclists from riding on the sidewalks, there was an exception for children under the age of ten. *Annotated Consolidated Laws of*

the State of New York, Vol. III (New York: The Banks Law Publishing Company, 1917), 3241.

6. *General Statistics of Cities: 1915* (Washington, DC: Government Printing Office, 1916), 18; "National Advertising for Bicycles," *Printer's Ink*, February 19, 1920, 26–28.

7. Peter Nye, *Hearts of Lions: The History of American Bicycle Racing* (New York: Norton, 1988), 101–3, 116–17, 119; "Columbatto Victor in Long Bike Race," *New York Times*, May 31, 1922. Although New York hosted more than its fair share of races, New Jersey was another hub of racing. For more on that history, see Michael C. Gabriele, *The Golden Age of Bicycle Racing in New Jersey* (Charleston, SC: The History Press, 2011).

8. "Bike Stars to Race," *New York Times*, May 29, 1922; "Bike Riders Made Debut at Coney," *New York Times*, July 20, 1930; Nye, *Hearts of Lions*, 101–2.

9. British Pathé, *Six Day Bicycle Race in New York* (1937), 1:08, YouTube video, posted by British Pathé, April 13, 2014, https://www.youtube.com/watch?v=RoIUL5QHNXA; "Fifteen Teams Scheduled to Start Long Cycling Grind in the Garden Tonight," *New York Times*, November 28, 1937; "Kilian-Vopel Take Six-Day Bike Race," *New York Times*, December 5, 1937; Nye, *Hearts of Lions*, 129, 132. For a humorous short film depicting a six-day race at Madison Square Garden in 1934, see A Van Beuren Production, *Six Day Grind*, 10:20, YouTube video, posted by Christopher Seufert, November 14, 2011, https://www.youtube.com/watch?v=l3Ivf8Zwfas.

10. Bruce Epperson, "Historical Statistics of the American Bicycle Industry, 1878–2013. Version 1.0" (unpublished spreadsheet, 2018); "Bicycles More Numerous," *New York Herald Tribune*, July 24, 1938; "Dos and Don'ts of Bicycling," *Popular Mechanics*, August, 1939, 248–51, 116–17A; "1937: The Biggest Bicycle Year of All Time," *American Bicyclist and Motorcyclist*, January 1938, 13.

11. "A Message to Every Cyclist in the United States," *Cycling Herald*, June 1938; "The Amazing Return of the 'Bikes,'" *Popular Mechanics*, January 1935, 62–64; Edward H. Albert, "A Dark Day in Sunnyside: A Bike-Obsessed Life of Damage and Redemption" (unpublished manuscript, 2015), 41. For more on the League of American Wheelmen in this period, see John S. Allen, "The League of American Wheelmen/Bicyclists in the 20th Century," in *Cycle History 20: Proceedings of the 20th International Cycle History Conference* (Cheltenham, UK: John Pinkerton Memorial Fund, 2010), 114–22.

12. Margaret Guroff, *The Mechanical Horse: How the Bicycle Reshaped American Life* (Austin: University of Texas Press, 2016), 117–20; David V. Herlihy, *Bicycle: The History* (New Haven, CT: Yale University Press, 2004), 355–58; James Longhurst, *Bike Battles: A History of Sharing the American Road* (Seattle: University of Washington Press, 2015), 125–28.

13. "Bicyclists Have Their Day Again as Pedals Fly in Park Mall Parade," *New York Times*, April 12, 1936; "Cyclists Hark Back to Gay Nineties; Demand Paths Like Horsemen Get," *Brooklyn Daily Eagle*, May 10, 1936.

14. Elizabeth A. Liebman, "Catherine Littlefield's Bicycle Ballet and the 1940 World's Fair," *Dance Chronicle* 36, no. 3 (2013): 326–51. Popular films and plays also reinforced the sense that bicycles were a definitional aspect of the "Gay Nineties." For an excellent, albeit somewhat later example, see *In the Good Old Summertime*, DVD, directed by Robert Z. Leonard (1949; Warner Home Video, 2004). Thanks to Paul Naish for pointing out this reference.

15. "Bicycle Paths for Two," *Brooklyn Daily Eagle*, August 29, 1938. There were still instructors offering riding lessons for those uninitiated in the practice. See, for example, "Parkways to Open on Upper West Side," *New York Times*, October 11, 1937.

16. "For the Women," *Cycling Herald*, December 1938; "Now the 'Bike' Train," *New York Times*, April 26, 1936; "Sports Trains Start," *New York Times*, April 18, 1937; "Bicycle Trains Proving Popular," *Cycling Herald*, June 1938; "Many City Folks Enjoy Bicycling in the Country via Cycle Trains," *American Bicyclist and Motorcyclist*, January 1938; "Cycling Steamers Set Excursion Schedules," *Cycling Herald*, June 1938; "Cyclists Hark Back to Gay Nineties; Demand Paths Like Horsemen Get," *Brooklyn Daily Eagle*, May 10, 1936.

17. New York City Department of Parks, *Program of Proposed Facilities for Bicycling* (New York, 1938). This alleged first bicycle cop arrest of a driver did not make the papers at the time, but other arrests did. On Long Island City's Jackson Avenue, Ewers set up a speed trap, counting the seconds as lead-footed motorists blazed past paced-off markers. In one bizarre case, a driver whose car moved like a "ball of fire" had to have his wealthy friend put up an entire building in Manhattan in order to secure his release. "1st City Bicycle Cop Who Nabbed 'Speeder' In Queens, Retires" *Brooklyn Daily Eagle*, July 9, 1938; "Chauffeur Fined $10," *Brooklyn Daily Eagle*, October 22, 1907; "75,000 House as Bail," *Brooklyn Daily Eagle*, November 18, 1907.

18. "New York Opens Cycle Path," *American Bicyclist and Motorcyclist*, August 1938, 35; "Parade Will Open Cycle Path Today," *New York Times*, July 9, 1938; "Cyclists' Byways Planned by Moses," *New York Times*, July 10, 1938; William Latham to Ernest MacAdam, 30 June 1938, Box 102410, Folder 43, Records of the Department of Parks, Parks Commissioner and General Files, Municipal Archives, New York, NY.

19. Philip J. Cruise, memorandum, 23 May 1939, Box 102468, Folder 46, Records of the Department of Parks, Parks Commissioner and General Files, Municipal Archives, New York, NY; "Bicycle Paths for Two," *Brooklyn Daily Eagle*, August 29, 1938; "Parade Will Open Cycle Path Today," *New York Times*, July 9, 1938; New York Department of Parks, *Press Release*, July 8, 1938, http://home2.nyc.gov/html/records/pdf/govpub/41921938_press_releases.pdf; Caro, *The Power Broker*, 492, 557–60; "Cyclists' Byways Planned by Moses," *New York Times*, July 10, 1938; Robert L. McCullough, *Old Wheelways: Traces of Bicycle History on the Land* (Cambridge, MA: MIT Press, 2015), 280; Marta Gutman, "Equipping the Public Realm: Rethinking Robert Moses and Recreation," in *Robert Moses and the Modern City*, ed. Ballon and Jackson, 77; "Cyclists Hark Back to Gay Nineties; Demand Paths Like Horsemen Get," *Brooklyn Daily Eagle*, May 10, 1936; "Cyclists Ask for Park Paths," *New York Tribune*, March 3, 1938.

20. Thomas Kessner, *Fiorello H. La Guardia and the Making of Modern New York* (New York: Penguin, 1991), 294–303; Caro, *The Power Broker*, 453–55; "Recreational Facilities of City Trebled Since January, 1934," *New York Herald Tribune*, October 10, 1937; Mason B. Williams, *City of Ambition: FDR, La Guardia, and the Making of Modern New York* (New York: Norton, 2013), 175–211. For more on the impact of WPA funding in terms of recreational opportunities in the city, see Judith Anne Davidson, "The Federal Government and the Democratization of Public Recreational Sport: New York City, 1933–43," (PhD diss., University of Massachusetts, 1983).

21. "California Recreation," 1937, File 69.56, Records of the Work Projects Administration, Series Motion Picture Films, 1931–1937, National Archives, College Park, MD, accessed November 7, 2016, https://catalog.archives.gov/id/12369.

22. An earlier feasibility study had proposed an even more remarkable 78.8 miles of paths. William Latham to Ernest MacAdam, 30 June 1938, Box 102410, Folder 43, Records of the Department of Parks, Parks Commissioner and General Files, Municipal Archives, New York, NY; Executive Officer to Tom Wallace, 29 November 1947, Box 102740, Folder 31, Records of the Department of Parks, Parks Commissioner and General Files, Municipal Archives, New York, NY; "Cyclists Hark Back to Gay Nineties; Demand Paths Like Horsemen Get," *Brooklyn Daily Eagle*, May 10, 1936; "City's Cyclists Hold Their Own," *New York Times*, October 28, 1928. One press report indicated that the Coney Island Cycle Path was still "exclusively for bicyclists only for two hours in the morning, from six to eight." "Adding City Cyclists," *New York Times*, August 14, 1938. For more on the long history of the Coney Island Cycle Path, see McCullough, *Old Wheelways*, 228–32.

23. *Program of Proposed Facilities for Bicycling*.

24. *Program of Proposed Facilities for Bicycling*; "Robert Moses, Pedal Pusher?" *Wall Street Journal*, June 25, 2012; Peter D. Norton, *Fighting Traffic: The Dawn of the Motor Age in the American City* (Cambridge, MA: MIT Press, 2008), 5. The state highway law was amended in 1909, carving out an exception for the New York City Department of Parks, enabling that body to regulate bicycles within its jurisdiction. Legally, it was much easier to control if, how, and where bicycles moved within the parks and on the parkways in comparison to ordinary city roads. *Laws of the State of New York*, 1890, Chapter 568, Section 163; *Laws of the State of New York*, 1909, Chapter 30, Section 327. For more on the late-nineteenth-century laws related to cyclists' right to the road, see Evan Friss, *The Cycling City: Bicycles and Urban America in the 1890s* (Chicago: University of Chicago Press, 2015), 63–81.

25. *Program of Proposed Facilities for Bicycling*; William Latham to Anthony Mestice, 15 March 1939, Box 102412, Folder 18, Records of the Department of Parks, Parks Commissioner and General Files, Municipal Archives, New York, NY. Controlling cyclists and their behavior was at the heart of an unsuccessful Moses-backed effort to mandate that New Yorkers register their bicycles. Moses figured the requirement would make it easier to enforce park prohibitions. Robert Moses, memorandum, 1 March 1941, Box 102540, Folder 21, Records of the Department of Parks, Parks Commissioner and General Files, Municipal Archives, New York, NY.

26. "Auto Deaths Here off 25% in August," *New York Times*, September 19, 1938; "Bicycle Casualties Rise Here; 8 Killed in Year's First 8 Months," *New York Times*, September 25, 1939; "Commissioner Mealey Warns Bicycle Riders," *New York Amsterdam News*, May 20, 1939.

27. *Program of Proposed Facilities for Bicycling*.

28. "New York Plans 58 Miles of Cycle Paths!" *American Bicyclist and Motorcyclist*, September 1938, 10–11; "Cycle Paths," *American Bicyclist and Motorcyclist*, September 1938, 9; "A Bicycle Trail and Rental Stand Created in a Municipal Park," *American Bicyclist and Motorcyclist*, January 1939, 26–27.

29. William Latham to Harry Cohen, 7 March 1939, Box 102412, Folder 18, Records of the Department of Parks, Parks Commissioner and General Files, Municipal Archives, New York, NY; "Cut in WPA Perils New York Bike Path Plan," *Cycling Herald*, May 1939; "N.Y. Park Paths Program Jeopardized," *Cycling Herald*, May 1939; "Bicycle's Comeback," *New York Herald Tribune*, July 21, 1940; McCullough, *Old Wheelways*, 277–90.

30. "Belt Parkways Path is Bikers' Paradise," *Brooklyn Daily Eagle*, July 13, 1941.

31. Clifton Fadiman to Robert Moses, 23 January 1941, Box 102540, Folder 21, Records of the Department of Parks, Parks Commissioner and General Files, Municipal Archives, New York, NY; Robert Moses to Clifton Fadiman, 27 January 1941, Box 102540, Folder 21, Records of the Department of Parks, Parks Commissioner and General Files, Municipal Archives, New York, NY; William Latham to Anthony Mestice, 15 March 1939, Box 102412, Folder 18, Records of the Department of Parks, Parks Commissioner and General Files, Municipal Archives, New York, NY. For more on Moses and the transformation of Central Park more generally, see Roy Rosenzweig and Elizabeth Blackmar, *The Park and the People: A History of Central Park* (Ithaca, NY: Cornell University Press, 1992), 439–63. For a fun memoir about Fadiman and his writer/daughter, see Anne Fadiman, *The Wine Lover's Daughter: A Memoir* (New York: Farrar, Straus and Giroux, 2017).

32. Clifton Fadiman to Robert Moses, 23 January 1941, Box 102540, Folder 21, Records of the Department of Parks, Parks Commissioner and General Files, Municipal Archives, New York, NY; Park Engineer, memorandum, 2 June 1941, Box 102540, Folder 21, Records of the Department of Parks, Parks Commissioner and General Files, Municipal Archives, New York, NY; "A Taxpayer" to Robert Moses, 22 April 1938, Box 102410, Folder 43, Records of the Department of Parks, Parks Commissioner and General Files, Municipal Archives, New York, NY; Robert Moses, memorandum, 1 March 1941, Box 102540, Folder 21, Records of the Department of Parks, Parks Commissioner and General Files, Municipal Archives, New York, NY; Clarence Edward Heller to The Editor of the *Brooklyn Eagle*, 7 August 1944, Box 102653, Folder 21, Records of the Department of Parks, Parks Commissioner and General Files, Municipal Archives, New York, NY. While there was certainly some talk about what women should wear when riding and how they should ride, in this period, unlike in the 1890s, there was hardly a heated debate.

33. Neil Langley to Robert Moses, 28 November 1939, Box 102412, Folder 17, Records of the Department of Parks, Parks Commissioner and General Files, Municipal Archives, New York, NY (underline in original); Alice M. Elting et al. to Robert Moses, 19 October 1939, Box 102467, Folder 90, Records of the Department of Parks, Parks Commissioner and General Files, Municipal Archives, New York, NY; Joan Joy to Robert Moses, 26 November 1939, Box 102468, Folder 46, Records of the Department of Parks, Parks Commissioner and General Files, Municipal Archives, New York, NY.

34. Robert Moses to Joan Baker, 29 November 1939, Box 102468, Folder 46, Records of the Department of Parks, Parks Commissioner and General Files, Municipal Archives, New York, NY; *Annotated Consolidated Laws of the State of New York*, 1917, Chapter 655, Section 19.

35. William Latham and Kenneth Franklin, memorandum, 30 September 1939, Box 102468, Folder 46, Records of the Department of Parks, Parks Commissioner and General Files, Municipal Archives, New York, NY; Howard Dunk to William Latham, 21 December 1939, Box 102468, Folder 46, Records of the Department of Parks, Parks Commissioner and General Files, Municipal Archives, New York, NY; William Latham to Harold Dunk, 22 December 1939, Box 102468, Folder 46, Records of the Department of Parks, Parks Commissioner and General Files, Municipal Archives, New York, NY.

36. Robert Moses to Joan Baker, 29 November 1939, Box 102468, Folder 46, Records of the Department of Parks, Parks Commissioner and General Files, Municipal Archives, New York, NY; Robert Moses to Charles Merz, 21 August 1939, Box 102412, Folder 17, Records of the Department of Parks, Parks Commissioner and General Files, Municipal Archives, New York, NY.

37. Press Release, 11 July 1940, Box 102480, Folder 25, Records of the Department of Parks, Parks Commissioner and General Files, Municipal Archives, New York, NY.

38. Throughout the 1940s, Moses continued to suggest that the city was invested in building paths, particularly along new parkways. Robert Moses to Alexander Rothstein, 7 October 1949, Box 102807, Folder 5, Records of the Department of Parks, Parks Commissioner and General Files, Municipal Archives, New York, NY; "Roosevelt Spurs War for Freedom on 'Grim' Fourth," *New York Times*, July 5, 1942; "Rationing of Bicycles Begun in New York; Defense and War Workers Can Get Them," *New York Times*, July 10, 1942; "'Gas' Ban Clears Highways; OPA Hails Motorists' Spirit," *New York Times*, May 24, 1943; Longhurst, *Bike Battles*, 130–51; Robert Moses to Jacob Horowitz, 28 May 1942, Box 102591, Folder 24, Records of the Department of Parks, Parks Commissioner and General Files, Municipal Archives, New York, NY; Robert Moses to Mrs. Everett Chase, 4 December 1956, Box 102896, Folder 31, Records of the Department of Parks, Parks Commissioner and General Files, Municipal Archives, New York, NY. For more on the impact of war on bicycles and bike production, see James Longhurst, "Reconsidering the Victory Bike in World War II: Federal Transportation Policy, History, and Bicycle Commuting in America," *Transportation Research Record*, August 26, 2018.

39. New York City Department of Parks, *Recreational Facilities for New Yorkers* (New York: Dept. of Parks), 1946; *Recreational Facilities for New Yorkers*, 1948; *Recreational Facilities for New Yorkers*, 1953; *Recreational Facilities for New Yorkers*, 1956.

40. Robert Kanigel, *Eyes on the Street: The Life of Jane Jacobs* (New York: Vintage, 2016), 134–35.

41. W. McQ., "(Get A Bike!)," *Architectural Forum*, April 1956, 43, 51; Kanigel, *Eyes on the Street*, 134–35.

42. For those cycling references, see Jane Jacobs, *The Death and Life of Great American Cities* (New York: Vintage, 1961), 87, 110, 267; David Byrne, *Bicycle Diaries* (New York: Viking, 2009), 2. For more on the unique ways cyclists experience the city and a phenomenological take on the practice, see Jesús Illundáin-Agurruza and Michael W. Austin, eds., *Cycling: Philosophy for Everyone: A Philosophical Tour de Force* (Malden, MA: Wiley-Blackwell, 2010); Janez Strehovec, "Cycling as Reading a Cityscape: A Phenomenological Approach to Interface-Shaped Perception," *Indo-Pacific Journal*

of Phenomenology 10, no. 3 (October 2010): 1–11; Robert Rao, "Urban Cycling as the Measure of the City: Experience, Policy and the Cultural Politics of Mobility" (master's thesis, Simon Fraser University, Spring 2010), esp. 47–52.

43. "Mayor Breaks Ground for Eastchester Housing Project," *New York Times*, September 29, 1948; Marlene Sciascia to John Lindsay, 20 October 1966, Box 103295, Folder 53, Records of the Department of Parks, Parks Commissioner and General Files, Municipal Archives, New York, NY. For more on Moses's role in the city's housing projects and urban renewal more generally, see Samuel Zipp, *Manhattan Projects: The Rise and Fall of Urban Renewal in Cold War New York* (New York: Oxford University Press, 2010).

44. "Bicycles Fill the Bill," *American Bicyclist and Motorcyclist*, March 1942, 18; Marlene Sciascia to John Lindsay, 20 October 1966, Box 103295, Folder 53, Records of the Department of Parks, Parks Commissioner and General Files, Municipal Archives, New York, NY.

45. Ira S. Robbins to Harry Levy, 20 April 1962, Box 62C7, Folder 5 (Robbins: Bicycle Paths), Records of the New York City Housing Authority, La Guardia and Wagner Archives, New York, NY; Harry Levy to Ira S. Robbins, 20 June 1962, Box 62C7, Folder 5 (Robbins: Bicycle Paths), Records of the New York City Housing Authority, La Guardia and Wagner Archives, New York, NY.

46. Turpin, " 'Our Best Bet is the Boy' " chapter 6; "A Bike for Christmas?" *American Bicyclist and Motorcyclist*, November 1953, 25; "Seasons Greetings from Schwinn," advertisement, *American Bicyclist and Motorcyclist*, November 1953. For more on wartime bicycle production and consumption, see Longhurst, *Bike Battles*, chapter 4.

47. Phyllis McGinley, "A Certain Age," *New Yorker*, November 1955, 46. When the *New York Times* reported in 1955 that a tariff on imported bicycles had been imposed, the writer concluded that "American parents will have to pay about 10 per cent more." "Tariff Will Raise Price of Bicycles," *New York Times*, August 20, 1955.

48. Alan Goldman to Robert Wagner, 2 February 1958, Box 102957, Folder 21, Records of the Department of Parks, Parks Commissioner and General Files, Municipal Archives, New York, NY. For more on the Cross-Bronx Expressway and its effect on the Bronx, see Caro, *The Power Broker*, 850–94.

49. Executive Officer to C. G. Peker, 3 December 1940, Box 102529, Folder 39, Records of the Department of Parks, Parks Commissioner and General Files, Municipal Archives, New York, NY; Caro, *The Power Broker*, 1062–65, 1086–1114; *Program of Proposed Facilities for Bicycling*; "Moses Outlines 4-Million Park on Site of Fair," *New York Herald Tribune*, August 15, 1940.

50. "New York World's Fair Awarded 1964 Olympic Team Tests," *USOC News Letter* 2, no. 5, Century Road Club Association Records, New York, NY. The 1960 Olympic trials were also held in New York.

51. Flushing Festival Flyer, 1963, Century Road Club Association Records, New York, NY; "Bicycle Track in Queens Will be Dedicated Today," *New York Times*, July 19, 1964; Nye, *Hearts of Lions*, 223; "Champion on Wheels," *Ebony*, September 1967, 108, 110, 112–13. In 1964, the track was dedicated as the Siegfried Stern Memorial Bicycle Track in honor of a local philanthropist and "manufacturer of bird food."

52. Joshua Freeman, interview by the author, January 2018.

53. "U.S. Bicycle Racing Championships Wheel into Town Thursday for 4-Day Run," *New York Times*, August 16, 1970; Freeman, interview.

54. With many thanks to Edward Albert for sharing his fine manuscript on Dick Power and the New York bike racing scene. Albert, "A Dark Day in Sunnyside"; Freeman, interview.

55. Albert, "A Dark Day in Sunnyside." Nye's book and an oral history with a member of the club suggests that the Century Road Club Association still prohibited blacks from joining in the 1960s. But archival records show that the requirement to be white was lifted in 1948. Perhaps the ban remained in spirit. Freeman, interview; Nye, *Hearts of Lions*, 213–15; "National By-Laws of the Century Road Club Association, Revised and Adopted, February 1, 1912," Century Road Club Association Records, New York, NY; "Century Road Club Association National By-Laws as Revised and Adopted, 1954," Century Road Club Association Records, New York, NY; "Interview by Mrs. Lisa Thayer of Louis Maltese," March 1983, Century Road Club Association Records, New York, NY.

56. Albert, "A Dark Day in Sunnyside," 9; Freeman, interview.

57. "100,000 Cars Cross Verrazano Bridge in First 24 Hours," *New York Times*, November 23, 1964. The opening festivities also stoked the ambition of then eighteen-year-old Donald Trump. As he recalled in a later interview, "All I'm thinking about is that all these politicians who opposed the bridge are being applauded. Yet in a corner, just standing there in the rain, is this man, this 85-year-old engineer who came from Sweden and designed this bridge, who poured his heart into it, and nobody even mentioned his name. I realized then and there that if you let people treat you how they want, you'll be made a fool. I realized then and there something I would never forget: I don't want to be made anybody's sucker." "Trump: The Development of a Manhattan Developer," *New York Times*, August 26, 1980.

58. "Great Link is Acclaimed," *New York Times*, July 12, 1936.

59. Another of the first-to-cross races featured a close call, in which a "Negro" beat out a pair on a tandem bicycle. "200,000 Rush to Use New Bridge by Auto, Bus, Cycle, and on Foot," *New York Times*, July 12, 1936; "31,000 Vehicles a Day Use Triborough Bridge," *New York Times*, August 12, 1936; "Great Link is Acclaimed," *New York Times*, July 12, 1936.

60. Harry Taylor to Charles Fier, 2 March 1938, Records of the TBTA, MTA Bridge and Tunnels Archive, New York, NY; Charles Fier to Robert Moses, 26 February 1938, Records of the TBTA, MTA Bridge and Tunnels Archive, New York, NY; Nellie Hankins, e-mail message to author, November 1, 2016; "Mayor to Open Bronx-Queens Bridge Today," *New York Times*, April 29, 1939. The toll rate for bicycles was lowered on the Marine Parkway Bridge to five cents in 1939. Robert Moses to Bernard Giffler, 3 February 1939, Records of the TBTA, MTA Bridge and Tunnels Archive, New York, NY; Harry Taylor, memorandum, 2 February 1939, Records of the TBTA, MTA Bridge and Tunnels Archive, New York, NY; "Ferries Cut Toll Below Bridge Rate," *New York Times*, November 7, 1931.

61. The Henry Hudson Bridge was completed in 1936. In 1939, Moses wrote that bicycles were prohibited on the bridge, but it is not clear if that had always been the policy. Tellingly, when engineers reconfigured the seven-year-old Bronx-Whitestone Bridge to strengthen the structure in 1946, they added more vehicle lanes and eliminated the

bridge's walkway. Robert Moses, memorandum, 3 February 1939, Records of the
TBTA, MTA Bridge and Tunnels Archive, New York, NY; "TBTA Toll Rates," c. 1940,
Records of the TBTA, MTA Bridge and Tunnels Archive, New York, NY; Nellie Han-
kins, e-mail message to author, November 1, 2016; Moses to Giffler, 3 February 1939.

62. Jerome Case to Robert Moses, 17 August 1940, Box 102529, Folder 39, Records of the
Department of Parks, Parks Commissioner and General Files, Municipal Archives,
New York, NY; Robert Moses to Jerome Case, 19 August 1940, Box 102529, Folder
39, Records of the Department of Parks, Parks Commissioner and General Files,
Municipal Archives, New York, NY.

63. Robert Moses, memorandum, 1 February 1939, Records of the TBTA, MTA Bridge
and Tunnels Archive, New York, NY; Harry Taylor, memorandum, 2 February 1939.

64. "Trunk Line Travel Rose Here in 1936," *New York Times*, April 5, 1937; Port of New
York Authority and Triborough Bridge and Tunnel Authority, *Joint Study of Arterial
Facilities: New York-New Jersey Metropolitan Area* (New York, 1955), 13–16; Harry
Taylor, memorandum, 2 February 1939.

65. Longhurst, *Bike Battles*, 160. "Dr. White's Bike Plan Wouldn't Be Easy Here," *New
York Herald Tribune*, February 26, 1956. Long-distance cyclists noticed the changing
polices too. As Joe Mariniello, a seventy-seven-year-old aspiring transcontinental bicycle
rider, reported in 1960: "It's got so now you have to have a car go along to carry you
across the bridges. . . . You run into toll bridges everywhere these days and they won't
let you ride a bike across them any more. . . . They phone somebody and you sit and
wait until that somebody comes. They don't hurry either." "Mariniello 77, Still Finds
Pleasure in Cycling," *New York Herald Tribune*, March 13, 1960.

66. Port of New York Authority and Triborough Bridge and Tunnel Authority, *Joint Study
of Arterial Facilities*, 20–26.

67. "150 Cycle to Fair in Rules Protest," *New York Times*, May 18, 1964; Robert Moses
to Louis Rosenberg, 5 January 1968, Records of the TBTA, MTA Bridge and Tunnels
Archive, New York, NY.

68. Steven F. Faust, "A Bicycle/Pedestrian Path for the Verrazano-Narrows Bridge: A
Demand and Feasibility Study," November 1976, accessed September 14, 2016, http://
home.earthlink.net/~sfaust1534/vnb/index.html; "100,000 Cars Cross Verrazano
Bridge in First 24 Hours," *New York Times*, November 23, 1964.

69. Many of the initial complaints about the Verrazano stemmed from the lack of pedestrian (not bike) access. "100,000 Cars Cross Verrazano Bridge in First 24 Hours," *New
York Times*, November 23, 1964. For more on the history (including some terrific
images) of the Verrazano Bridge, see Gay Talese, *The Bridge: The Building of the
Verrazano-Narrows Bridge* (New York: Bloomsbury, 2014).

70. "City Aiding the Cyclist," *New York Times*, October 1, 1939.

4. The Ban

1. Randi Taylor-Habib, interview by the author, February 2018.
2. Taylor-Habib, interview.

3. That same year Tom Wolfe published *Bonfire of the Vanities* (New York: Farrar, Straus and Giroux, 1987), expertly capturing the zeitgeist of 1987 New York. As wealth accumulated on Park Avenue by way of Wall Street, poverty, crime, and injustice permeated neighborhoods that sat nearby, but seemed a world away from the life that Wolfe's protagonist, bond trader Sherman McCoy, knew.

4. "Buckley Proposes to Gut Cars in City," *New York Times*, October 28, 1965.

5. "Central Park Drives to be Shut to Cars Sunday Mornings," *New York Times*, June 10, 1966; "Park Bans Cars for Saturday Cycling," *New York Times*, April 19, 1967; "Mayor and Wife Help to Start Central Park's Cycling Season," *New York Times*, May 18, 1969. For more on John Lindsay, see Vincent J. Cannato, *The Ungovernable City: John Lindsay and His Struggles to Save New York* (New York: Basic Books, 2001).

6. No. 55, *Local Laws of the City of New York*, 1967.

7. Adam Rome, *The Genius of Earth Day: How a 1980 Teach-In Unexpectedly Made the First Green Generation* (New York: Hill and Wang, 2013), ix–x; "In the Aftermath of Earth Day: City Gains New Leverage," *New York Times*, April 24, 1970.

8. John Lindsay, "Earth Day Speech," April 22, 1970, 7:04, from "Happy Earth Day— Now Move Your Car," NYPR Archives and Preservation, http://www.wnyc.org/story /happy-earth-day-move-your-car/; "Pedaling to be Pushed by Mayor Wednesday," *New York Times*, September 14, 1970; "Cycling Lane Likely for a Major City Street," *New York Times*, September 17, 1970; New York City Transportation Administration, *Bicycles in New York City* (New York: Office of Comprehensive Planning of the New York City Transportation Administration, 1973), 26.

9. New York City Transportation Administration, *Bicycles in New York City*, 41–43, appendix C. For more on bike policy and infrastructure in Davis, California, see Bruce D. Epperson, *Bicycles in American Highway Planning: The Critical Years of Policy-Making, 1969–1991* (Jefferson, NC: McFarland, 2014), 96–106.

10. Introductions, No. 710, October 26, 1971, *Proceedings of the Council of the City of New York*, Box 50377, 478, LaGuardia and Wagner Archives, New York; "Bicyclists Denied a Push by Mayor," *New York Times*, September 26, 1971.

11. The bikeway program was actually already under way. New York City Transportation Administration, *Bicycles in New York City*, 18–19. For more on the history of bikeways, see James Longhurst, *Bike Battles: A History of Sharing the American Road* (Seattle: University of Washington Press, 2015), 200–215.

12. Robert K. Herzfelder to Thomas Cuite, 25 October 1971, Box 50610, Records of The Council of the City of New York, La Guardia and Wagner Archives, New York.

13. New York City Transportation Administration, *Bicycles in New York City*, 1–2; Bruce Epperson, "Historical Statistics of the American Bicycle Industry, 1878–2013. Version 1.0" (unpublished spreadsheet, 2018). For more on the history of the bike boom of the early 1970s, see Epperson, *Bicycles in American Highway Planning*, 72–76; David V. Herlihy, *Bicycle: The History* (New Haven, CT: Yale University Press, 2004), 362–70; Longhurst, *Bike Battles*, 188–94; New York City Transportation Administration, *Bicycles in New York City*, 5.

14. Calvin Trillin, "U.S. Journal: Manhattan Fun's Over," *New Yorker*, October 9, 1971, 120–27. For more on the Moulton bicycle, see Bruce D. Epperson's fascinating book,

The Moulton Bicycle: A History of Innovative Compact Design (Jefferson, NC: McFarland, 2018).

15. Trillin, "U.S. Journal: Manhattan Fun's Over," 120–27.

16. New York City Transportation Administration, *Bicycles in New York City*, 7; Trillin, "U.S. Journal"; Rafael Macia, *The New York Bicycler* (New York: Simon and Schuster, 1972), 60–64.

17. Rivvy Neshama, "Transportation Alternatives: Memories and Organizational History," (unpublished manuscript, 2013), Microsoft Word file; Transportation Alternatives, *2012–2013 Annual Report* (New York: Transportation Alternatives, 2013), 2.

18. "Ride & Rally" (poster) from the collection of Transportation Alternatives, New York; Rivvy Berkman to Honorable Thomas J. Cuite, 26 April 1973, Records of The Council of the City of New York, Box 50610, La Guardia and Wagner Archives, New York; Transportation Alternatives, *2012–2013 Annual Report*, 2.

19. The Bring Back the Bicycle Committee to Councilman Thomas J. Cuite, 18 March 1974, Box 417, Records of The Council of the City of New York, La Guardia and Wagner Archives, New York.

20. New York City Transportation Administration, *Bicycles in New York City*, 8.

21. New York City Transportation Administration, *Bicycles in New York City*, 47. Especially important in shaping the debate about where cyclists belonged on city streets was John Forester's *Effective Cycling* (Cambridge, MA: MIT Press, 1976).

22. New York City Transportation Administration, *Bicycles in New York City*, 45, 49, appendix.

23. "Truck and Car Fall as West Side Highway Collapses," *New York Times*, December 16, 1973; Charles Komanoff, interview by the author, January 2018.

24. President Ford never used the actual words, "Drop Dead." "Ford to City: Drop Dead," (New York) *Daily News*, October 30, 1975. For an excellent study of New York during the fiscal crisis, see Kim Phillips-Fein, *Fear City: New York's Fiscal Crisis and the Rise of Austerity Politics* (New York: Metropolitan Books, 2017).

25. For a good biography of Koch, see Jonathan Soffer, *Ed Koch and the Rebuilding of New York City* (New York: Columbia University Press, 2012).

26. "Koch, in Inaugural, Asks that 'Pioneers' 'Come East' to City," *New York Times*, January 2, 1978.

27. "Metropolitan Briefs," *New York Times*, July 14, 1978; "Avenue of Americas and Broadway to Get a Special Bike Lane," *New York Times*, July 7, 1978.

28. "Mid-Manhattan Bikeways a Cyclist's Wish Coming True," *New York Times*, August 7, 1978; "To Aid Cyclists," *New York Times*, January 29, 1979.

29. La Guardia and Wagner Archives, *Mayor Ed Koch's 1980 Visit to China and the Creation and Destruction of NYC Bike Lanes*, 3:26, April 20, 2012, vimeo video, https://vimeo.com/62174609; Soffer, *Ed Koch and the Rebuilding of New York City*, 211.

30. "Koch Unveils Traffic Control Plan for Use if Transit Employees Strike," *New York Times*, March 25, 1980; "Bike Riders Gearing for Transit Strike," *New York Times*, March 26,1980.

31. Carl Hultberg, interview by the author, February 2018.

32. New York City Department of Transportation, *Bicycle Safety Education Program Final Report* (New York: New York City Department of Transportation, 1983), 13.

33. "Bicycling is Double Level Before Strike," *New York Times*, May 4, 1980; New York City Department of Transportation and Police Department, *Improving Bicycle Safety in New York City* (New York: New York City Department of Transportation and Police Department, 1980), 1–5, appendix.

34. New York City Department of Transportation, *Bicycle Safety Education Program Final Report*, 4, A–12, A–33, A–67, A–61. While an earlier law already required schools to offer bicycle safety instruction, the implementation of such programs was uneven at best.

35. Samuel I. Schwartz, memorandum, 29 August 1980, Reel 41124, Box 262, Folder 6, Edward Koch Papers, Departmental Correspondence, Municipal Archives, New York; Molly McArdle, "This Transportation Engineer Won't Give Up on Moving New York City," Next City, May 2, 2016, https://nextcity.org/features/view/move-ny-plan -transportation-plan-gridlock-sam-schwartz. For more on Schwartz, see Samuel I. Schwartz, *Street Smart: The Rise of Cities and the Fall of Cars* (New York: Public Affairs, 2015).

36. David Gurin, memorandum, 15 September 1980, Reel 41124, Box 262, Folder 6, Edward Koch Papers, Departmental Correspondence, Municipal Archives, New York; "New Bike Lanes: Perils of Progress," *New York Times*, September 24, 1980; "Koch Opens 2 Bike Lanes Already Used to Cyclists," *New York Times*, October 16, 1980. For Koch's own take on how he prepared for his inaugural ride, see Mayor Koch Oral History, June 25, 2010, 08.010.0515 OH, LaGuardia and Wagner Archives, New York. The only difference between the route of the 1980 lanes and those painted in 1978 was that the 1978 southbound lane started on Broadway, while the 1980 lane began on Seventh Avenue. They both crossed over to Fifth Avenue via Broadway.

37. David Gurin, memorandum, 15 September 1980, Reel 41124, Box 262, Folder 6, Edward Koch Papers, Departmental Correspondence, Municipal Archives, New York; "New Bike Lanes: Perils of Progress," *New York Times*, September 24, 1980; "Koch Opens 2 Bike Lanes Already Used to Cyclists," *New York Times*, October 16, 1980.

38. "Koch Says He's Prepared to Get Rid of Bicycle Lanes," *New York Times*, November 12, 1980; "New Bike Lanes: Perils of Progress," *New York Times*, September 24, 1980; "Bike lane $$$Speed Past New York City Blacks," *New York Amsterdam News*, November 15, 1980.

39. It is not clear exactly when the city conducted its November traffic count, but the weather was unusually bitter following Koch's November 11 announcement that he was going to consult with city staff about the future of the lanes. On the day of Koch's warning, the high temperature reached only 35 degrees, more than 20 degrees below average. It was also raining. Temperatures warmed slowly over the next couple of days but remained below normal. "Koch Says He's Prepared to Get Rid of Bicycle Lanes," *New York Times*, November 12, 1980; "Bike Lanes' Removal Ordered by Mayor," *New York Times*, November 14, 1980.

40. "Koch Says He's Prepared to Get Rid of Bicycle Lanes," *New York Times*, November 12, 1980; "Koch Opens 2 Bike Lanes Already Used to Cyclists," *New York Times*, October 16, 1980; "New Bike Lanes: Perils of Progress," *New York Times*, September 24, 1980; Charlie McCorkell, "Central Park—Not Seeing the Cars for the Congestion," *City Cyclist*, January–February 1983.

41. Samuel I. Schwartz, "On-Street Protected Bike Facilities Boost Mobility While Lessening Congestion," *intransition Magazine*, Winter 2011, http://www.intransitionmag.org/winter_2011/protected_bike_lanes.aspx; StreetFilms, *Gridlock Sam on NYC's 1980 Bike Lanes*, 5:44, YouTube video, posted by StreetFilms, November 10, 2006, https://www.youtube.com/watch?v=awfNxaoqjjk; "Koch Says He's Prepared to Get Rid of Bicycle Lanes," *New York Times*, November 12, 1980.

42. "Work Crews Remove Bike-Lane Barriers," *New York Times*, November 15, 1980.

43. Ed Koch, memorandum, 28 November 1980, Reel 41124, Box 262, Folder 7, Edward Koch Papers, Departmental Correspondence, Municipal Archives, New York; Department of Transportation, City of New York, "New York City's Bicycle Program," March 1983 (NYC DOT); Schwartz, interview; "Muggings Rise on Brooklyn Bridge as More Bicyclists Make Use of It," *New York Times*, July 22, 1980.

44. New York City Department of Parks, *Program of Proposed Facilities for Bicycling* (New York, 1938).

45. "About New York," *New York Times*, August 4, 1976. For more on very early messengers, see Gregory J. Downey, *Telegraph Messenger Boys: Labor, Technology, and Geography, 1850–1950* (New York: Routledge, 2002).

46. Jeffrey L. Kidder, *Urban Flow: Bike Messengers and the City* (Ithaca, NY: Cornell University Press, 2011), 39; Shelly Mossey, interview by the author, February 2018.

47. "Steppin' into Tough Turf," *Crain's New York Business*, July 27, 1987.

48. "Pedaling for Profit," *Newsday* (NY), June 14, 1985; Kidder, *Urban Flow*, 7–11; Jack M. Kugelmass, "I'd Rather be a Messenger," *Natural History* 90, no. 8 (August 1981): 67–68, 72.

49. "Courier Service Caters to the Image-Conscious," *Crain's New York Business*, August 24, 1987; Mossey, interview.

50. "Bikes Taking us for Ride," *New York Daily News*, August 10, 1987; Kugelmass, "I'd Rather Be a Messsenger," 66–68; Dinitia Smith, "Fast Company," *New York Magazine*, January 13, 1986, 40; Peter Sutherland, *Pedal*, 2001, 52:13, YouTube video, posted by "Mr. Fixie," May 28, 2013, https://www.youtube.com/watch?v=EyitrLKUUJI. The $100 a day figure, according to one scholar, remained the norm for messengers for many years to come, effectively reducing the real value of messengers' wages. Kidder, *Urban Flow*, 28, 34. Using the Consumer Price Index, $13,500 equals roughly $30,000 in 2018 dollars.

51. "Ban on Bikes Could Bring More Mopeds," *New York Times*, August 25, 1987; Kugelmass, "I'd Rather be a Messenger," 69–71.

52. Kidder, *Urban Flow*, 15, 91; Sutherland, *Pedal*; Taylor-Habib, interview; "10 Famous People Who Used to be Bike Messengers," *Bicycling*, March 26, 2015, https://www.bicycling.com/culture/people/10-famous-people-who-used-be-bike-messengers; Marky Ramone (with Rich Herschlag), *Punk Rock Blitzkrieg* (New York: Touchstone, 2015).

53. Kugelmass, "I'd Rather be a Messenger," 69–70; Smith, "Fast Company," 40–42.

54. Kugelmass, "I'd Rather be a Messenger," 67.

55. Smith, "Fast Company," 40; Kidder, *Urban Flow*, 65–69.

56. Smith, "Fast Company," 40; "Fastest is Best as Messengers Pedal in Pursuit of a $100 Day," *New York Times*, December 2, 1983.

57. National Geographic Explorer, "Big City Bike Messengers," July 27, 1986, 14:50, You-Tube video, posted by Barbara Ross, August 23, 2012, https://www.youtube.com /watch?v=MGIp5ajmBGU.

58. National Geographic Explorer, "Big City Bike Messengers." Another female messenger reported few instances of sexism, with the notable exception of an incident in which a male courier undressed himself in her presence. Taylor-Habib, interview.

59. Charles Komanoff, interview by the author, January 2018; George Bliss, interview by the author, February 2018; Carl Hultberg, *Garden of Eden: The Eco Eighties in NYC Parts 1–5* (N.p.: Ragtime Society Press, 2016).

60. (Cover), *Newsweek*, December 31, 1984; *Do the Right Thing*, DVD, directed by Spike Lee (1989; Universal Pictures, 2009). With thanks to Dylan Gottlieb for pointing me to the *Newsweek* cover.

61. Steve Stollman, interview by the author, February 2018; Bliss, interview.

62. Bliss, interview.

63. Charles Komanoff, interview by the author, January 2018; Mossey, interview.

64. "New York Day by Day," *New York Times*, January 18, 1983. Proposals came in different shapes and from different directions. Even Isaac Asimov weighed in with a limerick, throwing his support behind a Bicycle Transportation Action plan to increase enforcement and education. Bicycle Transportation Action, memorandums, 5 January, 19 March, and 25 April 1984, Reel 41096, Box 209, Folder 8, Edward Koch Papers, Departmental Correspondence, Municipal Archives, New York; Isaac Asimov to Roger Herz, 24 May 1983, Reel 41096, Box 209, Folder 8, Edward Koch Papers, Departmental Correspondence, Municipal Archives, New York.

65. Carol Greitzer to Paul Dalnoky, 4 February 1983, Box 51215, Records of The Council of the City of New York, La Guardia and Wagner Archives, New York; "New York Day by Day," *New York Times*, January 18, 1983; Larry Reilly to Roger Herz, 21 June 1984, Reel 41096, Box 209, Folder 8, Edward Koch Papers, Municipal Archives, New York; Bicycle Transportation Action, memorandum, 26 June 1984, Reel 41096, Box 209, Folder 8, Edward Koch Papers, Municipal Archives, New York; "Safety, Comfort, and Convenience," *New York Times*, June 4, 1984; Bicycles, I.D., Int. No. 679-A, Box 051424, Folder 1, Records of the Council of the City of New York, La Guardia and Wagner Archives, New York; No. 47, *Local Laws of the City of New York*, 1984.

66. Jack Lusk, memorandum, 19 July 1985, Reel 41028, Box 71, Folder 6, Edward Koch Papers, Departmental Correspondence, Municipal Archives, New York; Jeremy Travis to Jack Lusk, 11 July 1985, Reel 41028, Box 71, Folder 6, Edward Koch Papers, Departmental Correspondence, Municipal Archives, New York.

67. New York City Department of Transportation, *Bicycle Safety Education Program Final Report*, D–7.

68. *Quicksilver*, DVD, directed by Thomas Donnelly (1986; Sony Pictures Home Entertainment, 2002). For more on Vails, see Stephane Gauger, "Cheetah: The Nelson Vails Story," 1:06:03, YouTube video, posted by One World Media Group, April 11, 2015, https://www.youtube.com/watch?v=VjLnzbzuNhE.

69. Benjamin Ward to Joseph Sadler, 6 October 1986, Reel 41052, Box 120, Folder 8, Edward Koch Papers, Departmental Correspondence, Municipal Archives, New York;

"Anti-Bicyclist Movement Gets Rolling," *Newsday* (NY), December 24, 1986; "Pol Rips City on Dead-End Bike Law," *New York Post*, April 17, 1987; Edward Koch, memorandum, 20 April 1987, Reel 41108, Box 2321, Folder 8, Edward Koch Papers, Departmental Correspondence, Municipal Archives, New York.

70. *Review of Bicycle Operation in New York City with Recommendations for Additional Safety Measures,* Reel 41108, Box 2321, Folder 8, Edward Koch Papers, Departmental Correspondence, Municipal Archives, New York; "New York to Ban Bicycles on 3 Major Avenues," *New York Times*, July 23, 1987; "Collisions and Fatalities in NYC," in *Bicycle Blueprint: A Plan to Bring Bicycling into the Mainstream in New York City,* ed. Michele Herman (New York: Transportation Alternatives, 1993), table 17.

71. The comparisons to stabbing and air conditioner-related deaths are anecdotal and imperfect. "Man Riding a Bicycle on Coney I. is Beaten and Stabbed to Death," *New York Times*, May 29, 1986; "Man Stabbed to Death While Delivering Pizza," *New York Times*, 1988; "Air-Conditioner Falls, Killing a Pedestrian," *New York Times*, October 27, 1988; "Collisions and Fatalities in NYC," table 17.

72. *Review of Bicycle Operation in New York City with Recommendations for Additional Safety Measures,* Reel 41108, Box 2321, Folder 8, Edward Koch Papers, Departmental Correspondence, Municipal Archives, New York.

73. "New York to Ban Bicycles on 3 Major Avenues," *New York Times*, July 23, 1987.

74. While it is not clear exactly who, someone (perhaps the mayor himself) thought that the original restrictions proposed in a police department report might be too harsh. The originally proposed four-month window was shortened to three, four restricted avenues were shrunk to three, and the time restrictions eased from seven hours a day to six. "New York to Ban Bicycles on 3 Major Avenues," *New York Times*, July 23, 1987; Ross Sandler, memorandum, 17 March 1988, Reel 41127, Box 267, Folder 1, Edward Koch Papers, Departmental Correspondence, Municipal Archives, New York; *Review of Bicycle Operation in New York City with Recommendations for Additional Safety Measures,* Reel 41108, Box 2321, Folder 8, Edward Koch Papers, Departmental Correspondence, Municipal Archives, New York.

75. Barbara Gunn and Benjamin Tucker, memorandum, 24 August 1987, Reel 41016, Box 40, Folder 13, Edward Koch Papers, Departmental Correspondence, Municipal Archives, New York.

76. "City to Seek a Licensing Law for the Commercial Cyclist," *New York Times*, December 8, 1987; "For Bikers, It's a No-Go," July 23, 1987, *New York Daily News*; Smith, "Fast Company," 43; New York City Department of Transportation, *Bicycle Safety Education Program Final Report*, F–3; "Beyond a Bicycle Ban," *New York Times*, August 1, 1987; Barbara Gunn and Benjamin Tucker, memorandum, 24 August 1987, Reel 41016, Box 40, Folder 13, Edward Koch Papers, Departmental Correspondence, Municipal Archives, New York; *Review of Bicycle Operation in New York City with Recommendations for Additional Safety Measures,* Reel 41108, Box 2321, Folder 8, Edward Koch Papers, Departmental Correspondence, Municipal Archives, New York. Children eighteen years old or younger were the ones most likely to be killed while riding a bicycle, not the messengers, who were largely in their twenties. New York City Department of Transportation, *Bicycle Safety Education Program Final Report*, A–66.

77. Mary Frances Dunham, "Fifth, Park and Madison," in *Bicycle Blueprint: A Plan to Bring Bicycling into the Mainstream in New York City*, ed. Michele Herman (New York: Transportation Alternatives, 1993), 107–9; Charles Komanoff, "The Bicycle Uprising: Remembering the Midtown Bike Ban 25 Years Later," 2012, http://www.komanoff.net/bicycle/Bicycle_Uprising.pdf; "Traffic Bikemare Hits City Again," *New York Post*, July 31, 1987; "Pedalers' Protest: 1,000 Pedal to Protest Bicycle Ban," *Newsday* (NY), August 13, 1987.

78. "Ban on Bikes Could Bring More Mopeds," *New York Times*, August 25, 1987; "Bikers See Red Over Ban in Midtown," *New York Post*, July 23, 1987; "It's a Holdup—Of Traffic," *New York Daily News*, August 27, 1987.

79. Charlie McCorkell, "The Truth About the Bike Ban," *City Cyclist*, Oct–Nov 1987, 8–10; Roger Herz, memorandum, 6 August 1987, Box 40, Folder 13, Edward Koch Papers, Departmental Correspondence, La Guardia and Wagner Archives, New York; "Vicious Cycles?" *New York Daily News*, July 23, 1987.

80. Dragan Ilic, *Fifth, Park, and Madison*, 1987, 38:49 YouTube video, posted by Time's Up Environmental Group, September 25, 2012, https://www.youtube.com/watch?v=GfsQkiwkldg.

81. Dragan Ilic, *Fifth, Park, and Madison*, 1987, 38:49 YouTube video, posted by Time's Up Environmental Group, September 25, 2012, https://www.youtube.com/watch?v=GfsQkiwkldg; Charles Komanoff, "The Man Who Saved NYC Cycling," Streetsblog, December 18, 2015, http://www.streetsblog.org/2015/12/18/the-man-who-saved-nyc-cycling/; "Traffic Bikemare Hits City Again," *New York Post*, July 31, 1987; "Pedalers' Protest: 1,000 Pedal to Protest Bicycle Ban," *Newsday* (NY), August 13, 1987.

82. Ilic, *Fifth, Park, and Madison*; Komanoff, "The Man Who Saved NYC Cycling"; "Traffic Bikemare Hits City Again," *New York Post*, July 31, 1987; "Pedalers' Protest: 1,000 Pedal to Protest Bicycle Ban," *Newsday* (NY), August 13, 1987.

83. Ilic, *Fifth, Park, and Madison*; "Ban on Bikes Could Bring More Mopeds," *New York Times*, August 25, 1987; "Bikers See Red Over Ban in Midtown," *New York Post*, July 23, 1987; "It's a Holdup—Of Traffic," *New York Daily News*, August 27, 1987.

84. Stollman, interview; Charles Komanoff, interview by the author, January 2018; Katie Lemanczyk, "Transportation Alternatives, A History" (unpublished manuscript, 2008).

85. Hultberg, *Garden of Eden*; Hultberg, interview.

86. Charles Komanoff, interview by the author, January 2018; Charles J. McCorkell, memorandum, 8 August, 1987, Box 40 Folder 13, Edward Koch Papers, Departmental Correspondence, La Guardia and Wagner Archives, New York.

87. Dunham, "Fifth, Park and Madison," 107; McCorkell, "The Truth About the Bike Ban," 8–10; Komanoff, interview.

88. Even some of those who opposed the bike ban admitted that messengers tried to scare pedestrians. In a letter to the editor of *Newsday*, a Long Island man who worked in the city derided the Bike Ban proposal as "unfair and unconstitutional," while reporting that messengers had nearly run him over a dozen times. And even Athineos never denied that certain messengers behaved badly, but he differentiated those "youngsters" (kids inspired by *QuickSilver*) who worked when school let out from the real professionals. "Hell on Wheels," *New York Post*, August 3, 1987; Gerard Sentochnik, letter to the editor, *Newsday* (NY), August 6, 1987; "Bikes Taking us for Ride," *New York*

Daily News, August 10, 1987. For another journalistic account of a day in the life of a bike messenger, albeit in Toronto, see "Life in the Curb Lane," *The Globe and Mail*, August 19, 1988. For a fuller account from a messenger in a later period and in Chicago, see Travis Hugh Culley, *The Immortal Class: Bike Messengers and the Cult of Human Power* (New York: Villard, 2001).

89. Lou Venech to Jack Lusk, 23 April 1984, Reel 41096, Box 209, Folder 8, Edward Koch Papers, Departmental Correspondence, Municipal Archives, New York; "Easy, Riders: This Bike Rule Helps Everyone," *Crain's New York Business*, August 3, 1987.

90. Frank Trippett, "Scaring The Public to Death," *Time*, October 5, 1987; "What do they Want?" *Village Voice*, August 11, 1987; "The Post Asks: Should all Bicycles be Banned in Midtown?" *New York Post*, July 23, 1987; "Will Koch's Midtown Bike Ban Make You Feel Safer," *New York Daily News*, July 23, 1987; "Back the Bike Ban," *New York Daily News*, July 24, 1987.

91. McCorkell, "The Truth About the Bike Ban," 8–10; Stollman, interview; Barbara Gunn and Benjamin Tucker, memorandum, 24 August 1987, Reel 41016, Box 40, Folder 13, Edward Koch Papers, Department Correspondence, Municipal Archives, New York. At the time, there was no explicit discussion about implementing the Bike Ban as a means to stop and search people of color, but, as John Bloom points out in the case of Washington, DC, bike-related ordinances and initiatives have been used as a pretext for stopping and searching cyclists who have been "racially targeted." John Bloom, "'To Die for a Lousy Bike': Bicycles, Race, and the Regulation of Public Space on the Streets of Washington, DC, 1963–2009," *American Quarterly* 69, no. 1 (March 2017): 47–70.

92. "Koch Must Resign" *New York Amsterdam News*, August 1, 1987; "City Sends Message to Pit Bulls on Bikes," *New York Daily News*, July 24, 1987.

93. "Bike Ban Birth is 'Painless,'" *New York Post*, August 25, 1987.

94. "Bikers Beat Ban. What Next?" *City Cyclist*, Oct–Nov 1987, 1, 15.

95. Barbara Gunn and Benjamin Tucker, memorandum, 24 August 1987, Reel 41016, Box 40, Folder 13, Edward Koch Papers, Departmental Correspondence, Municipal Archives, New York; Gabriel Taussig, memorandum, 21 August 1987, Reel 41016, Box 40, Folder 13, Edward Koch Papers, Departmental Correspondence, Municipal Archives, New York.

96. New York City Department of Transportation and Police Department, *Improving Bicycle Safety in New York City*, 5; Evan Friss, *The Cycling City: Bicycles and Urban America in the 1890s* (Chicago: University of Chicago Press, 2015), 102–15.

97. Association of Messenger Services v. City of New York, 136 Misc.2d 869 (Sup. Ct., NY Co. 1987); "Judge Voids Ban on Bikes on 3 Avenues," *New York Times*, September 10, 1987.

98. "A Better Way to Tame Bikers," *New York Times*, January 12, 1988; "City Pushes Messenger Licensing," *City Cyclist*, July–August 1988, 1; Bob McGlynn, "Messengers: Licensing = Apartheid," *City Cyclist*, 8–9; "City to Seek a Licensing Law for the Commercial Cyclist," *New York Times*, December 8, 1987; Edward Koch, memorandum, 25 September 1987, Reel 41016, Box 40, Folder 12, Edward Koch Papers, Departmental Correspondence, Municipal Archives, New York.

99. "Delivery Slowdown Seen," *New York Daily News*, July 31, 1987; Charles Komanoff, interview by the author, January 2018; "How to Solve the Bicycle Messenger Mess," *Crain's New York Business*, September 21, 1987; "Messenger Regulation Revisited," *Crain's New York Business*, December 21, 1987; Stollman, interview; "Koch on Pension Board, Bikes," *Crain's New York Business*, March 7, 1988.

100. Bicycle Transportation Action, memorandum, March 1988, Reel 41017, Box 41, Folder 5, Edward Koch Papers, Departmental Correspondence, Municipal Archives, New York; "Bikes Taking us for Ride," *New York Daily News*, August 10, 1987; Charles Komanoff, interview by the author, January 2018.

101. Resolution No. 1256, March 22, 1988, *Proceedings of The Council of the City of New York* (1988), 322.

102. "Boom! Bang! Waking Up to Tour de Trump," *New York Times*, May 8, 1989.

103. Edward Koch, memorandum, 25 July 1989, Henry Stern to Edward Koch, 28 July 1989, and Lewis Rudin to Edward Koch, 18 July 1989, Reel 41105, Box 226, Folder 11, Edward Koch Papers, Departmental Correspondence, Municipal Archives, New York.

104. "Campaign Matters; The Question Is, Does Koch Have Your Confidence?" *New York Times*, July 10, 1989; "Mayor Says Dinkins Would 'Run from the Flak,'" *New York Times*, July 26, 1989; "Mayoral Debate: Numbers Flow but Don't All Add Up," *New York Times*, August 7, 1989.

105. Edward Koch, memorandum, 19 September 1989, Henry Stern to Edward Koch, 11 October 1989, and Edward Koch to Henry Stern, 16 October 1989, Reel 41105, Box 226, Folder 11, Edward Koch Papers, Departmental Correspondence, Municipal Archives, New York.

106. Kidder, *Urban Flow*, 22–23, 49, 51, 98–122.

5. Bloomberg

1. For more on Bloomberg and his three terms in office as mayor, see Chris McNickle, *Bloomberg: A Billionaire's Ambition* (New York: Skyhorse Publishing, 2017). For a more critical take, see Julian Brash, *Bloomberg's New York: Class and Governance in the Luxury City* (Athens: University of Georgia Press, 2011).

2. Joe Garofoli, "Critical Mass Turns 10," *SFGATE*, September 26, 2002, accessed July 21, 2017, http://www.sfgate.com/politics/joegarofoli/article/Critical-Mass-turns -10-A-decade-of-defiance-2767020.php; *Return of the Scorcher*, directed by Ted White (1992; Oakland, CA; The Video Project), VHS video; Chris Carlsson, "King of the Road," *Boom: A Journal of California* 1, no. 3 (Fall 2011): 80–87. For an excellent overview of Critical Mass in San Francisco, see Jason Henderson, *Street Fight: The Politics of Mobility in San Francisco* (Amherst: University of Massachusetts Press, 2013), chapter 5.

3. *We aren't blocking traffic, we are traffic!*, directed by Ted White (1999; San Francisco, CA; Video Project), VHS video; Susan Blickstein and Susan Hanson, "Critical Mass: Forging a Politics of Sustainable Mobility in the Information Age," *Transportation*

28, no. 4 (November 2001): 352; Benjamin Shepard and Kelly Moore, "Reclaiming the Streets of New York (for a world without cars)," in *Critical Mass: Bicycling's Defiant Celebration*, ed. Chris Carlsson (Edinburgh: AK Press, 2002), 197; Critical Mass Ephemera, undated, Box 31, Printed Ephemera Collection on Organizations, Tamiment Library and Robert F. Wagner Labor Archives, New York. Cleverly, writers have described the phenomenon of printing and distributing advertisements for Critical Mass rides as a "xerocracy," or "rule through photocopying." Zack Furness, *One Less Car: Bicycling and the Politics of Automobility* (Philadelphia: Temple University Press, 2010), 82.

4. As Jason Henderson points out in *Street Fight*, environmentalists and antiwar protestors helped shape Critical Mass.

5. Time's Up Environmental Education and Direct Action, "Bicycle Cops Ride with Critical Mass NYC May 1999," May 1999, video, 2:57, October 11, 2010, https://www .youtube.com/watch?v=JPBSwWT9AOk&feature=player_embedded.

6. Jonathan Wald, "264 Arrested in NYC Bicycle Protest," CNN, August 28, 2004, http:// www.cnn.com/2004/ALLPOLITICS/08/28/rnc.bike.protest/.

7. "Preparing for the Convention: Protesters; 100 Cyclists are Arrested as Thousands Ride in Protest," *New York Times*, August 28, 2004; FluxRostrum Films, "Critical Mass: 8-24-04 NYC," August 24, 2004, video, 10:38, August 15, 2008, https://www.youtube .com/watch?v=LcGnEjPJ7Lc. Back in 2000, Critical Mass riders were arrested during an event held in conjunction with the Democratic National Convention in Los Angeles. Scott Svatos, "Ride a Bike, Go to Jail! Critical Mass DNC 2000," in *Critical Mass*, ed. Carlsson, 214–18.

8. Wald, "264 Arrested in NYC Bicycle Protest."

9. "Police Records Detail Large Presence at Critical Mass Rides," *City Room: Blogging from the Five Boroughs (New York Times)*, October 20, 2010, https://cityroom.blogs .nytimes.com/2010/10/20/police-records-detail-large-presence-at-critical-mass-rides /?mcubz=0; Charles Komanoff, "NYPD Has Spent $1.32M to Suppress a Monthly Bike Ride," StreetsblogNYC, November 16, 2006, http://nyc.streetsblog.org/2006/11 /16/nypd-spent-132m-to-suppress-monthly-bike-ride/; "City Pays $98,000 to Critical Mass Cyclists," *City Room: Blogging from the Five Boroughs (New York Times)*, March 30, 2010, https://cityroom.blogs.nytimes.com/2010/03/30/city-pays-98000-to -critical-mass-cyclists/?mcubz=0&_r=0; "Judge Rules Against Cyclists," *City Room: Blogging from the Five Boroughs (New York Times)*, February 16, 2010, https://city room.blogs.nytimes.com/2010/02/16/judge-rules-against-cyclists/?hp.

10. Furness, *One Less Car*, 98–100; Henderson, *Street Fight*, chapter 5; Adam Kessel, "Why They're Wrong about Critical Mass!" in *Critical Mass*, ed. Carlsson, 105–11; Dave Snyder, "Good for the Bicycling Cause," in *Critical Mass*, ed. Carlsson, 112–15; Chris Carlsson, "Cycling under the Radar—Assertive Desertion," in *Critical Mass*, ed. Carlsson, 81; Furness, *One Less Car*, 87.

11. McNickle, *Bloomberg*, 171; Jen Petersen, "Whose Streets? Paving the Right to the City" (PhD diss., New York University, 2011), 147–48, 109–13; Ryan Russo, interview by the author, April 2018. For Doctoroff's own take on this transformation, see Daniel L. Doctoroff, *Greater Than Ever: New York's Big Comeback* (New York: Public Affairs, 2017).

12. David Harvey, "From Managerialism to Entrepreneurialism: The Transformation in Urban Governance in Late Capitalism," *Goegrafiska Annaler. Series B, Human Geography* 71, no. 1 (1989): 3–17.

13. Rohit Aggarwala, "Seat of Empire: New York, Philadelphia, and the Emergence of an American Metropolis, 1776–1837" (PhD diss., Columbia University, 2002); "Mayor Bloomberg Announces Director of Long-Term Planning and Sustainability Rohit T. Aggarwala Stepping Down in June," April 1, 2010, http://www1.nyc.gov/office-of-the -mayor/news/141-10/mayor-bloomberg-director-long-term-planning-sustainability -rohit-t-aggarwala.

14. The City of New York, *PlaNYC: A Greener, Greater New York*, 85, 87.

15. The City of New York, *PlaNYC: A Greener, Greater New York*, 84–88, 144, 151.

16. Janette Sadik-Khan and Seth Solomonow, *Streetfight: Handbook for an Urban Revolution* (New York: Viking, 2016).

17. "Ms. Sadik-Khan Weds Mark Geistfeld," *New York Times*, July 15, 1990; "Orhan Idris Sadik-Khan" (Obituary), *Greenwich Time*, August 5, 2007, http://www.legacy.com /obituaries/greenwichtime/obituary.aspx?n=orhan-idris-sadik-khan&pid=92039387; Sadik-Khan and Solomonow, *Streetfight*, 12–13.

18. Sadik-Khan and Solomonow, *Streetfight*, xi.

19. Sadik-Khan and Solomonow, *Streetfight*, xiv. For a history of how streets became primarily conceived as motor thoroughfares, see Peter D. Norton, *Fighting Traffic: The Dawn of the Motor Age in the American City* (Cambridge, MA: MIT Press, 2008).

20. Ryan Russo et al., "Ninth Avenue Bicycle Path and Complete Street," accessed September 14, 2015, http://www.nyc.gov/html/dot/downloads/pdf/rr_ite_08_9thave.PDF. The plans also included bicycle traffic signals to mitigate the problem of turning cars.

21. Ryan Russo, interview by the author, April 2018.

22. American Association of State Highway and Transportation Officials, *Guide for the Development of Bicycle Facilities* (Washington, DC: 1999); Sadik-Khan and Solomonow, *Streetfight*, 29–30.

23. Sadik-Khan and Solomonow, *Streetfight*, 29–30; New York City Department of Transportation, *Press Release #09-024*, May 2009, http://www.nyc.gov/html/dot/html /pr2009/pr09_024.shtml; New York City Department of Transportation, *Street Design Manual* (2009), http://www.nyc.gov/html/dot/downloads/pdf/sdm_lores.pdf; National Association of City Transportation Officials, *Urban Bikeway Design Guide* (Washington DC: NACTO, 2011).

24. New York City Department of Transportation, *Street Design Manual*, 22, 24, 32; Sadik-Khan and Solomonow, *Streetfight*, chapter 6; Janette Sadik-Khan, "Eighth and Ninth Avenues Complete Street Extension Community Board 4," September 21, 2011, 22, http://www.nyc.gov/html/dot/downloads/pdf/201109_8th_9th_cb4_slides.pdf.

25. Petersen, "Whose Streets?" 152, 162; "On Daddy Day, Heck on Wheels," *New York Times*, October 12, 2014; "Brooklyn 100 Influencer: Paul Steely White, Transportation Alternatives," *Brooklyn*, March 13, 2017, http://www.bkmag.com/2017/03/13 /brooklyn-100-influencer-paul-steely-white-transportation-alternatives/.

26. Elizabeth Press, "Clowns Liberate Bike Lanes," video, 3:08, November 9, 2007, http://www.streetfilms.org/clowns-liberate-bike-lanes/; The Open Planning Project,

"PSA—Cab in a Crosswalk," video, :30, December 30, 2006, http://www.streetfilms .org/cab-in-a-crosswalk/; Petersen, "Whose Streets?" 179, 185.

27. New York City Department of Transportation, *Sustainable Streets: 2013 and Beyond* (New York: New York City Department of Transportation, 2013), 130.

28. Sadik-Khan and Solomonow, *Streetfight*, 154–55. For a beautifully illustrated, general history of bicycle planning in twentieth-century Europe, see Ruth Oldenziel, Martin Emanuel, Adri Albert de la Bruhèze, and Frank Veraart, eds., *Cycling Cities: The European Experience a Hundred Years of Policy and Practice* (Eindhoven, Netherlands: Foundation for the History of Technology, 2016).

29. Peter Tuckel and William Milczarski, "Bike Lanes + Bike Share Program = Bike Safety: An Observational Study of Biking Behavior in Lower and Central Manhattan," January 2014, http://silo-public.hunter.cuny.edu/62eaab1fad6c75d37293d2f2f6504a15adacd 5c6/Cycling_Study_January_2014.pdf.

30. For more on the Coney Island Cycle Path, see Robert L. McCullough, *Old Wheelways: Traces of Bicycle History on the Land* (Cambridge, MA: MIT Press, 2015), 220–32; Evan Friss, *The Cycling City: Bicycles and Urban America in the 1890s* (Chicago: The University of Chicago Press, 2015), 102–14.

31. New York City Department of Transportation, "Kent Avenue Traffic Calming & Bicycle Lanes," September 8, 2008, http://www.nyc.gov/html/dot/downloads/pdf/Kent -Ave-2008.pdf.; New York City Department of Transportation, "Kent Avenue Improvement Plan: Implementation Update," August 7, 2009, http://www.nyc.gov/html/dot /downloads/pdf/kent_ave.pdf; Sadik-Khan and Solomonow, *Streetfight*, 162–64.

32. Michael Idov, "Clash of the Bearded Ones: Hipsters, Hasids, and the Williamsburg Street," *New York*, April 11, 2010, http://nymag.com/realestate/neighborhoods/2010 /65356; Brian Ries, "Hasids and Bicyclists Debate Bedford Avenue Bike Lane," NBC New York, accessed August 1, 2017, http://www.nbcnewyork.com/news/local/Hasids -and-Bicyclists-Debate-Bedford-Avenue-Bike-Lane-82659062.html.

33. Thefacts (December 19, 2009), Kelinpeter (December 19, 2009), Snoopy (December 19, 2009), and Billdozer (December 19, 2009), comments on John Del Signore, " 'Topless' Bedford Bike Lane Protest Draws Media, Clothed Cyclists," *Gothamist*, http:// gothamist.com/2009/12/19/top-less_bedford_bike_lane_protest.php#; Tal Barziliai (December 9, 2009), PDub (December 9, 2009), and Isaac (December 8, 2009) comments on Sean Patrick Farrell, "Cyclists Redraw the Lines in Brooklyn," *City Room: Blogging from the Five Boroughs* (*New York Times*), December 8, 2009, https://city room.blogs.nytimes.com/2009/12/08/cyclists-redraw-the-lines-in-brooklyn/?_r=3.

34. Sadik-Khan and Solomonow, *Streetfight*, 164; "Cyclists Redraw the Lines in Brooklyn," *City Room: Blogging from the Five Boroughs* (*New York Times*); Del Signore, " 'Topless' Bedford Bike Lane Protest Draws Media, Clothed Cyclists"; Verena Dobnik, "Too Cold for Nude Protest, Bikers Switch Gears," NBC News, December 12, 2009, http://www.nbcnews.com/id/34495913/ns/us_news-weird_news/t/too-cold-nude -protest-bikers-switch-gears/#.WeoEshNSyfU.

35. "Cyclists Redraw the Lines in Brooklyn," *City Room: Blogging from the Five Boroughs* (*New York Times*); Ries, "Hasids and Bicyclists Debate Bedford Avenue Bike Lane," NBC New York; Streetsblog, "Gridlock Sam on NYC's 1980 Bike Lanes," video, 5:44, November 10, 2006, https://www.youtube.com/watch?v=awfNxaoqjjk.

36. "Cyclists Redraw the Lines in Brooklyn," *City Room: Blogging from the Five Boroughs* (*New York Times*).

37. "Dueling Protests Over a Brooklyn Bike Lane," *City Room: Blogging from the Five Boroughs* (*New York Times*), October 21, 2010, https://cityroom.blogs.nytimes.com /2010/10/21/dueling-protests-over-a-brooklyn-bike-lane/.

38. Splashed across the cover of the March 28, 2011, print edition of *New York Magazine* was the word "bikelash." The magazine also featured a cover story on the subject. Matthew Shaer, "Not Quite Copenhagen" *New York*, March 20, 2011, http:// nymag.com/news/features/bike-wars-2011-3/#. See also "Bike Lanes Proliferate, And Protest Gets Louder," *New York Times*, November 23, 2010.

39. Louise Hainline to Christoph M. Kimmich, e-mail message, December 24, 2010, http://www.streetsblog.org/wp-content/uploads/2011/10/SchumerLevinGodfa therRedacted.pdf; Louise Hainline, Norman Steisel, and Iris Weinshall, "Letter to the Editor," *New York Times*, December 17, 2010; "Street Fighter," *New York Times*, March 6, 2011; "Judge Rejects Groups' Effort to Remove Bike Lane," *New York Times*, August 17, 2011.

40. "Bike Lane Lawsuit, A Bigger Traffic Challenge," *New York Times*, March 8, 2011; Sadik-Khan and Solomonow, *Streetfight*, 169; "Notice of Petition Pursuant to CPLR Article 78," Seniors for Safety and Neighbors for Better Bike Lanes vs. NYC DOT and Janette Sadik-Khan, Supreme Court of the State of New York, County of Kings, March 7, 2011.

41. The initial plans for the Prospect Park lane stemmed from discussion about the need to calm traffic on Prospect Park West. The lawsuit alleged that the community board approved the plan for the lane in part because of misleading statistics about the traffic problem before the lane was installed. The board approved the lane, the suit alleged, because of a "misplaced reliance on the truth and accuracy of DOT's data." "Notice of Petition Pursuant to CPLR Article 78," Seniors for Safety and Neighbors for Better Bike Lanes vs. NYC DOT and Janette Sadik-Khan. For the data in question, see NYC DOT, "Prospect Park West: Bicycle Path and Traffic Calming Update," January 20, 2011, http://www.nyc.gov/html/dot/downloads/pdf/20110120_ppw.pdf; "Answers about Cycling in New York, Part I," *City Room: Blogging from the Five Boroughs* (*New York Times*), May 14, 2008, https://cityroom.blogs.nytimes.com/2008/05/14 /answers-about-cycling-in-new-york-part-1/. Initially, a judge ruled that the statute of limitations had passed and dismissed the lawsuit (Seniors for Safety and Neighbors for Better Bike Lanes vs. NYC DOT and Janette Sadik-Khan, August 15, 2011, Index No. Index No. 5210/11, Part 8 of the Supreme Court of the State of New York, http: //www.nyc.gov/html/dot/downloads/pdf/ppw_decision.pdf; "Judge Rejects Groups' Efforts to Remove Bike Lane," August 17, 2011, *New York Times*). But one of the lingering issues was whether or not the lane had been installed on a trial basis. If the plaintiffs could prove that the original path had only been meant as a pilot, the statute of limitations would not have passed. An appeals court granted a review of the case in 2012, and in 2016 a hearing took place. By September 2016, the lawsuit was dropped. Seniors for Safety v. New York City DOT, 101 A.D.3d 1029 (2012); Nathan Tempey, "It's Alive: Judge Revives 5-Year-Old Prospect Park Bike Lane Lawsuit," *Gothamist*, March 15, 2016, http://gothamist.com/2016/03/15/judge_revives_prospect

_park_west_bi.php; Raphael Pope-Sussman, "The Prospect Park West Bike Lane Legal War is OVER," *Gothamist*, September 21, 2016, http://gothamist.com/2016/09/21/ppw_bike_lane_lawsuit.php.

42. "How One New York Bike Lane Could Affect the Future of Cycling Worldwide," *Guardian* (Bike blog), March 9, 2011, https://www.theguardian.com/environment/bike-blog/2011/mar/09/new-york-bike-lane-cycling.

43. "Bike Lane Lawsuit, A Bigger Traffic Challenge," *New York Times*, March 8, 2011; John Cassidy, "Battle of the Bike Lanes," *New Yorker*, March 8, 2011, https://www.newyorker.com/news/john-cassidy/battle-of-the-bike-lanes; John Cassidy, "Bike Lanes II: The Condemned Motorist Speaks," *New Yorker*, March 9, 2011, https://www.newyorker.com/news/john-cassidy/bike-lanes-ii-the-condemned-motorist-speaks; John Cassidy, "Bike Lanes III: A Closing Word," *New Yorker*, March 10, 2011, https://www.newyorker.com/news/john-cassidy/bike-lanes-iii-a-closing-word.

44. Shaer, "Not Quite Copenhagen"; Louise Hainline, interview by the author, April 2018.

45. "Community Survey Results on Prospect Park West Reconfiguration," October 2010, http://bradlander.nyc/ppwsurvey; "Survey Finds Support, but a Bike-Lane Debate Continues," *City Room: Blogging from the Five Boroughs* (*New York Times*), December 7, 2010, https://cityroom.blogs.nytimes.com/2010/12/07/survey-finds-support-but-a-bike-lane-debate-continues/; "New Yorkers Support Bicycle Lanes, Poll Finds," *City Room: Blogging from the Five Boroughs* (*New York Times*), March 18, 2011, https://cityroom.blogs.nytimes.com/2011/03/18/new-yorkers-support-bicycle-lanes-poll-finds/.

46. DOT leaders certainly understood that community boards were not perfect proxies for neighborhood sentiment, but taking the pulse of a neighborhood is never easy. And there were plenty of instances when community boards stifled well-intentioned DOT proposals. For better or worse, the DOT decided that working through the boards was the best way to move forward. Hainline, interview; Minutes of Brooklyn Community Board 6, General Board Meeting, June 9, 2010; Russo, interview.

47. Shaer, "Not Quite Copenhagen"; New York City Department of Transportation, "Prospect Park West: Bicycle Path and Traffic Calming Update," January 2011, http://www.nyc.gov/html/dot/downloads/pdf/20110120_ppw_data.pdf.

48. Shaer, "Not Quite Copenhagen."

49. Howard Wolfson, memorandum, 21 March 2011, http://www.nyc.gov/html/om/pdf/bike_lanes_memo.pdf; (Cover), *New York*, March 28, 201; Howard Wolfson (@howiewolf), "Piece forgot to mention that the local CB trans comm voted recently for the bike lane 'NY Liberals Battle a Bike Lane' http://on.wsj.com/g1Ohc7," Twitter, March 26, 2011, https://twitter.com/howiewolf/status/51618082363408384; Howard Wolfson, "Bike Lanes: A Choice, Not a Metaphor," *HuffingtonPost*, March 22, 2011, https://www.huffingtonpost.com/howard-wolfson/bike-lanes-a-choice-not-a_b_839076.html.

50. "Residents Face Off Over Brooklyn Bike Lane," *New York Times*, March 10, 2011. Many critics of congestion pricing labeled it a regressive tax that would hurt working-class New Yorkers, but others emphasized the way the plan would force people to change their behavior. One editorial, for example, went so far as to suggest that congestion pricing would "curtail civil liberties." A. K. Gupta, "Congestion Pricing: Don't

Trust Mayor Mike," *The Indypendent*, July 24, 2007, https://indypendent.org/2007/07
/congestion-pricing-dont-trust-mayor-mike/.

51. "Brooklyn Bike Lane is Scuttled (No, Not That One)," *City Room: Blogging from the
Five Boroughs* (*New York Times*), April 12, 2011, https://cityroom.blogs.nytimes.com
/2011/04/12/brooklyn-bike-lane-is-scuttled-no-not-that-one/?_r=0.

52. Sadik-Khan and Solomonow, *Streetfight*, 184–85; Alex Davies, "3 Charts that Explain
the Massive Success of NYC's Bike Share Program," Business Insider, March 7, 2014,
http://www.businessinsider.com/3-charts-explain-nyc-bike-share-success-2014-3; New
York City Department of Transportation, *Press Release #01-064*, November 23, 2010,
http://www.nyc.gov/html/dot/html/pr2010/pr10_060.shtml.

53. Oldenziel, Emanuel, de la Bruhèze, and Veraart, eds., *Cycling Cities*, 182–85, 187–88,
191; Susan A. Shaheen, Stacey Guzman, and Hua Zhang, "Bikesharing across the
Globe," in *City Cycling*, ed. John Pucher and Ralph Buehler (Cambridge, MA: MIT
Press, 2012), 183–210.

54. "Bike Share Program May Mean More Accident Suits Against the City, Liu Warns,"
New York Times, June 23, 2012; "Bicycles? Tough Sit!" *New York Post*, April 19, 2013;
John Del Signore, "West Village Residents File Lawsuit to Stop Citi Bike," *Gothamist*,
April 30, 2013, http://gothamist.com/2013/04/30/west_village_nimbys_file_futile_law
.php; Mary Johnson, "Residents Say Bike-Share Site Near UN Creates Safety Risk,"
dnainfo, June 18, 2012, https://www.dnainfo.com/new-york/20120618/midtown-east
/residents-say-bike-share-site-near-un-creates-safety-risk/; "Bike Sharing? Sure. The
Racks? No Way," *New York Times*, May 14, 2014.

55. *Wall Street Journal*, "Opinion: Death by Bicycle," video, 4:59, May 31, 2013, https://
www.wsj.com/video/opinion-death-by-bicycle/C6D8BBCE-B405-4D3C-A381
-4CA50BDD8D4D.html; *The Daily Show with Jon Stewart*, "Full Pedal Racket—
Citi Bike," video, 5:34, June 6, 2013, http://www.cc.com/video-playlists/kw3fjo/the
-opposition-with-jordan-klepper-welcome-to-the-opposition-w—jordan-klepper
/2432gv.

56. "Citi Bike Data 2013—Launch thru Sept 2013," accessed July 12, 2017, http://cf
.datawrapper.de/pe6k4/2/; "Flooding Apparently Damaged Equipment for Bike-Share
Program," November 15, 2012, *New York Times*; NYC Bike Share, "June 2013 Monthly
Report," accessed October 19, 2017, https://s3.amazonaws.com/Citi Bike-regunits
/pdf/2013_06_June_Citi_Bike_Monthly_Report.pdf.

57. Roxanne Palmer, "Citi Bike Launches in NYC, But Will it Reach New Yorkers Who
Aren't Rich and White?" *International Business Times*, June 1, 2013, http://www
.ibtimes.com/citi-bike-launches-nyc-will-it-reach-new-yorkers-who-arent-rich-white
-1284617; *The Daily Show with Jon Stewart*, "Full Pedal Racket—Citi Bike"; "Bike
Sharing? Sure. The Racks? No Way," *New York Times*, May 14, 2014.

58. "Bike Sharing? Sure. The Racks? No Way," *New York Times*, May 14, 2014.

59. NYC Bike Share, "September 2017 Monthly Report," accessed October 19, 2017, https:
//d21xlh2maitm24.cloudfront.net/nyc/September-2017-Citi-Bike-Monthly-Report
.pdf?mtime=20171018154130.

60. "Citi Bike System Data," https://www.Citi Bikenyc.com/system-data; Alex Goldmark,
"The Three (and a Half) Citi Bike Usage Patterns," WNYC, July 28, 2013, http://www
.wnyc.org/story/307846-chart-three-and-half-citi-bike-usage-patterns/; Joe Jansen,

"What Factors Influence Citi Bike Usage," December 30, 2013, https://www.joejansen .co/blog/2013/12/29/what-factors-influence-citi-bike-usage; Sarah Kaufman, "Citi Bike and Gender," New York University Rudin Center for Transportation, accessed October 31, 2017, https://wagner.nyu.edu/rudincenter/2014/05/citi-bike-and-gender. See also, "Is Bike Share the Bloomer of the 21st Century?" velojoy, June 19, 2014, https:// velojoy.com/2014/06/19/bike-share-and-gender-data/; Michael Guerriero, "Interactive: A Month of Citi Bike," *New Yorker*, July 26, 2013, http://projects.newyorker.com /story/citi-bike.html; Todd W. Schneider, "A Tale of Twenty-Two million Citi Bike Rides: Analyzing the NYC Bike Share System," January 13, 2016, http://toddwschnei der.com/posts/a-tale-of-twenty-two-million-citi-bikes-analyzing-the-nyc-bike-share -system/; Sara Robinson, "Analyzing NYC Biking Data with Google BigQuery," Google Cloud Platform, December 7, 2016, https://cloud.google.com/blog/big-data/2016/12 /analyzing-nyc-biking-data-with-google-bigquery. Relatively, women were more likely to ride for reasons other than commuting. Still, between 2010 and 2014, they accounted for only 35 percent of total adult cyclists. A. Getman, L. Gordon-Koven, S. Hostetter, and R. Riola, *Safer Cycling: Bicycle Ridership and Safety in New York City* (New York: NYC DOT, 2017); Tuckel and Milczarski, "Bike Lanes + Bike Share Program = Bike Safety"; "Commuting Characteristics by Sex: American Community Survey 5-Year Estimates," U.S. Census Bureau, 2010–2016. There are many theories that account for the gender disparity, including issues of safety, income level, parenting responsibilities, and others. See, for example, Lauren Evans, "Why Do So Few Women Bike in NYC?" *Gothamist*, July 7, 2015, http://gothamist.com/2015/07/07/citi_bike_women _problem.php; "Women, Uneasy, Still Lag as Cyclists," *New York Times*, July 4, 2011; Mona Chalabi, "Why Women Don't Cycle," FiveThirtyEight, June 16, 2014, https:// fivethirtyeight.com/features/why-women-dont-cycle/; Carolyn Szczepanski "Bike Share's Gender Gap," The League of American Bicyclists: News From the League, June 27, 2014, http://www.bikeleague.org/content/bike-shares-gender-gap; Sarah Goodyear, "Is There Such a Thing as a 'Feminine' Way to Ride a Bike?" CITYLAB, April 16, 2014, https://www.citylab.com/transportation/2014/04/there-such-thing -feminine-way-ride-bike/8886/; Eillie Anzilotti, "What Will It Take to Close the Gender Gap in Urban Cycling?" *Fast Company*, November 27, 2017, https://www.fastcompany .com/40488970/what-will-it-take-to-close-the-gender-gap-in-urban-cycling; Sydney Brownstone, "NYC Bike Share Riders Are Overwhelmingly 30-Something Dudes, But the Gap Is Narrowing," *Fast Company*, April 14, 2014, https://www.fastcompany.com /3028926/nyc-bike-share-riders-are-overwhelmingly-30-something-dudes-but-the-gap-is -narrowing; Jan Garrard, Susan Handy, and Jennifer Dill, "Women and Cycling," in *City Cycling*, 211–34.

61. Ian Parker, "Hacking the Citi Bike Points System," *New Yorker*, December 4, 2017. Calvin Trillin noticed the same phenomenon back in 1971: "I have never been able to rid myself of the notion that downtown is downhill." Calvin Trillin, "U.S. Journal: Manhattan Fun's Over," *New Yorker*, October 9, 1971, 126.

62. NYC Bike Share, "December 2012 Monthly Report," accessed November 15, 2017, https://s3.amazonaws.com/Citi Bike-regunits/pdf/2013_12_December_Citi_Bike _Monthly_Report.pdf; "A Success, but Wobbly from the Start," March 27, 2014, *New York Times*.

63. New York City Department of Transportation, *Press Release #14-087*, October 28, 2014, http://a841-tfpweb.nyc.gov/dotpress/2014/10/citi-bike-program-in-new-york-city/; Sarah Kessler, "Love Citi Bike? You have a Real Estate Developer to Thank," *Fast Company*, January 12, 2016, https://www.fastcompany.com/3055168/love-citi-bike-you-have-a-real-estate-developer-to-thank. Early on, some wealthy residents resisted the notion of Citi Bike stations near their place of residence. "City Moves Citi Bike Stations from Richest Areas While Letting Other Contested Racks Stay," *New York Post*, June 23, 2013, https://nypost.com/2013/06/23/city-moves-citi-bike-stations-from-richest-areas-while-letting-other-contested-racks-stay/.

64. Peter Tuckel and William Milczarski, "Bike Lanes + Bike Share Program = Bike Safety: An Observational Study of Biking Behavior in Lower and Central Manhattan," January 2014, http://silo-public.hunter.cuny.edu/62eaab1fad6c75d37293d2f2f6504a15ada cd5c6/Cycling_Study_January_2014.pdf; "Tips and Fear on Wheels," *New York Times*, March 4, 2012; Getman, Gordon, Hostetter, and Riola, *Safer Cycling*.

65. For more on inequities, see, for example, Melody Hoffman, *Bike Lanes Are White Lanes: Bicycle Advocacy and Urban Planning* (Lincoln: University of Nebraska Press, 2016); she argues that "white upwardly mobile people" used "their cultural privilege and power to control how their advocacy will materialize in cities." For other critiques highlighting some of the failures associated with recent bicycle advocacy attempts, see Adonia E. Lugo, "Body-City-Machines: Human Infrastructure for Bicycling in Los Angeles" (PhD diss., University of California, Irvine, 2013); Adonia E. Lugo, *Bicycle/Race: Transportation, Culture, & Resistance* (Portland, OR: Microcosm Publishing); John G. Stehlin, "Business Cycles: Race, Gentrification, and the Making of Bicycle Space in the San Francisco Bay Area" (PhD diss., University of California, Berkeley, 2015).

66. Lawrence Solomon, "Ban the Bike! How Cities Made a Huge Mistake in Promoting Cycling," *Financial Post*, December 1, 2017, http://business.financialpost.com/opinion/lawrence-solomon-ban-the-bike-how-cities-made-a-huge-mistake-in-promoting-cycling; Jeremiah Moss, *Vanishing New York: How a Great City Lost Its Soul* (New York: HarperCollins, 2017), 210, 324; Tuckel and Milczarski, "Bike Lanes + Bike Share Program = Bike Safety." For a smart take on the relationship between cycling and gentrification see Stehlin, "Business Cycles: Race, Gentrification, and the Making of Bicycle Space in the San Francisco Bay Area."

67. Michael Crowley, "Honk, Honk, Aaah," *New York*, March 17, 2009, http://nymag.com/news/features/56794/; Michael Bloomberg, review excerpt on book jacket, Sadik-Khan and Solomonow, *Streetfight*.

68. Samuel Zipp and Nathan Storring, eds., *Vital Little Plans: The Short Works of Jane Jacobs* (New York: Random House, 2016), 275.

69. Crowley, "Honk, Honk, Aaah."

70. Crowley, "Honk, Honk, Aaah."

71. The percentage increase in the number of regular bicycle commuters is staggering, but the total number, roughly 1.2 percent of all commutes by 2015 (earning a 24th place ranking in terms of percentage) was still small. Also, roughly three-quarters of New Yorkers never rode a bicycle, and many of the new riders and much of the new infrastructure were not equally distributed among the boroughs. NYC DOT, "Cycling in

the City: Cycling Trends in NYC, January 2017," 2017, http://www.nyc.gov/html/dot /downloads/pdf/cycling-in-the-city.pdf; "2015 ACS Large Cities," The League of American Bicyclists, accessed October 21, 2017, http://bikeleague.org/sites/default/files /2015ACSlargecities.pdf; NYC DOT, "Bicycle Network Development: Lane Miles by Borough & Type," accessed October 19, 2017, http://www.nyc.gov/html/dot/down loads/pdf/bike-route-details.pdf; NYC DOT, "East River Bridge Counts," accessed October 14, 2017, http://www.nyc.gov/html/dot/downloads/pdf/east-river-bridge -counts-24hrs-1980-2016.pdf; New York City Department of Transportation, *Press Release #14-069*, September 3, 2014, http://www.nyc.gov/html/dot/html/pr2014/pr14 -069.shtml. On streets with protected bike lanes, cyclists rode in greater numbers and suffered fewer injuries. New York City Department of Transportation, *Sustainable Streets*, 30.

72. Janette Sadik-Khan, "The Bike Wars Are Over, and the Bikes Won," *New York*, March 8, 2016, http://nymag.com/daily/intelligencer/2016/03/bike-wars-are-over-and -the-bikes-won.html. Protected bike lanes totaled 36.4 miles across nearly two dozen projects by the end of 2013. "Protected Bike Lane Week," People for Bikes, accessed October 19, 2017, https://s3-us-west-2.amazonaws.com/static.peopleforbikes.org/pro tected-bike-lane-week-lg.jpg; "Protected Bike Lanes" (spreadsheet), October 10, 2017, https://docs.google.com/spreadsheets/d/11HogArHx06kMop1I18yMcq7Arb NrwaGBLmIXgqI1Gjk/edit#gid=3.

73. "Bicycle Lanes Draw Wide Support Among City Residents," *New York Times*, August 22, 2010; New York City Department of Transportation, *Sustainable Streets*, 85.

74. "Protected Bike Lanes" (spreadsheet); "De Blasio Offers Ideas in Policy Book for Election," *New York Times*, June 19, 2013.

75. Ian Dille, "2014 Top 50 Bike-Friendly Cities," accessed September 21, 2015, http://www .bicycling.com/culture/advocacy/2014-top-50-bike-friendly-cities; "2014 Top 50 Bike-Friendly Cities," August 29, 2014, *Bicycling*, https://www.bicycling.com/culture/advo cacy/2014-top-50-bike-friendly-cities; New York City Department of Transportation, *Press Release #14-069*, September 3, 2014, http://www.nyc.gov/html/dot/html/pr2014 /pr14069.shtml; "Tour de New York," *New York Times*, March 23, 1997.

Epilogue

1. "Catherine Potter Obituary," *Charlottesville Daily Progress*, May 12, 2013, http://www .legacy.com/Obituaries.asp?Page=LifeStory&PersonId=164739194.

2. Sidewalk Labs, accessed June 14, 2018, https://www.sidewalklabs.com/; Elizabeth Woyke, "A Smarter Smart City," MIT Technology Review, February 21, 2018, https:// www.technologyreview.com/s/610249/a-smarter-smart-city/.

3. New York City Press Office, "Mayor de Blasio and NYPD Announce Plans to Crack Down on Improper Use of Electric Bikes," October 19, 2017, http://www1.nyc.gov /office-of-the-mayor/news/666-17/mayor-de-blasio-nypd-plans-crack-down-improper -use-electric-bikes#/0; Brad Aaron, "Shameful Scenes from de Blasio's Crackdown on Delivery Workers Who Use Electric Bikes," StreetsblogNYC, January 16, 2018, https://

nyc.streetsblog.org/2018/01/16/shameful-scenes-from-de-blasios-crackdown-on
-delivery-workers-who-use-electric-bikes/; New York City Press Office, "Mayor de Blasio Announces New Framework to Clarify Legality of Pedal-Assist Bicycles," April 3,
2018, https://www1.nyc.gov/office-of-the-mayor/news/165-18/mayor-de-blasio-new
-framework-clarify-legality-pedal-assist-bicycles. For an interesting take on what
e-bikes mean for the state of cycling, see Thomas Beller, "The Electric-Bike Conun-
drum," *New Yorker*, August 18, 2017, https://www.newyorker.com/culture/culture
-desk/the-electric-bike-conundrum.

4. Regina R. Clewlow and Gouri Shankar Mishra, "Disruptive Transportation: The
Adoption, Utilization, and Impacts of Ride-Hailing in the United States," Institute
of Transportation Studies, University of California Davis, October 2017; "Uber,
Surging Outside Manhattan, Tops Taxis in New York City," *New York Times*, October 12, 2017; Bruce Schaller, "Unsustainable?: The Growth of App-Based Ride Services
and Traffic, Travel and the Future of New York City," Schaller Consulting, February 27, 2017; Bruce Schaller, "The New Automobility: Lyft, Uber and the Future of
American Cities," Schaller Consulting, July 25, 2018.

5. "Uber Gets into Bike-Share Business with Deal to Buy Jump," *Washington Post*,
April 9, 2018; "New York City Limits Growth of Ride-Hailing," *New York Times*,
August 9, 2018; "Uber to Diversify into Electric Bikes and Scooters to Drive Growth,"
The Guardian, August 27, 2018, https://www.theguardian.com/technology/2018/aug
/27/uber-to-diversify-into-electric-bikes-and-scooters-to-drive-growth.

6. "Lyft Buys Bike-Share Giant in 2-Wheeled Race with Uber," *New York Times*, July 3,
2018; New York City Press Office, "Mayor de Blasio Announces That in Advance of
L Train Disruption, Citi Bike Will Increase Coverage in Many of Its Busiest Areas,"
June 27, 2018, https://www1.nyc.gov/office-of-the-mayor/news/332-18/mayor-de-blasio
-that-advance-l-train-disruption-citi-bike-will-increase-coverage; Schaller, "Unsustainable?;" Schaller, "The New Automobility: Lyft, Uber and the Future of American
Cities."

INDEX

Page numbers in italics refer to figures.